In *Creature of the Word* you will learn  it is about Jesus and how to live all o: for Him. This is a foundational, practical, and helpful book for both Christians and church leaders.

—Mark Driscoll, pastor, Mars Hill Church, Seattle, Washington

I love Matt Chandler, his heart for the gospel and his love for the church. I am so glad that he, Josh Patterson, and Eric Geiger wrote this book addressing the fact that God's Word should be the foundation of the Church rather than the latest trend that seems to be working in the world. This book provides a fresh challenge for all of us and will help us establish a biblical foundation in regard to the ONE THING that Jesus promised He would build!

—Perry Noble, senior pastor, NewSpring Church, South Carolina, and author of *Unleash!: Breaking Free from Normalcy*

Our homes, communities, cities, and nations need churches that are immersed in the gospel and fueled by the gospel. Why? Because the good news of Jesus Christ changes everything! I am encouraged and excited by the strong gospel challenge found in *Creature of the Word: The Jesus-Centered Church*. Matt, Josh, and Eric provide a clarion call for our churches to recapture their awe for Jesus and His perfect work accomplished on our behalf. They help us see how the beautiful bride of Christ can be possessed by both a doctrine and a culture centered on Jesus. This is the kind of book the Church has needed for a long time.

—Daniel L. Akin, president, Southeastern Baptist Theological Seminary, Wake Forest, North Carolina

Creature of the Word is a crystal clear call to the Church to recenter around Jesus and the gospel. Practical yet theological, I recommend this book as essential reading for anyone who would lead or plant a church.

—Matt Carter, pastor, Preaching and Vision at The Austin Stone Community Church, Austin, Texas

Too often Jesus Christ is central to our theology but not to the way we do church. This book serves as a needed reminder and a powerful corrective for those of us who must continually recalibrate our ministry *for* Jesus with the person and work *of* Jesus.

—Larry Osborne, pastor, North Coast Church,
Vista, California, and author of *Sticky Church*

When a church goes vertical, it's the small adjustment that leads to a major renovation. It's an active, hard-hats-only construction zone where every decision has just one goal: to honor God. When we get that right, God Himself shows up and *builds*. My friend Matt Chandler and his colaborers Josh and Eric are calling us to make church about Jesus, again.

—Dr. James MacDonald, senior pastor, Harvest Bible Chapel,
Chicago, Illinois, and author of *Vertical Church*

Be careful if you read this book. *Creature of the Word* will make you rethink much of what you think you know about the Church, its message, and its mission. Matt Chandler, Josh Patterson, and Eric Geiger have conspired to write a book that will make you think more faithfully about the church and what it means for Christ's people to be formed by the gospel. I welcome the conversations this book will spark.

—R. Albert Mohler, Jr., president, The Southern Baptist
Theological Seminary, Louisville, Kentucky

Lately many books are coming out with a title that has "gospel" in it. As you begin to read the philosophical and allegorical talk about the gospel, there is a disconnect from the Word of God. However, what is phenomenal about *Creature of the Word* is that it is gospel-centered and rooted in the Word of God with uncanny readability. I hope that this work will devotionally impact the whole people of God and increase our intimacy with our God.

—Eric Mason, lead pastor, Epiphany Fellowship, Philadelphia, Pennsylvania

The Bible has been referred to as the "Him Book" because it's all about Him. In *Creature of the Word,* we will be challenged to keep everything Jesus centered. This commitment always leads us into His work.

Johnny Hunt, pastor, First Baptist Church, Woodstock, Georgia

There is no greater need for church leaders than for the reality of the person and work of Christ to permeate our entire being. This not only results in personal holiness but spills out all over the people to whom we minister. *Creature of the Word* will change you and those you shepherd.

—Darrin Patrick, lead pastor of The Journey Church in St. Louis, Missouri, and author of *Church Planter*

Godly leaders from my generation have prayed and deeply desired for a new generation of church leaders to lead His bride well. Works like *Creature of the Word* are an answer to our prayers. I am excited and hopeful for the local church after reading the encouragement and challenges Matt, Josh, and Eric offer. What an incredible book by three incredible leaders!

—Thom S. Rainer, president and CEO, LifeWay Christian Resources, Nashville, Tennessee

I look for five things when reading a book: readable, accessible, practical, helpful, and fresh. This book by Chandler, Patterson, and Geiger scores highly on all counts. It is a book church leaders should read, but it would be a great pity if the target audience was limited to that select group. Whatever your role or place among the people of God, do not hesitate to pick up this book and be refreshed by the insights, observations, and challenges you'll find here. But primarily, the fresh encouragement to us to focus on, and be all about, Jesus.

—Steve Timmis, director for Acts 29 (Western Europe)
and coauthor of *Total Church*

Creature of the Word excites me because I know the result of churches centering themselves on Jesus, and His redemptive mission will result in God's people engaging in kingdom work. Church leaders and staff teams should read and discuss this book in community.

—Ed Stetzer, lead pastor of Grace Church,
president, Lifeway Research

Creature of the Word paints a compelling and exciting picture of what a church can be under the gospel of our Lord Jesus Christ. Matt, Josh, and Eric offer sound and practical insight that will encourage and challenge church leaders. How refreshing it is in a model-driven church world to read the call to all to be a Jesus-centered church! This alone makes me want to shout!

Dr. Ronnie W. Floyd, senior pastor, Cross Church, Fayetteville,
Arkansas, and author of *Our Last Great Hope*

CREATURE OF THE WORD

THE JESUS-CENTERED CHURCH

MATT **CHANDLER** · JOSH **PATTERSON** · ERIC **GEIGER**

B&H
PUBLISHING GROUP
NASHVILLE, TENNESSEE

978-1-4336-7862-2

Published by B&H Publishing Group
Nashville, Tennessee

Dewey Decimal Classification: 269.2
Subject Heading: CHURCH \ EVANGELISTIC WORK \ BIBLE.
N. T. GOSPELS

2 3 4 5 6 7 8 9 • 16 15 14 13 12

DEDICATION

From Matt~

*To The Village Church: there is nowhere I would rather
spend the days of my life than in glad service
to Jesus alongside of you.*

From Josh~

*For my sweet wife, Natalie.
I cannot get over the fact that you said, "Yes."
You are a thousand graces to me.*

From Eric~

*For my bride, Kaye.
Your faithfulness and goodness to me is
a constant reminder of God's grace.*

ACKNOWLEDGMENTS

From Matt:

It has been a joy to work with Josh and Eric on this project. To be given by God kindred spirits is no small thing. It's been my joy to think, dialogue, laugh, and love this project with both of you.

I want to thank the elders of The Village Church for allowing me the time to think and write. Laboring with you for the glory of Christ and the good of our people is a joy. Your love and care for me and my family is evidence of God's grace on our lives.

To my family, thank you for allowing me precious time to write, review, and work on what would normally have been your time.

Finally, what a gift it has been to partner with LifeWay on this project. Working with you has been easy and fun. Jedidiah Coppenger is a man-child and has been incredible to work with throughout the entirety of this project.

From Josh:

I am truly humbled to have labored alongside Matt and Eric on this project. Matt, you are on the short list of people who have most impacted my life. I am honored to be in this fight with you and to call you friend. I love you, brother. Eric, who knew what would materialize from our first meeting in New Orleans. God has used you profoundly at key seasons to significantly shape my leadership and ministry. Not only that, you have pushed me to be a better husband and dad. You are a dear friend and brother that I love.

To the elders of The Village Church, thank you for being a covering and encouragement. You men are worthy to be emulated. To the The Village staff, our partnership in the gospel ministry is one of the greatest joys of my life. To the people of The Village, thank you for loving my family so well. It is an honor to serve you. I am wholly undeserving.

A special thanks to Jeremy Treat for his invaluable insights and suggestions. Your influence is throughout this book. Jeremy Pace, your "house analogy" brings clarity to a concept. Andrea Bowman, your administrative gift results in peace and order.

Michael Bleecker, Matt Chandler, Jason Holleman, and Trevor Joy are friends worthy of mention. You consistently encourage, sharpen, and shape me in the gospel as a husband, father, friend, and pastor. I am deeply indebted to each of you.

Finally, what a gift it has been to partner with LifeWay on this project. Your desire to steward gospel opportunities has been an encouragement to us. In particular, I want to thank Jedidiah Coppenger for his incredible work throughout the entirety of this project. You are clutch.

From Eric:

I am honored to write this book alongside two godly leaders I respect: Matt and Josh. God has used their faith to build mine, and I am grateful for the friendship. I am thankful for a small group of friends of lead/executive pastors who have sharpened me in recent years: Josh, Kevin Peck, David Thompson, and Steve Miller. Working alongside several great theological and publishing minds at LifeWay has served me well already. Thanks to Trevin Wax, Michael Kelley, Sam O'Neal, Alyssa Jones, Micah Carter, and Daniel Davis for your feedback and editing help. In particular, I want to thank Jedidiah Coppenger for his tireless work and commitment to this project.

CONTENTS

CHAPTER 1: A People Formed. 1

CHAPTER 2: The Creature Worships. 22

CHAPTER 3: The Creature in Community. 45

CHAPTER 4: The Creature Serves. 64

CHAPTER 5: The Creature Multiplies. 82

CHAPTER 6: Jesus-Centered Culture. 94

CHAPTER 7: Preaching the Word 119

CHAPTER 8: Pulpit to Preschool (and Puberty Too) 137

CHAPTER 9: The Jesus-Centered Leader. 157

CHAPTER 10: Jesus-Centered Flower Committee 177

CHAPTER 11: Jesus-Centered Contextualization 198

CHAPTER 12: Jesus-Centered Ministry 213

Conclusion. 235

Notes 237

CHAPTER 1

A PEOPLE FORMED

It is the promises of God that make the church, and not the church that makes the promises of God.

~ MARTIN LUTHER[1]

PASTOR BARRY PULLS INTO HIS driveway at exactly 12:21 early Sunday afternoon, wondering, *How is it that I always arrive home from church at the exact same time every single week?*

His day thus far has occurred with the same clockwork precision as all his other Sundays. He rose early to look over his sermon notes. Kissed his kids good-bye shortly after they woke. Hustled off to church for his morning routine: a brief sound check, a walk around the facility, a time of customary prayer with a few men in the church before leading his "pastor's class."

And though he prayed with several more friends immediately before the worship service, he'd be embarrassed to admit he didn't really expect anything special to happen that morning. Just preaching his usual sermon to the usual people—same as last week, same as every week—people who seem unmoved, a church that appears to be barren.

After the worship services, he stood in the back and shook the hands of people he loves and others he tolerates, receiving the same type of casual compliments he hears every week, along with the same few hugs and the same few suggestions.

The same. The same. Always the same.

Even sitting here in his driveway like this, staring at these same green numbers on the same dashboard clock, having plodded his way again through the same routine, everything's playing out the same as every other Sunday. Everything except this . . .

He would usually be out of the car and inside by now, if the pattern held true. But today, something's different. The passage he'd just preached this morning is still resonating in his heart, lingering more powerfully than usual. Matthew 16—about Jesus' promise to build His church, punctuated by the phrase: "the gates of Hades will not overcome it" (v. 18 NIV). That line, that thought, still messing with his mind.

When Jesus spoke of His Church withstanding the gates of Hades, surely this is not what He envisioned—a church without life.

Barry thinks back to his first encounters with Matthew 16 as a young pastor, back when he was convinced that the churches he'd be called to lead throughout his ministry would become unstoppable movements of grace, threatening the very gates of Hades. But today his youthful belief seems replaced by a sinking feeling in his gut, enough that he's started to seriously consider doing something else with his life—not because his love for Jesus has waned, but just because this is not what he envisioned when he committed to pastoring.

He longs for life. And this, well . . . this just feels dead. Like he's no longer alive. Inspiring little passion for God among the people in his church, little hunger to worship, little compassion for those in the community. Just a continual cycle of the same lifeless motions.

Why?

Several hours later, across town in a newer neighborhood, Pastor Chase pulls into his driveway. He's been running on adrenaline all day. Huge crowd at church this morning—a big response to the new teaching series his staff has been planning for weeks, one with an edgy title, a tightly produced sermon bumper video, and a crisp assortment of mass marketing packages. It's been a full, bustling day already.

Yet he feels empty inside. Because if next week is anything like past history, the attendance for Part Two of his splashy new teaching series will be way down, and the staff will immediately want to start strategizing for another big launch. Probably on sex. He wonders if his church will set the record for the number of sex series in one year.

Why does it take that? he wonders. *Why does everything have to be so forced, so fabricated, built on hype instead of substance? Why this emptiness inside after all the energy they'd generated in the past few hours?*

As he sits in his driveway, looking down at his cell phone, friends from his networks are already texting to see how "the big day" went. He knows what they're wanting to hear. Success in ministry still seems defined by Sunday attendance. And based on that scale, his is a growing ministry with attention from all around the country.

Why then does he feel so empty?

He thinks about some of his earlier teaching messages, ones where he knocked and rebuked empty religion and dead rituals. He wonders if his current ministry is just a newer, cooler version of what he once hated. Has he learned how to give the appearance of life without actually being alive? The outside looks so good. Lots of people. Lots of activity. But on the inside he senses minimal life change, minimal spiritual growth. And whatever little there is, it almost seems to happen accidentally amid all the buzz.

On the outside, Chase and Barry could not be any more different. One is wearing jeans with his shirt untucked; the other is still in his suit and tie. One is in an SUV with Coldplay blaring in the background; the other recently noticed the speakers have gone out in his old Camry. One enjoys sushi late at night; the other prefers meat and potatoes—at six, on the dot.

Yet they have much more in common than they realize.

Both men walk into their homes longing for more. One is tired of the deadness; the other is tired of the empty activity.

And what both men need, as well as both of their churches, is a return. They need to return to their first love. A simple, yet significant return to Jesus.

As God said to the church at Ephesus:

> I know your works, your labor, and your endur-
> ance, and that you cannot tolerate evil. You have tested
> those who call themselves apostles and are not, and you
> have found them to be liars. You also possess endurance
> and have tolerated many things because of My name
> and have not grown weary. But I have this against you:
> You have abandoned the love you had at first. Remem-
> ber then how far you have fallen; repent, and do the
> works you did at first. (Rev. 2:2–5 HCSB)

Like the church at Ephesus, Barry and Chase are good men for the most part. Both are faithful to their wives. They invest in their children. They work hard and are morally above reproach. Both have continued in the ministry despite difficult days, criticism, and disappointment.

But both of these pastors have slowly lost their awe for Jesus and His finished work. Intellectually, of course, they still hold firmly to the gospel. Each could easily share a snapshot of its truths without think-ing hard—a brief, biblical presentation of Jesus and His gracious gift of salvation. Yet they've both learned to rely on other things to form the center of their daily work, to motivate the life and activity of their churches. Their drift has not been one of overt rebellion but of an inner twisting of the heart, a loss of appreciation for the gospel and all its ramifications. Both could articulate the gospel well, but they don't view the essence of the gospel as the foundation for all of ministry.

And that's a huge difference—the difference between knowing the gospel and being consumed by the gospel, being defined by the gospel, being driven by the gospel. It's one thing to see the gospel as an important facet of one's ministry. It's quite another to hold firmly to it as the centerpiece for all a church is and does, to completely orbit around it.

The gospel. Though such a glorious thing, it's also such a simple thing—so simple we almost overlook it. Such a basic thing, we're tempted to feel as if we've somehow graduated beyond it. And yet without this simple thing, this basic thing—without the life-giving gospel driving and defining both us and our churches—there really isn't much of anything that makes us distinct and alive, nothing that other people, groups, and organizations aren't already doing.

And that's where our lives begin to intersect with these two men—where Barry and Chase's names dissolve into the name that's etched on the front of our own Bibles, the name of the guy who uses our deodorant every morning. Us. You. In your heart perhaps—if you're being very honest—you sense a loss of awe for the gospel, a failure to connect its power to your entire ministry. You'd admit you've become distracted by other motivators, impressed by other ways of measuring success and discerning direction.

There is a solution to the death and emptiness. A way back to where we started. But only by returning to a fascination with Christ.

And that's where we all can begin again.

"We were born," Tertullian explained, "for nothing but repentance."[2] As Martin Luther said, "To progress is always to begin again."[3] So here at this place of recognition and regret, we meet together to start a fresh journey into the heart of the gospel, prepared to be newly amazed by it, resolved to let its principles begin shaping how our churches worship, serve, and operate. For just as an individual must continually return to the grace of Jesus for satisfaction and sanctification, a local church must continually return to the gospel as well. Our churches must be fully centered on Jesus and His work, or else death and emptiness is certain, regardless of the worship style or sermon series. Without the gospel, everything in a church is meaningless. And dead.

Distributaries of Death

The 137-mile long Atchafalaya River is a distributary of the Mississippi River that meanders through south central Louisiana and empties into the Gulf of Mexico, serving as a significant source of income for the region because of the many industrial and commercial opportunities it offers. Yet as scenic, productive, and enriching as this river is, it owes all its strength—all of it—to the mighty Mississippi.

That's because a distributary doesn't have its own direct water source; it is an overflow of something else. So when the Mississippi is high, the Atchafalaya is high; and when the Mississippi is low, the Atchafalaya is low. What the Atchafalaya accomplishes depends wholly on something other than itself.

The Church is a lot like the Atchafalaya River. Anything of value she accomplishes is always tied to her source. So if she somehow loses connection with it—with her first love, the Living Word—she loses all power. She dries up and empties. If any church becomes fed by a less potent source, by some other supply system than the gospel of Christ, her level of transformative power is directly affected. It's like trying to overflow the banks of a river with a twelve-ounce bottle of water. Impossible. Pointless.

The Bible, of course, gives us good and right teaching on everything from sex to parenting to money to morals. All good things. Wonderful things. God's design and desire for all of life. But our ability to walk in these truths with freedom and joy—and our church's ability to lead people into this ongoing, abundant-life experience for themselves—is dependent on something else: an accurate and deep understanding of the gospel. *That is our Mississippi.*

Without a proper understanding of the gospel, people will miss the big biblical picture and all the joyful freedom that comes from living it. They will run from God in shame at their failures instead of running toward Him because of His mercy and grace.

Just as the river forms distributaries, the gospel forms the Church. The distributaries do not form the river, just as the Church does not form the gospel. When a church confuses the order, she loses her true effectiveness. When a church chooses something other than the river of the gospel as the driving force behind her teaching, programming, staffing, and decisions, she empties herself of all power. Instead of becoming a distributor of life, she becomes a distributary of death. She doesn't really have anything else to offer.

That's why we've felt a significant amount of joy in watching what appears to be a resurgence in gospel thinking, writing, and preaching in recent days. When Michael Horton, Trevin Wax, J.D. Greear, Tullian Tchividjian, Greg Gilbert, and a host of others write books explicitly on the gospel, we're encouraged to think we're once again focusing on what is of "first importance."

In addition to books like these, we're seeing connections formed around initiatives like the Gospel Coalition, Together for the Gospel, and endless blogs and banter about the gospel. In all of this, we do need to be careful not to see the term *gospel* as a sort of junk drawer that holds any and every piece of our theology. Although the gospel does impact everything, everything is not the gospel. If everything about Jesus and the Bible becomes "the gospel" to us, then we end up being gospel-confused rather than gospel-centered. That's why we've chosen to use "The Jesus-Centered Church" instead of "The Gospel-Centered Church" as the subtitle of this book. The gospel centers us on Jesus' person and work or it isn't the gospel . . . and it isn't where our first love should be. Ultimately, the gospel is not a nebulous or ethereal concept, but Jesus Himself.

The gospel. What is it, really? In its simplest form, *the gospel is God's reconciling work in Christ—that through the life, death, and resurrection of Christ, God is making all things new both personally for those who repent and believe, and cosmically as He redeems culture and creation from its subjection to futility.*

And that's what this book is about—the Church and the huge implications of this glorious gospel upon her.

Sadly, as in the case with Pastor Barry and Pastor Chase, a big gap exists between understanding the gospel and understanding what the gospel means for the Church. Perhaps this is largely because we tend to think of the gospel as an *individual* message that causes *individual* transformation—which is partially true. But the gospel is much more than that. The gospel also forms the church. Scripture says Jesus "gave himself up" for the Church (Eph. 5:25 ESV), buying the Church "with his own blood" (Acts 20:28 ESV), in order "to redeem us from all lawlessness and to purify for himself a people for his own possession who are zealous for good works" (Titus 2:14 ESV). The gospel needs to be seen in this total perspective.[4]

The gospel is, of course, for individuals—yes—and it should and ultimately does cause transformation in the life of every person who believes on the Lord Jesus. However, that's only part of what God is accomplishing in His plans to make all things new. And we cannot afford to forget it.

Watching the Story Unfold

When I (Matt) was six years old, my dad took us to see *The Empire Strikes Back,* the second installment in the original *Star Wars* trilogy. I have no memory of seeing the first film, which might have given me some context for what I was seeing, but this one just confused me. It seemed like the bad guys were winning at every turn, and Luke (the eventual hero) actually bothered me more than he inspired me. Even at the age of six, I was turned off by his whiny attitude and easily breakable spirit. He almost had me rooting for the Empire instead. I found myself pulling for the ruthless, powerful Darth Vader to hurry up and kill Luke so that Han Solo (the far more manly and capable of the two) could emerge as the new hero. Little did I know I was being set up for another movie that would come out three years later (followed by three more, of course, two *decades* later).

Genesis 3 is kind of like *The Empire Strikes Back*—a heartbreaking chapter of the Bible where the bad guys appear to have won a decisive victory. Sin has fractured the "shalom" of the universe. Everything that God had declared "good" is now broken and tainted, and the crown jewel of creation is in outward rebellion, hopelessly broken.

But Genesis 3 is not how the story ends.

God had told Adam and Eve they would die if they ate from the tree of the knowledge of good and evil, yet they ate its fruit anyway, bringing spiritual and physical death into the creative order. But not only did God provide a way to clothe their shame and nakedness by slaughtering an animal and crafting garments for them to wear, He also added the whisper of a promise within this dark chapter, declaring that He would one day make all things right again.

God said to the serpent (to Satan, the embodiment of evil, deceit, and death), "I will put enmity between you and the woman, and between your offspring and her offspring; he shall bruise your head, and you shall bruise his heel" (Gen. 3:15 ESV). A man would come, God promised, born of woman, who would crush the head of the enemy once and for all. Yes, this man would be wounded in the process. But the "heel strike" He endured would be nothing compared to the death blow inflicted on His enemy's head.

Time went on and the story continued with God unfolding more and more of how His restoration of all things would occur. In Genesis 12, He came to a man named Abram to give this startling command and promise:

> "Go from your country and your kindred and your
> father's house to the land that I will show you. And I

> will make of you a great nation, and I will bless you and
> make your name great, so that you will be a blessing. I
> will bless those who bless you, and him who dishonors
> you I will curse, and in you all the families of the earth
> shall be blessed." (vv. 1–3 ESV)

Make sure you don't miss this, because it's very significant. God spoke and through His Word formed a "nation"—a people!—not just individuals but an entire community of faith. Yes, His promised One was still set to come at a definite point in history to crush the head of the enemy and restore peace to creation, but He would do so by first creating a covenant community of faith, a people of His own possession.

Israel was to be a picture of what life should look like when a group of people submit with gladness to God. He would govern everything for them through His law, lining them up with how He designed the universe to work, allowing the rest of the nations to see their joy and to recognize His glory. God gave His people laws about marriage, business, relationships, sex, parenting, worship, and even agriculture, not merely as isolated points of emphasis but as insights into His larger purposes and plans, to unify their corporate lives around His grand story of redemption.

Continuing along in the Old Testament, we see Israel unable to follow God's good and right commands—rebelling against Him, refusing Him, in certain seasons even mocking and belittling Him. God rightly judged and disciplined His dearly loved people, as all good fathers do, but He never strayed from the promise He made to Abraham: that all the families of the earth would be blessed through Israel. This was an early hint of the gospel "mystery" that was there for the understanding to anyone "with ears to hear." Repeatedly throughout the Old Testament, God would remind His people through the prophets that the salvation coming to them was intended for all nations, not just the Jewish people. Consider Isaiah 60:3–5:

> And the Gentiles shall come to thy light, and kings
> to the brightness of thy rising. Lift up thine eyes round
> about, and see: all they gather themselves together, they
> come to thee: thy sons shall come from far, and thy
> daughters shall be nursed at thy side. Then thou shalt
> see, and flow together, and thine heart shall fear, and
> be enlarged; because the abundance of the sea shall be
> converted unto thee, the forces of the Gentiles shall
> come unto thee. (KJV)

Israel, of course, was thinking nationally and ethnically much like some still think of the gospel today, primarily in individual terms. Yet God was reminding His ancient people they were thinking way too small. Which means we think even smaller. Truly, God's plan of redemption is about more than me and you and our neighbor down the street. It's about men and women from every tribe, tongue, and nation on earth becoming a part of His covenant community.

This story of reconciliation continued rolling forward as Jesus was born, fulfilling all the prophetic words of who the Messiah would be: born in the line of David (2 Sam. 7:12) by way of Abraham (Gen. 49); born of a virgin (Isa. 7:14) in Bethlehem (Micah 5:2); ministering primarily from Galilee (Isa. 9:1); acquainted with suffering and sorrow (Isa. 53); and finally resurrected in glory (Ps. 16:8–11). "These are my words that I spoke to you while I was still with you," Jesus said before returning to the Father, "that everything written about me in the Law of Moses and the Prophets and the Psalms must be fulfilled" (Luke 24:44 ESV). And even as He spoke these words, "He opened their minds to understand the Scriptures" (v. 45 ESV), showing the men on the road to Emmaus that the Old Testament promises of a Messiah—not only to Israel but to all peoples of the earth—were fulfilled in Him.

Stop for a second now and think about Luke 24 in the context of Genesis 3—a bit of time-travel my six-year-old mind couldn't pull off while watching the Empire strike back "a long time ago in a galaxy far, far away." God promised in Genesis 3 to restore what was broken from the fall. And as biblical history revealed, He would do it through a man who came into a community of faith to serve and reflect the glory of God to the rest of the world, fulfilling all the law of Moses, the words of the prophets, and the expressions of the Psalms along the way.

Ask yourself: Does this sound like a logical place then for this enormous, redemptive plan of the ages to suddenly become a purely individualistic pursuit, somehow separate from a body of people who are called into eternal, covenantal unity with Him?

What happens next answers that question for us.

A Creature of the Word

After Jesus' ascension, the disciples went into an upper room. And prayed. And waited. Waited and prayed. While they were praying, on the day of Pentecost, the Holy Spirit came upon them . . . and all heaven broke loose. This mob of misfits who had struggled to understand what Jesus had taught and explained, this cluster of cowards who had fled when Jesus was arrested and tried, this pack of junior-varsity rejects who had argued with Jesus were laid low by the manifesting power of the Spirit. The wind and fire of that divinely inspired Pentecost removed much of what had hindered them from boldly following Him, and they began "to speak in other tongues as the Spirit gave them utterance" (Acts 2:4 ESV).

The Bible goes on to describe a chaotic scene that most of us wouldn't welcome on Sunday morning in our quaint, little services, and fewer of us can fully get our minds around—Jews from "every nation under heaven" (v. 5 ESV) hearing this rough band of Galileans (a region not known as a hotbed of intellectual insight) speaking in the languages of everyone present. It was enough to leave the people "amazed and astonished" (v. 7 ESV)—or certain that these followers of Jesus had been soaking their sadness in an early-morning binge of adult beverages.

Into the middle of this messy scene, Peter (who else?) stood up to address the crowd, informing the Jewish throng in town for an otherwise staid religious observance that the disciples were most definitely not drunk. Rather, this was the fulfillment of what God had spoken through the prophet Joel, who said that in these "last days" God would "pour out" His Spirit on His people (v. 17 ESV). And by the time Peter finished his impassioned sermon, complete with a fitting explanation for the recent death and resurrection of Christ—a gospel message—some three thousand people were "cut to the heart" (v. 37 ESV), repented of their sins, received the Holy Spirit, and were baptized.

And look what naturally followed . . .

> They devoted themselves to the apostles' teach-
> ing and the fellowship, to the breaking of bread and
> the prayers. And awe came upon every soul, and
> many wonders and signs were being done through the
> apostles. And all who believed were together and had all
> things in common. And they were selling their pos-
> sessions and belongings and distributing the proceeds
> to all, as any had need. And day by day, attending the
> temple together and breaking bread in their homes,
> they received their food with glad and generous hearts,
> praising God and having favor with all the people. And
> the Lord added to their number day by day those who
> were being saved. (Acts 2:42–47 ESV)

Yes, they clearly repented and believed as individuals, but the Scriptures immediately begin to talk of them as a group:

- They devoted themselves to teaching.
- Awe came on every soul, on the whole gathering.

- All who believed came together, sharing all things in common.
- They attended the temple together.
- They shared meals together.

That's because the Word, the gospel, creates not just *people* individually, but *a people,* collectively. The gospel isn't just individual and cosmic; it is also deeply corporate.

There's a reason why teachers are drawn to this text when the topic of biblical community comes up. Whether we're talking about Sunday school, small groups, missional communities, or just a gathering of people with spiritual intent, what we see in Acts 2:42–47 becomes the hope of what our fellowships could and should look like. The deepest hope of many Christian leaders is that our people would engage one another at this level, knowing that God never intended us to grow our faith in isolation but rather within a community of faith called "the church."

With their individual gifts, resources, and levels of faith, these early believers built one another up into maturity. They encouraged one another, blessed one another, rebuked one another, disciplined one another, outdid one another in showing honor, taught one another, and trained one another in the gospel. All over the ancient world, churches were planted in an eerily similar way: "Repeatedly in Acts, the growth of the Church is attributed to the fact that 'the word of God spread' and 'prevailed' (Acts 6:7; 13:49; 19:20)."[5] So like Israel before it, the Church became the picture of what life should look like when a group of people submit with gladness to how God designed the universe to work. By carefully watching what happens in Acts 2 and beyond, we see it's really not all that different from what God was already talking about in Genesis 12. He had stayed with His plan to reconcile all things to Himself individually and cosmically through His Son—and through a people.

In Acts 2, the Word of God formed a people yet again.

This awesome reality—the fact that God spoke the Church into existence—would later lead the Reformers to call the Church "the Creature of the Word." What they meant was that the Church is not a human invention or institution; it was birthed from God's Word. God spoke and created the universe. God spoke to Abraham and created Israel; and in the same way, God created the Church through the proclaimed gospel of the revealed Word, Jesus Christ.

Martin Luther spoke and wrote passionately about this truth, instilling in those who heard him an understanding that the Church did not form the gospel but was formed (and must be continually formed) by the gospel. He wrote:

> The church was born by the word of promise through faith, and by this same word is nourished and preserved. That is to say, it is the promises of God that make the church and not the church that makes the promise of God. For the Word of God is incomparably superior to the church, and in this Word the church, being a Creature, has nothing to decree, ordain, or make, but only to be decreed, ordained, and made. For who begets his own parent?[6]

Without the Word of God, we don't have a covenant community of faith. The gospel precedes the Church, informs the life of the Church, and sustains the growth of the Church. Michael Horton helps us understand how the Word gives birth not only to us but also to the Church, when he writes:

> The new birth, as part of the new creation, is effected *in* the church (i.e., through its ministry of the Word), but not *by* the church. The individual does not give birth to him- or herself, nor does the community give birth to itself; both are born from above (John 3:3–5). The origin and source of the church's existence

is neither the autonomous self nor the autonomous church: "So then it depends not on human will or exertion, but on God, who has mercy" (Rom. 9:16). Where there is God's Word and Spirit, there is faith, and where there is faith there is a church.[7]

The Word of God went out in Holy Spirit power, granting the gift of faith in the hearts of men to believe in the grace offered in Jesus. When that gift of faith was extended, men were saved and the Church was formed.

The Creature Sustained and Shaped

A big question needs to be answered before we can move on. And if we can't answer it, we're in big trouble. This is it: What makes the Church able to succeed where the Israelites so often failed? Martin Luther and Tim Keller explain:

> It is an absolute and unique teaching in all the world to teach people, through Christ, to live as if there were no law or wrath or punishment. In a sense, they [these laws] do not exist any longer for the Christian but only total grace and mercy for Christ's sake. Once you are in Christ, the law is the greatest guide for your life, but until you have Christian righteousness, all the law can do is show you how sinful and condemned you are.[8]

The Church now has the power of the Holy Spirit and the manifest grace of Christ, having been set free from guilt and shame by the imputed righteousness and wrath-absorbing death of Christ. So no longer should the fear of rejection and God's vengeance be the motivating factors in our pursuit of holiness, but rather the delight of being loved, pursued, and saved by a gracious Father whose "kindness leads us to repentance" (Rom. 2:4 ESV).

That's a gospel difference.

Like children whose father delights in them, we can run to our Father knowing that nothing can "separate us from the love that is in Christ Jesus" (Rom. 8:38–39 HCSB). We can approach His throne with confidence—not confidence in ourselves but in Christ, who has fulfilled the requirements of the law for us. And this is why the Church succeeds, maturing by the power of God's Spirit working in and through the Word as He massages it deeply into the life of His body. A church is alive and full when she is sustained by the sacrifice and resurrection of Christ and is drawn back to that precious reality again and again, every time she gathers.

So . . . if challenged to give an answer for why we've lost a great deal of our power as the Church, one of the major reasons we'd give is this: our misunderstanding about what the gospel actually does. We seem to have developed gospel amnesia, forgetting that the gospel not only creates and sustains the Church but also deeply shapes the Church. Present and future.

All of the Epistles in the New Testament were written to Christians, and they each contain a heavy emphasis on the gospel and its implications for the people of God. This suggests that for churches who *believe* the gospel, the Spirit of God repeatedly wants to bring them *back* to the gospel. It means the Church is gospel-centric in its existence. She must not move on from the gospel, must never graduate from the gospel. The gospel, in fact, provides our ongoing, day-by-day motivation to pursue holiness and to experience the reality of what God claims we already are in Christ: perfect, spotless, and blameless.

How does the gospel do this, though—not only save but also sanctify? The pattern we see in Scripture is an *indicative/imperative* pattern. Notice that whenever a command is given in the Scriptures (an imperative)—in either the Old or New Testament—it is attached to a "why" (an indicative) for obeying that command. Here are some examples:

Leviticus 20:7–8 (ESV): "Consecrate yourselves, therefore, and be holy [*imperative*], for I am the LORD your
God [*indicative*]. Keep my statutes and do them [*imperative*]; I am the LORD who sanctifies you [*indicative*]."

Luke 6:36 (NIV): "Be merciful [*imperative*], just as
your Father is merciful [*indicative*]."

1 John 4:12 (ESV): "If we love one another [*imperative*], God abides in us, and his love is perfected in us
[*indicative*]."

Hebrews 10:19–25 (NIV): "Therefore, brothers,
since we have confidence to enter the Most Holy Place
by the blood of Jesus, by a new and living way opened
for us through the curtain, that is, his body, and since
we have a great priest over the house of God [*indicative*], let us draw near to God with a sincere heart in
full assurance of faith, having our hearts sprinkled to
cleanse us from a guilty conscience and having our bodies washed with pure water. Let us hold unswervingly
to the hope we profess, for he who promised is faithful.
And let us consider how we may spur one another on
toward love and good deeds. Let us not give up meeting
together, as some are in the habit of doing, but let us
encourage one another—and all the more as you see the
Day approaching [*imperative*]."

1 Peter 2:9 (ESV): "But you are a chosen race, a
royal priesthood, a holy nation, a people for his own
possession [*indicative*], that you may proclaim the excel-
lences of him who called you out of darkness into his
marvelous light [*imperative*]."

1 Peter 2:10–12 (ESV): "Once you were not a
people, but now you are God's people; once you had
not received mercy, but now you have received mercy

[*indicative*]. Beloved, I urge you as sojourners and exiles to abstain from the passions of the flesh, which wage war against your soul. Keep your conduct among the Gentiles honorable, so that when they speak against you as evildoers, they may see your good deeds and glorify God on the day of visitation [*imperative*]."

2 Peter 1:3–7 (ESV): "His divine power has granted to us all things that pertain to life and godliness, through the knowledge of him who called us to his own glory and excellence, by which he has granted to us his precious and very great promises, so that through them you may become partakers of the divine nature, having escaped from the corruption that is in the world because of sinful desire [*indicative*]. For this very reason, make every effort to supplement your faith with virtue, and virtue with knowledge, and knowledge with self-control, and self-control with steadfastness, and steadfastness with godliness, and godliness with brotherly affection, and brotherly affection with love [*imperative*]."

1 John 4:19 (ESV): "We love [*imperative*] because he first loved us [*indicative*]."

This pattern becomes incredibly important for the Church, always to be viewed through the lens of the gospel. If we don't see this pattern, we are at risk of buying into a false gospel that seems adequate to save us but then sends us back to the law to be sanctified or made holy.

Our motivation to obey the commands (or imperatives) of Scripture can finally become a delight when we see that the reasons (the indicatives) almost always center around God's love and provision for us in Christ. Through the gospel, the Holy Spirit empowers our motivations so that we are driven with gladness, not guilt, being ever reminded of our forgiveness in the gospel, not our failures in the law. It is God's ability, not ours. Again and again . . . and always.

We are created by, sustained by, and empowered by something other than ourselves. *By the gospel of Christ.* What the Mississippi River is to the Atchafalaya River, the gospel is to the Church.

> At issue is the kingdom of God among us. Because the kingdom of God has the concrete form of fellowship with God and others, the gospel as the message of reconciliation to God must everywhere lead to the founding of congregations that have among themselves a fellowship that provisionally and symbolically represents the world-embracing fellowship of the kingdom of God that is the goal of reconciliation. The fellowship of the church that the gospel establishes is thus a sign and a provisional form of the humanity that is reconciled in the kingdom of God—the humanity that is the goal of the event of reconciliation in the expiatory death of Jesus Christ. The gospel thus takes precedence over the church. . . . Though the gospel is proclaimed in the church and by its leaders, it is not a product of the church; rather, the gospel is the source of the church's existence. The proclamation of the gospel, then, is not merely one thing among others in the church's life. It is the basis of the church's life. The church is a Creature of the Word.[9]

"The Church is a Creature of the Word . . ."

Yes, a Creature. She is alive. A living, breathing movement of God's people redeemed and placed together in collective community. But she is not alive in her own doing. She has been made alive by the Word. God spoke her into existence through the declaration of the gospel—His righteousness on our behalf.

The more a church is tapped into the gospel, the more transformative power will be present by the Holy Spirit in that church. But the more that church gets away from the centrality of the gospel, the more a church will run on fumes, seeing people conformed to a pattern of religion rather than transformed by the Spirit of God.

All that the Lord commands is good and right. There is no word wasted in the inerrant Word of God. But we must always proclaim the Scripture with the gospel at its heart or we will set people up for failure, teaching them to continue trying to earn what's already been freely given.

Try this sentence on for size. A church that understands where its power comes from is a place *where individuals are transformed and empowered to join God's corporate family and participate in God's plan to reconcile all things to Himself.* Did you see all the pieces there? Individual salvation and transformation leads to a corporate identity, which is then used by God to redeem, restore, and reconcile all things in heaven and on earth by making peace through the blood of His cross.

And all by the gospel.

In the first half of this book, we will look at what the gospel does to the hearts of people, their relationships, and how they understand their position and purpose. We will discover that the Creature God formed—the Church—is a Creature that worships, lives in community, serves, and multiplies, while God simultaneously sanctifies His Church more and more as she practices these things. In His wisdom, God has ordained worship, community, service, and multiplication that is centered on Jesus to mature and develop His people.

After we have encountered the beauty of this " Creature" centered on Jesus, we will move on in the second half to what a Jesus-centered culture looks like, how it is formed and sustained. A church that is centered on Jesus looks more and more like Jesus. And since Jesus is the perfect Prophet-King-Priest, the church will begin to more faithfully and effectively carry out these prophetic-kingly-priestly functions. While these roles should not be utilized in a way that excludes one from another, they do provide a helpful and biblical framework for shaping a "Jesus-Centered Church." By God's grace, we will offer practical thoughts on letting the gospel shape the life of a local church so that we might be more aligned with the mighty, life-giving river of the gospel.

Let's continually return to our first love.

To our Christ and His gospel.

CHAPTER 2

THE CREATURE WORSHIPS

Hallelujah!

~ Psalm 150 (HCSB)

On May 27, 2009, the world's largest worship venue opened in Arlington, Texas, a suburb of Dallas. With close to 30,000 parking spaces, the ability to hold 110,000 people, a state-of-the-art sound system, and a gigantic center-hung, high-definition television screen that measures 160 x 72 feet, it is the perfect location to gather, sing, shout, cry, clap, and feel the energy that occurs when that many souls come together with the same hope in mind.

What church does this massive edifice belong to? It must be the Baptists or charismatics, right? Who else has that kind of coin? No, the owner of this $1.33 billion monster in Arlington with its retractable roof and almost limitless possibilities for usage is none other than Jerry Jones, owner of the Dallas Cowboys. And all year long, whether for a concert, motocross event, tractor pull, or football game, men and women flood into the stadium ready to support and cheer on their favorite team, band, or player. They've come for one reason and one reason alone. They have come to . . . *rejoice!*

Rejoice is a simple yet serious word, meaning to celebrate, cheer, exult, or delight in. One synonym for rejoice is *worship*, and we were each created by God to do so, hardwired by our Creator for it. And thus, even those men and women who don't enjoy worshipping their Maker can sometimes be seen with their bodies painted in team colors, becoming emotionally affected for hours, sometimes days, by how the game went on a particular Saturday or Sunday, or Monday night, or Thursday night. They're ready for worship any day of the week—morning, noon, or evening. But, their hearts are yielded to lesser things.

Because we humans are worshippers, we are rejoicers. It's what we do. Every single person, whether religious or irreligious, actively worships. They have identified something bigger than themselves that they believe is worthy of their money, time, and the meditations of their hearts. In many ways, they have offered themselves as sacrifices to that "something," whatever it is. It comes naturally to them. Easily. Enjoyably.

But in our sinfulness, this tendency to worship things other than God is an exercise in disappointment. It offers us nothing but temporary satisfaction while simultaneously bringing down God's judgment upon us (Eccl. 11:9). Since we are worshippers by God's design, the problem is not that we rejoice but rather that we rejoice wrongly. In the book of Romans, Paul writes:

> For although they knew God, they did not honor him as God or give thanks to him, but they became futile in their thinking, and their foolish hearts were darkened. Claiming to be wise, they became fools, and exchanged the glory of the immortal God for images resembling mortal man and birds and animals and

creeping things. . . . They exchanged the truth of God
for a lie, and worshiped and served something created
instead of the Creator who is forever praised. (Rom.
1:21–23, 25 ESV and HCSB)

Simply put, we prefer creation to the Creator.

So in essence, sin is a fundamental failure to rejoice in what we
should rejoice in. Our worship has to be redeemed and rescued from
futile things. Rather than rejoicing in our Creator—the Creator of all
that exists—we rejoice in and serve shallow, temporary things that are
here one moment and gone the next. The reason some of us swing from
elation to despair so easily is that we rejoice wrongly. Our worshipping
is in the wrong place. We spend too much of our energy and vitality
on the wrong thing.

Yet God, because He created us for worship, pursues our worship.
The first commandment listed in the Ten Commandments is God
instructing His people to worship only Him. He said to the Jewish
people in Exodus 20 (with major implications to all of us):

"I am the LORD your God, who brought you out
of Egypt, out of the land of slavery. You shall have no
other gods before me. You shall not make for yourself
an idol in the form of anything in heaven above or on
the earth beneath or in the waters below. You shall not
bow down to them or worship them; for I, the LORD
your God, am a jealous God." (vv. 2–5 NIV)

Out of slavery. Delivered into freedom. By His own gracious hand.
Sounds a lot like the gospel, doesn't it.

Prior to giving the command to have "no other gods," God
reminded the people who He is and what He has done. His demand
and desire for worship were based on His character and the fact that
He had rescued these people from bondage. He was worthy, He said,
of their rejoicing in Him.

Martin Luther articulated that the first commandment appears first because it is the foundation for all the other commandments. He said that if we keep the first commandment, we will keep all the others. And if we break another commandment, it is because we have already broken the first commandment.[1] For example, if you break the commandment to "not give false testimony," it is because you have rejoiced in something other than God, something that seems worthy of your lies. If you break the commandment not to covet, you have first elevated the thing you are coveting as the object of your affection. You have made it your god. Luther wrote, "Under every behavioral sin is the sin of idolatry."[2] When we sin, we are ultimately worshipping something other than God, placing an idol on the throne of our lives.

We tend to think of idolatry as expressing adoration to false gods, bowing down to carved, graven images. Perhaps when you hear the word *idolatry*, you conjure up images of people in distant lands singing and dancing before their statues. And that is certainly part of it. But idolatry is more relevant to us and our own experiences than we like to believe. Puritan pastor David Clarkson, in his sermon entitled "Soul Idolatry," identified the presence of external idols (those we outwardly bow to) and inward idols (those we revere in our heart).[3] Our inward idols—be they greed, lust, prestige, or whatever—are the ones that are most offensive to God because He is ultimately concerned about who we are on the inside. He insists on being the center of our hearts, the One in whom we rejoice.

Throughout this chapter, we'll look at this issue of Jesus-centered worship by taking notes from Jesus' encounter with the woman at the well in John 4, where He begins to reveal the barriers that keep us from genuine, soul-satisfying, awe-inspiring, eternal worship of God. By the Spirit's power, may we learn to avoid the pitfalls of lifeless, manipulative worship, or of leading our people into worship based on anything less than gospel realities. May we realize more clearly Who we worship, why He calls us to worship, and how we can achieve greater freedom as a church in expressing our worship.

Barrier #1: The Wrong Wells

The Samaritan woman had a question or two for Jesus when He offered her a taste of water more refreshing and long lasting than the water that came from this particular well. "Are You greater than Jacob?" she seemed to say. "Are You too good for this well? Jacob and his sons drank from this well. Aren't You a Jew? The livestock of Your people for generations have drunk from this well. All that Israel was built upon drank from this well. Are You better than that?"

Truth is, Jesus basically said, there were flaws with this well. "It doesn't work long-term. It only helps for a moment, then you have to come back for more." The contrast was simple: her well never quenched her thirst for long; His well, however, would satisfy forever. Then as now, drinking from the wrong well becomes a serious problem of supply and demand.

In our Western culture, we consistently dip our buckets into three wells that promise to leave us feeling satisfied. And even though we know they're lying to us—every time—we keep coming back, hoping against hope they'll finally be telling us the truth.

The most predominant is the well of *money and comfort*. Not just money, because very few people hoard money just for money's sake. It's money *and* comfort.

New stuff is nice. Almost intoxicating, isn't it? We feel an emotive response to trinkets and toys, to new gadgets and gear. But especially in our day and age, when new becomes old very, very quickly, the high of a new purchase barely has time to wear off before we want to feed it something newer. So we go from trinket to toy, to trinket to toy, from new thing to new thing. We keep drawing from that well. It feels good for a second. Those new clothes, that new house, that new car, whatever we collect. Everything that's unsettled in our soul feels settled for a moment. But deep inside, we know we're holding the stuff of future garage sales. We know we're drinking sand. The well of money and comfort always does that to us. It's never enough.

The second is the well of *relationships and sex*. These desires, of course, are not intrinsically evil or wrong. Like money and comfort, they are gifts from a good God. But like everything, they can steer us off track when we elevate them beyond what God created them for, when the gifts become gods.

That's what we've done with sex and relationships. We have perverted these blessings from God, the Author and Creator of these gifts, and have elevated them beyond their assigned place, leaving nothing for ourselves but heartache and disappointment.

We simply ask too much of our relationships. Women—you'll never find a man who completes you. Regardless of what the TV shows and movies promise you, no one can fix what's broken in your heart. If you had a man who thought of nothing but you, how to romance you, how to love and encourage you, you would still be empty. If you came home every day to rose petals on the floor, a house your husband had cleaned while you were away, his chiseled physique leaning over the changing table finishing up the care of another dirty diaper, you would eventually think, "Gah, why does he keep doing this with the roses? Does he think I'm an idiot? He doesn't think I can even change a diaper?" You'd begin to wish he would be somebody else, would do things differently.

No man is enough. You need a Savior.

And men—if you came home each evening to a woman who was skimpily dressed, presenting you a platter with a freshly grilled steak, having sequestered the kids to their rooms so you could watch football uninterrupted till bedtime, you would still be empty if you thought you could find all your satisfaction in her . . . because your heart is broken. And over time, you would begin to fantasize about a salad and some other woman.

She can't fix you. No woman can. You need a Savior. None of us can go to this well expecting to find the answers to our deepest thirsts.

A third empty well we commonly employ is that of *respect and success*. We want approval. We want acceptance. We want other people to look at us and be impressed by what they see. We want to be pointed to as the example. We want to be shown respect. We feel like we are entitled to it. *We love this well.*

But that little pat on the back from other people is fleeting. The same guy who pats you on the back today will turn around and stab you in the back tomorrow. The encouragement we received from that girlfriend of ours will quickly turn into gossip about our weaknesses. This well just doesn't hold up.

When Jesus extended the offer of water that would quench thirst once and for all, He was offering us affirmation, acceptance, and approval that goes far beyond what any human can give. What more affirmation do we need than the cross of Jesus Christ? How insignificant is a "good job, buddy," compared to the fact that God, knowing the absolute truth about you and your motivations, died on the cross for you. Man can approve and accept you without any knowledge of your motives. He may never spot the shady, sinful, selfish motives that lead you to perform your "good deeds." But God knows your wicked heart. And still, He died on the cross for you.

That's gospel truth.

That's worship material.

Your approval before God is woven into the life and sacrifice of Jesus Christ on the cross, not what other men and women think about you. In fact, living your life trying to please them becomes a form of slavery. Jesus went so far as to warn us, "Woe to you, when all people speak well of you, for so their fathers did to the false prophets" (Luke 6:26 ESV). "Be nervous," He was sort of saying, "if everyone loves you. They persecuted Me, and they persecuted the prophets. This is what happens when you make a stand—what happened to Me. People get angry. They don't like you anymore." Jesus didn't need the approval of man, "for He Himself knew what was in man" (John 2:25 HCSB)—insincerity, false flattery, selfish interests, the fickle winds of change. *Never enough water to satisfy us.*

In the wisdom literature of the Bible, we find two stories that are vitally important to us in today's climate. The first is in the book of Job, where this righteous man loses everything, yet finds that God is enough. The second is from the book of Ecclesiastes, where King Solomon *gets* everything and finds that obtaining all you desire doesn't solve any soul issues.

Solomon's voice should be an alarm for us today. We should hear him screaming, "It doesn't work, I tell ya! I had three hundred wives—a different one for nearly every day and night of the year—and yet I was miserable! I built houses for all of them, I built my own mansion, I planted forests, I owned ranches and hilltop estates, I threw parties so big they were sung about and written about, and it was meaningless! All of it—meaningless!"

We will probably never be Job or Solomon. Our lives will most likely fluctuate somewhere between the extreme experiences of these two men. Most of us, for example, are never going to be wealthy or powerful enough to come to Solomon's conclusion on our own. We will always have something more to pursue, something new to acquire, some ungranted wish we're trying to crank up out of that well in hopes that it will bring us life.

But it's not going to work. The wrong wells never do. And our worship suffers because we keep going back to them.

Barrier #2: Unconfessed Sin

Not only do we have the tendency to drink from empty wells, we also have the proclivity to live with unconfessed sin. In the woman at the well, we see our own foolish ability to deny the impact of our sin, hold on to our sin, and try to cover up our sin.

> Jesus said to her, "Go, call your husband, and come here." The woman answered him, "I have no husband." Jesus said to her, "You are right in saying, 'I have no

husband'; for you have had five husbands, and the one
you now have is not your husband. What you have said
is true." The woman said to him, "Sir, I perceive that
you are a prophet." (John 4:16–19 ESV)

With each of our kids, we have played the game "Hide and Seek."
We count to a certain number while they run off to "hide" in different
places, then at the announced moment, we "seek" to find them. But
all of our children have made a similar mistake over the years. They
have simply plopped down under a blanket on the floor or under a
chair that is fully exposed, closed their eyes, and assumed that because
they couldn't see *us*, we couldn't see *them*. As fathers, of course, we
play along and ask, "Where are you? Are you over here? Are you over
there?" The truth is, however, they're in plain sight and are hardly
hidden at all.

We often make the same mistake with God. Most of us try to
avoid the thought that God knows and sees everything about us. But
like a reality show star, we don't have any secrets. There is no place we
can go, not even in our own thoughts, where He is not present. And
to the natural-thinking mind, this is a problem. How are we supposed
to react to this invasive, 24/7 nature of God's knowledge about us?
We don't like it. We feel impinged by it. And therefore, we have this
hot-and-cold relationship with God—all because we've lost sight of the
gospel and have failed to understand its implications.

Sometimes being obedient to the commands of God seems fairly
easy. Temptation is manageable. We don't feel called upon to flex our
faith muscles much at all. We just trust Him. Following His direction
at times like these is not particularly difficult or weighty. But then
there are other times—times when we feel like God is asking us to do
the impossible, leading us to places we don't want to go. So instead of
trusting in His goodness and wisdom, we refuse like a strong-willed
child. Instead of finding our security and comfort in His sovereign

power, we run away from Him and try finding comfort in other things that don't ask so much of us.

It's important that you see the two-step movement here: running *from* Him while simultaneously running *toward* things that make matters worse—soothing the heat of conviction with accomplishments, food, movies, porn, whatever you think will give you temporary relief. Then when you feel like you're doing better, you'll run *back* to God, hoping He's forgotten what He originally told you to do. This ends up being a sad cycle for many of us.

But this cycle can stop for you because . . . (read this next sentence slowly) . . . *God has made provision for our sin in Christ.* So when we struggle to believe and obey, we should run *to* Him, not *from* Him— the opposite of our pattern, in contradiction to our feelings. Why? *Because He already knows!*

See, the gospel just keeps changing everything.

The cross should continually testify to us that God fully knew we would need to be justified. Therefore, unconfessed sin is actually the foolish decision to run *away from* our healing and growth rather than *toward* it. We hang on to things we believe will satisfy us, thinking we need those more than what God offers to provide.

But how can we rejoice in and worship the majesty of a loving and forgiving God if in practice we don't believe He loves and forgives, if in practice we don't believe the gospel? How can our churches rejoice and worship corporately when our collective energy is expended carrying around the saddle of unconfessed sin and shame? When people walk in honesty about their fears, shortcomings, and needs—not in thoughtless disobedience but in grace-based freedom and forgiveness—they reveal a deep understanding of the gospel. To confess our sins to one another is to violently pursue our own joy and the glory of God . . . and to exponentially increase our rejoicing and worship, both individually and corporately.

Barrier #3: Ignorance

Seeking satisfaction in the wrong wells and harboring unconfessed sin prohibit the worship that honors God and replenishes our souls. So, too, does ignorance. Jesus confronts and corrects this problem in the life of the Samaritan woman:

> "Our fathers worshiped on this mountain, but you say that in Jerusalem is the place where people ought to worship." Jesus said to her, "Woman, believe me, the hour is coming when neither on this mountain nor in Jerusalem will you worship the Father. You worship what you do not know; we worship what we know, for salvation is from the Jews." (John 4:20–22 ESV)

Most of us find the God of the Bible to be a bit too edgy for modern sensibilities. So instead of submitting to Him, we're drawn toward creating a "God" we like better, choosing to be ignorant of who He really is. We pull back on the wrathful, vengeful stuff, for instance—the God who's angry toward sin every day (Ps. 7:11). We feel that Jesus needs better PR—something along the lines of an "extreme makeover." Make Him friendlier, a bit whiter, give Him a happier disposition. He's not going to flip tables over anymore. He's not coming back with a tattoo on His thigh (Rev. 19:16), wielding a sword and filling the streets with blood. People don't want that kind of stuff—maybe in their movies, but not in their Maker. For many, Jesus is more like a masculine Tinker Bell, sprinkling pixie dust of love on everyone He meets. And who doesn't feel safe with Tinker Bell?

The problem, however, is that if we strip Jesus of His deity, we also strip Him of His authority and power. If we change our perception of who He actually is, we cannot be free to worship Him genuinely. We end up missing out on real depth of relationship with Him. Our churches end up with a God who is safe, but weak; domesticated, but limited.

So why do we do it, then? Why do people choose to be ignorant of the one true God, even at the cost of authentic, grateful worship?

The underlying motivation in creating a God other than the One we see in Scripture always boils down to the same, wishful falsehood: "I'm not as bad as the Bible says I am; besides, God would never really judge anyone because that would be wrong." And, sorry, that's just not gospel.

Worship always suffers when man is exalted and God is belittled. If you remove the fact that you're a sinner, if you elevate yourself to a more righteously entitled place, if you exalt yourself and think, "I'm not really all that bad; I'm kind of a good person," then your worship is going to suffer. If your church doesn't understand the nature of their sinful condition, they will be stunted in their adulation of salvation. By stripping away aspects of His power, we worship a God who isn't real. Every time we stray from the revealed Word of God—from the Mississippi River that fuels our spiritual power—we attest that we actually believe some aspects of these foolish statements.

Yet here's the paradoxical reality: *you are a rebellious, wicked sinner, and God has loved you in Christ.* In the gospel, these opposites go together. You retain no secrets from Him, and yet He has still pursued and saved you.

The people we serve need to be constantly reminded of that.

Jesus confronted the woman at the well with the fact that secrecy is a myth. God knows and yet has still chosen to extend mercy and grace in the cross. Worship flourishes when people know this—when we know who we are, know who He is, and then stare into that massive, terrifying gap that Jesus has filled with blood-bought grace and forgiveness. As Thomas Merton powerfully writes, "When sin becomes bitter, then Christ becomes sweet." Worship explodes from the nucleus of that reality, when the gospel truly informs our worship. It compels us to put no other god before Him . . . to magnify Him to the extinction of all rivals.

The more we hear and receive the gospel, the more the Spirit sanctifies us from empty wells, unconfessed sin, and deceptive ignorance. The more we become worshippers of the one true living God.

All-Around Worship

During His encounter with the woman, Jesus declared:

> "But the hour is coming, and is now here, when the true worshipers will worship the Father in spirit and truth, for the Father is seeking such people to worship him. God is spirit, and those who worship him must worship in spirit and truth." (John 4:23–24 ESV)

God is seeking people who will worship Him "in spirit and truth"—with both *inflamed hearts* and *informed minds*[4]—two things that seem almost opposed to each other, as if they were mutually exclusive. And yet when they are infused by the gospel, God causes them to nourish one another, both within ourselves and within our churches. We need (and can have) both.

Most people do typically have a disposition toward either end of this spectrum, toward either heart or mind, toward spirit or truth. Some are more intellectual, wanting a theological grid that lines out how God works, where we fit into His plan, and how all of life should function. They're not prone to emotions or to giving themselves over to expressive affections. In fact, they often view emotions as a danger that must be suppressed to a manageable level. They say things like, "What we need is truth, not feelings."

Other people have the opposite disposition. They say, "Are you kidding me? What we need to do is to hold hands, sing, and worship together. You guys always want to talk about doctrine and theology, which is all so cold and dead. That's what your problem is. You read too much. God never asked me to be a theologian. I just want to love Jesus with my whole heart."

Easy to go there and feel so justified in bashing theology, but the reality is that everybody is a theologian; some of us have just unwittingly become heretics. Everybody has an idea about who God is and how He works. Some are just, well . . . they're wrong, that's all. Because just as God has never asked you to be a brainiac, neither has He asked you to simply guess what He's like. He calls us to worship Him from *both* of these perspectives—in "spirit" *and* in "truth"—from hearts inflamed through minds informed by the revealed Word of God and the indwelling Holy Spirit.

By illuminating the text, the Spirit inflames our heart. And the inflamed heart then creates energy for the growing mind. Our intellect is not at odds with our faith, nor our faith at odds with our intellect. Understanding God's nature in a deep way should lead to an emotive response that creates an even deeper hunger to meditate on Him all the more. The mind and the heart feed each other. Mind to heart and then heart to mind.

And just as truth inspires spirit, and spirit calls for truth, our worship as *individuals* should constantly be seeking an outlet for worshipping *corporately*, which then leaves us wanting to worship everywhere we are.

Worship is in some ways organic and individualistic. After my (Matt's) conversion to Christ, a friend gave me a tape (that's right, a cassette tape—Google it) filled with songs of praise to God. I blared that thing in my car until my ears were ringing. Windows down. Hairdryer hotness whipping through my sleeves and messing up my hair. Sailing down the road, I just got after the Lord—just me and Him. No, my local church hadn't bought the tape for me. Giving them out to people wasn't some ministry program of theirs. It wasn't in my "membership covenant" with the church that I should turn up loud music in my car and worship the Lord at set times of the day. I was just a young guy being moved by the Spirit to enjoy Jesus, rejoice, and worship Him. Simple and natural as that.

And still today, I love worshipping God even when outside the typical corporate gathering of a church service. Almost every morning besides Saturday and Sunday, my wife and I get up, sit at our dining room table, and read, talk, and pray. *We worship.* At night before we go to bed, we gather our kids around the Bible as a family and read a chapter of it, sharing prayer requests. After prayer we all sing together—hosannas and praises and clapping hands and rejoicing. *Worshipping.* My local church doesn't drive that; my new heart in Christ is what drives it. But not only does this serve an individual purpose in my own, my wife's, and my children's lives, it continually connects us with times of corporate worship that expand our awe of Him more and more. Private worship excites us for times of public worship.

We can draw this parallel again from the woman at the well in John 4—

> So the woman left her water jar and went away
> into town and said to the people, "Come, see a man
> who told me all that I ever did. Can this be the Christ?"
> They went out of the town and were coming to him.
> (vv. 28–30 esv)

See the immediate change in her? This woman had been hiding for years in guilt and shame, as well as from the hostilities of other people in town. Imagine the things that must have been whispered about her as she walked through the streets—this five-timing woman, now with another on the side. Yet she met Jesus one day, who exposed her sin in a compassionate, forgiving way. Reborn, she was no longer inclined to hide anymore. Instead, she went running into town, rejoicing, free from bitterness and resentment toward those who had judged her harshly, entreating them to come, come hear the good news, saying to everyone who would listen, "You've got to come hear this guy. Let Him tell you what He told me. He told me everything about myself. You've got to come check this out." The whole state of her heart had shifted. She wasn't worshipping to hear herself worship. Worship was flowing out of her individually and leading her to herald it to others.

That's when something even more special occurred.

Many Samaritans from that town believed in him because of the woman's testimony, "He told me all that I ever did." So when the Samaritans came to him, they asked him to stay with them, and he stayed there two days. And many more believed because of his word. They said to the woman, "It is no longer because of what you said that we believe, for we have heard for ourselves, and we know that this is indeed the Savior of the world." (vv. 39–42 ESV)

Here we go. It's happening again. Right here in the fourth chapter of John. God is creating a people by the Word of the gospel, and their worship is flowing out of them and creating more worship, more rejoicing, leading to a gathering of that covenant community both by decree, design, and delight. This is the biblical pattern, the expected trajectory of the gospel. "Regular corporate seasons (or services) of worship that include the pursuit of full satisfaction in God through expressing dependence and longing for God, expressing gratitude for God's glory and gifts and expressing the delight of admiration and adoration to God, are normative in the Scriptures."[5]

God commands us today as His people to come together for worship. This is a part of His plan to care for, grow, and encourage us. We are not to gather in begrudging submission but in delightful obedience, knowing that when God's people make much of Jesus together, something spiritually profound happens. Corporate worship is a sustaining force in the life of individual believers. It's where our personal worship takes us—week after week, as often as we meet—and where our personal worship comes from as we leave to serve Him in other places.

King David, in one of his darkest seasons of his life, remembered times of corporate worship as a source of nourishing strength (Ps. 42:4). They can be equally special to us—times when we are reminded as a people that God is good and sovereign, that we are saved by His blood. But that's not all that happens when we meet together. First Corinthians 14:25 tells us that even unbelievers should be moved by what occurs in our gatherings. In the assembly of God's people, He gives the world a visible picture of steadfast joy in the midst of any and all circumstances of life—through the worship of His name by the people of His Word.

This "Creature of the Word" is an eclectic group. We are immature, but maturing. Struggling, yet with hope. Hypocrites, yet covered by grace. Some of us are sick and in pain, others of us are as healthy as can be. We are rich and poor, educated and uneducated, of all different ethnicities and backgrounds. And yet we've come together as a "city on a hill," as a "light to the world," showing what redeemed rejoicing looks like. The Creature of the Word exposes the weak, futile worship of the world by worshipping the only One who can satisfy every longing of the human heart.

The book of Psalms ends with Psalm 150, which includes the word "praise" a total of thirteen times. (Evidently the psalmist didn't get the memo about people not liking to repeat lyrics.) The word in the original language is *halle*, in the imperative tense, which means it's a command. *Hey, you—praise!*

How fitting that the editor of the Psalms—a body of ancient writing loaded with such gripping, diverse content—would choose to conclude the collection this way. In the Psalms, we hear godly people crying out in pain. We see them struggling against insurmountable odds and adversity. We hear them angry, joyful, discouraged, and grateful—practically every human emotion known to man. At times we detect their songs pointing prophetically to Jesus, hundreds of years before He was born. And in wrapping up all the rich content in the Psalms, the closing words leave us with this one command: "Praise the Lord!"

> Praise the LORD! Praise God in his sanctuary; praise
> him in his mighty heavens! Praise him for his mighty
> deeds; praise him according to his excellent greatness!

Praise him with trumpet sound; praise him with lute
and harp! Praise him with tambourine and dance; praise
him with strings and pipe! Praise him with sounding
cymbals; praise him with loud clashing cymbals! Let
everything that has breath praise the LORD! Praise the
LORD! (Ps. 150 ESV)

As you read Psalm 150, you see an array of instruments used;
trumpets, tambourines, strings, cymbals. This is no one-man-band.
It's a picture of a corporate worship gathering, same as many of the
psalms that come before it. Psalm 95, for example . . .

Oh come, let us sing to the LORD; let us make a
joyful noise to the rock of our salvation! Let us come
into his presence with thanksgiving; let us make a joyful
noise to him with songs of praise! (vv. 1–2 ESV)

The Creature worships. She gathers together. And as she does,
her worshipping presence allows individuals to do what the gospel
always intended us to do: see ourselves as "a people," not just a person.
Worshipping in spirit and in truth. All of us.

A church engaging regularly in collective worship also accomplishes two important things, which we'll consider for a brief moment:
worship *shadows eternity* and *provides supernatural encouragement*.

Shadow of Eternity

Right now, this very moment, God is being perfectly praised in
the heavens by angels and believers who have already entered His
eternal presence. And every time we gather to praise Him corporately,
our gathering is a foretaste of this eternal gathering. Our worshipping
together *shadows eternity*.

Then I looked, and I heard around the throne and
the living creatures and the elders the voice of many

angels, numbering myriads of myriads and thousands
of thousands, saying with a loud voice, "Worthy is the
Lamb who was slain, to receive power and wealth and
wisdom and might and honor and glory and blessing!"
(Rev. 5:11–12 esv)

The picture in heaven is one of "myriads of myriads" of people
gathering around the throne with "a loud voice," declaring how worthy God is. It's an amount beyond calculation—people who have
been forgiven because of the slain Lamb of God, Jesus the Christ—a
people from every tribe, tongue, and nation, each of them declaring
the praises of God. Heaven is filled with a people satisfied in the very
character of God, not just the benefits He gives.

Church people often make comments that cause one to think
they're not likely to enjoy heaven very much (assuming they're going).
Perhaps you've heard someone say, "I'm uncomfortable around people
from other cultures." Hmmm. Heaven might not be their cup of tea
then, because it will be forever filled with people from every people
group on earth.

Some church people approach worship with an apathetic attitude,
as if praising God is boring and unappetizing—a necessary chore
before heading out for Sunday lunch and an afternoon of NFL football. Heaven, though, is an eternal gathering of people *enthralled* with
praising God. Someone with no desire to corporately rejoice in Him
is not exactly prepping well for the eternal gathering that is to come.

When we and the people in our churches consider whether we
really want heaven or not, we must realize that we are not simply
asking ourselves if we prefer heaven to hell. Choosing one thing over
another doesn't necessarily mean we love the thing we choose. If given
the choice to eat spinach or broccoli, you may choose broccoli. But that
doesn't mean you love broccoli. It may only mean you don't want to eat
spinach. Heaven is not for people who just want to skip hell. Heaven is
reserved for those who love Jesus, who have been rescued by Him and

who long to praise Him. If someone doesn't have much use for praising Him now, it's foolish to think they're ready for heaven. Those set apart for the eternal corporate worship gathering enjoy the temporary gathering of the Church on earth.

Since our corporate gatherings here are a shadow of eternity, even our imperfect, incomplete expressions of worship as the people of God should foreshadow the perfect response that is to come. A church gathered for worship should embody a sense of awe and anticipation because of the One who has rescued the worshippers.

Supernatural Encouragement

Not only does our worship as rescued sinners reflect an eternal reality, God also supernaturally utilizes our corporate gatherings to mature and encourage His people in ways not available anywhere else. God designed our faith to be communal and interdependent—and markedly supernatural. When believers gather together as a worshipping community, we benefit from all the spiritual gifts of the body of Christ. Worship reminds us that the Church is bigger and more beautiful than any one person or a few leaders alone. Each of us, worshipping together, is used of God to build each other up in Jesus.

Notice the plural language throughout this passage from the writer of Hebrews.

> Therefore, brothers, since we have confidence
> to enter the holy places by the blood of Jesus, by the
> new and living way that he opened for us through the
> curtain, that is, through his flesh, and since we have a
> great priest over the house of God, let us draw near with
> a true heart in full assurance of faith, with our hearts
> sprinkled clean from an evil conscience and our bodies
> washed with pure water. Let us hold fast the confession
> of our hope without wavering, for he who promised

is faithful. And let us consider how to stir up one
another to love and good works, not neglecting to meet
together, as is the habit of some, but encouraging one
another, and all the more as you see the Day drawing
near. (Heb. 10:19–25 ESV)

"Let us draw near. . . . Let us hold fast. . . . Let us consider how to
stir up one another . . . encouraging one another." Worship brings us
together and is infused with supernatural power through the "blood
of Jesus" and the "new and living way" that He has given access for us
to enjoy and experience in Him.

Worship gatherings are not always spectacular, but they are always
supernatural. And if a church looks for or works for the spectacular,
she may miss the supernatural. If a person enters a gathering to be
wowed with something impressive, with a style that fits him just right,
with an order of service and song selection designed just the right way,
that person may miss the supernatural presence of God. Worship is
supernatural whenever people come hungry to respond, react, and
receive from God for who He is and what He has done. A church worshipping as a Creature of the Word doesn't show up to perform or be
entertained; she comes desperate and needy, thirsty for grace, receiving
from the Lord and the body of Christ, and then gratefully receiving
what she needs as she offers her praise—the only proper response to
the God who saves us.

Your Gatherings

Throughout the Old Testament, we see God expressing deep disgust with some of the empty gatherings and routine worship offered
to Him. At one point, He tells His people He hates their religious
feasts and won't listen to their showy, insincere offerings of worship
(Amos 5:21–24). In another place He asks His people to quit lighting
worthless fires on the altar (Mal. 1:10). In each case, the Lord knew

He didn't have the full hearts of His people. They were going through motions of worship without hearts melted by His grace, without being filled with awe by His greatness and His goodness.

Only the gospel can grip our hearts with this kind of ongoing, unending awe. Only the gospel can cause grateful praise to flow, and keep flowing, and never stop flowing from our lips. Therefore, your gatherings must be soaked in the gospel. Everything from the music, to the teaching, to the observance of the ordinances—all of it must unashamedly, explicitly, point people to Jesus and what He has done. Otherwise, the Creature suffers.

Music. As you consider selecting songs for your worship services, consider them in light of the truth of the gospel. Imagine the songs as teachers—*because they are!* If your people could understand your doctrine only through the music you sing, what would they know about God and His pursuit of us? If your people could understand your church's beliefs only through the music, what would they know? These are good questions to ask yourself in order to stay Jesus-centered.

Too often the songs we sing in many churches are bold declarations of what we can do for God, of what we have that we can offer Him. And while the character of God and His work on our behalf does demand an active response from us, we must be careful not to teach people unintentionally that the Christian faith is about our personal resolve and commitments. Choose songs instead that remind people about the greatness of God. Choose songs that boldly remind people of the gospel—how He found us in the hopelessness of our sin and redeemed us for His own pleasure and glory—because only the gospel can stir the Creature to worship authentically and live. Without consistent reminders of the gospel, our worship services quickly become empty religious feasts that (according to Scripture) disgust the Lord.

Teaching. We will address this in further detail later in the book, but as you prepare the teaching moments of the worship service—both the sermon and other instructive elements—be sure the gospel is the foundation for all that is said. Connect the imperatives of Scripture (things to do) with the indicatives of Scripture (what Christ has done). Don't mention the gospel only at the end of your messages, when you speak to those who are not yet Christian, accidentally teaching that the gospel is only for unbelievers. Instead, show how the gospel impacts all of life. Help your people feast on the gospel throughout the whole message, throughout the whole service.

Ordinances. As you prepare and lead people through the ordinances of communion and baptism, aggressively apply the gospel to the hearts of your people. These two ordinances were given to the Creature to remind her that she is alive because of the gospel.

Baptism is a visual statement of the gospel, a reminder that our sins were buried with Christ and that we have been made alive because of His resurrection. Communion, too, is an opportunity to surround ourselves with the powerful realities of gospel truth—the unleavened bread, a symbol of the purity and holiness of Jesus; the cup, the blood of the covenant, reminiscent of His great sacrifice as the pure and faultless Lamb of God.

We come together each week from our individual modes and manners of life to unite in shared worship not only of His majesty but also of His deep love—a love wholly undeserved and yet lavishly given. We don't just celebrate God; we celebrate His gospel. And, we celebrate as a community.

No other worship will satisfy.

CHAPTER 3

THE CREATURE IN COMMUNITY

True friendship calls you out of the darkness of personal privacy into the loving candor of mutual concern. It moves you from being a sealed envelope to being an open letter.

~ PAUL TRIPP[1]

"PERSONAL RELATIONSHIP WITH JESUS CHRIST . . ."

This phrase is used countless times each weekend when churches gather for worship across the United States and around the world. And while such wording is helpful in describing the intimacy of our fellowship with God, it is only part of the truth—because it neglects the reality that God's design is for believers to be deeply connected in community with other followers of Christ. If not carefully explained, this phrase could give the impression that the Christian faith is private— "just between you and God." For while our faith is indeed very personal, it is definitely not private. Private Christian faith is an oxymoron, like "white chocolate," "jumbo shrimp," and "ACC football." (Sorry.)

You have been individually saved by Christ, but you are not the only individual saved. God has always been building a *people* for Himself—a family of faith that unites across the dividing lines of race, nationality, politics, and economics. God Himself exists in community as Father, Son, and Spirit. And out of that divine community flows His design for humans to be involved in relationships with each other. He started with Adam and Eve, progressed to the nation of Israel, and now has established and is building His Church. Every tribe, tongue, nation, ethnicity, and socioeconomic status come together in this covenant body, declaring the praises of God and making much of Jesus Christ.

Since the day Adam searched for a suitable helper, people have always longed for community. So it would seem our era is a great one in which to live, seeing as how connectivity is so much easier now than it's ever been. Facebook currently claims more than 900 million active users who visit their social networking site at least once a month. Thanks to Twitter, we can constantly bombard each other with even the most boring details of our everyday lives. You can take a picture of the sampler you ordered at Applebee's, and then tweet it to all your friends so they can be jealous of your potato skins. Technology has enabled humanity to be more connected, more informed, and more social than at any other time in history.

But connectivity does not equate to community. Being able to make quick connections with people doesn't automatically require any depth to the relationship.

All you have to do is take a look inside your local Starbucks to see something strange going on in the midst of all these "connections." Starbucks was founded to be a gathering place for relationships. Sure, they serve a million combinations of coffee and pastries, but it was also intended as a place where people could get their coffee not "to go" but to stay. And stay together. Starbucks was built to capitalize on the intrinsic human desire to relate.

But as you look into your local Starbucks, notice that many people are in there—together in one place—but they're also alone. They're sitting at tables with their headphones on, working on their computers or fiddling with their phones. Not that it's the fault of Starbucks. This "all alone, all together" phenomenon is merely symptomatic of what's at play in human relationships throughout our culture.

So although we are more connected than we've ever been, we also feel more alone and unknown than at any other time in human history. We relate without relationships, all together but all alone. Thus, without the gospel forming community, we are doomed to connectivity and aloneness in the midst of crowds. Only the gospel forms deep community.

Gospel Forms Community

Paul wrote the book of Philippians as an encouraging letter to believers who were in community only because of the gospel. The Lord had formed a beautiful community among them by His grace, which is why Paul was confident they would continue to grow and mature "until the day of Christ Jesus" (1:6 NIV)—because of their "partnership in the gospel" (1:5 NIV).

But who *were* these people who were partners in the gospel? Acts 16 gives us a snapshot, as it records the apostle Paul's first visit to Philippi and the responses of people there to the good news of Jesus.

One of them was a woman named Lydia, who was a dealer in purple cloth, a high-end material for the wealthy. Lydia was evidently the kind of prominent, savvy businesswoman who today might travel first-class, enjoy expensive meals on her corporate card, and entertain with affluent colleagues. Yet her high-end lifestyle could never quite quench the deep longings of her soul. When she heard the good news of Jesus and His grace, she responded in faith.

But her next actions revealed something else about her, as well as the nature of the early church. She intrinsically knew that her faith was not private. She persuaded Paul and his companions to stay at her house while they shared the gospel in Philippi. Many scholars believe the church at Philippi met at her house.

The next person converted was a demon-possessed slave girl who made money for her owners by telling people their future. (Although the text does not explicitly mention the word *conversion*, we believe that the passage's context clearly implies that she was converted.) For many days, this girl had been following Paul while the spirit within her kept crying out, "These men are servants of the Most High God, who are telling you the way to be saved" (Acts 16:17 NIV). Paul allowed this irritation to continue for a while, but finally he'd had enough, and in the name of Christ demanded the evil spirit to leave the girl. "And it came out right away" (v. 18 HCSB).

This girl was most likely a runaway who had sold herself into slavery for food and bare essentials. She had a rough past, had seen more than a young girl should ever see, and was deeply wounded from her brief life history. But in Christ, she found healing—One who loved her regardless of her past. Good for her.

Her transformation, however, was not so good for her owners' business model. They were livid because of her conversion, knowing they wouldn't be making money off her anymore. So they dragged Paul and Silas to the authorities, who ordered that they be beaten and thrown into prison—the whole mob joining in the attack. In prison they were monitored heavily by one specific guard, a guy the authorities must have trusted because of his ability to follow orders and execute tasks. He was the hardworking, blue-collar type from the south side of town. He was a good family man when he wasn't cuffing criminals.

In prison, around midnight, as Paul and Silas were praying and singing out loud, God caused an earthquake to occur, that shook the prison violently, causing the shackles to fall off the prisoners' wrists and ankles and the doors to fly open. This particular guard who had been made personally responsible for Paul and Silas's confinement drew his sword to kill himself, thinking they had escaped, knowing he would be in serious trouble with his supervisors for letting them get free. But Paul yelled out to him, "We're here! Don't harm yourself!" Amazed by their fearless faith and the power of their God, the man fell down trembling before them, asking, "What must I do to be saved?" He and his entire family became Christians that night, trading their insufficient goodness for God's all-surpassing goodness.

So the little growing church in Philippi was now home to people like this: a wealthy, upscale businesswoman whose material success could never satisfy her; a slave girl with a deep, dark, wounded past; a tough-nosed jailer and his family, just to mention the few we know. So ask yourself: What else did these people have in common but the gospel? They never would have gone to the same restaurants, hung out in the same parts of town, or listened to the same music. But because God had radically transformed them, they shared a common bond deeper than anything that divided them. They were together only because of the gospel.

The gospel by its very nature forms community. D. A. Carson writes:

> The church is . . . made up of natural enemies. What binds us together is not common education, common race, common income levels, common politics, common nationality, common accents, common jobs, or anything else of that sort. Christians come together . . . because they have all been saved by Jesus Christ. . . . They are a band of natural enemies who love one another for Jesus' sake.[2]

Believers, as we know, have different careers, different political viewpoints, different parenting philosophies, different economic status, and different cultural backgrounds. We are different in many, many ways. Yet we are still drawn together in the body He calls the Church. Unity in the gospel is much deeper than surface uniformity.

The reason most community is shallow in our world is because it's built on temporary foundations. The reason most relationships don't last is because they're built on commonalities that change over time. When the common bond changes, the relationship changes.

If you're married, you see this happen immediately when you have kids. You once had friends you would hang out with late at night, but now you can't do that. Even if you get a babysitter, you're not staying up till 1:00 in the morning, because your kids are waking up at 6:30 and you'll be exhausted.

If you play sports with a group of guys, and if nothing deeper than your love of basketball binds you together, that community will weaken and likely disappear if you blow out a knee and can't play anymore. If relationships aren't built on something deeper than finding good restaurants, working at the same company, or having kids in the same activities, they will change whenever the common bond is no longer there. Community is only as strong as what it's built upon.

And nothing is as strong as the gospel.

The gospel is the deepest foundation for community. What connects believers is the reality that we were all very messed-up people, broken before a holy God, yet rescued and given new life in Christ. What unites believers is deeper than anything that can divide.

The Christmas Truce of 1914 is one familiar example—a true story that has captured hearts for nearly a hundred years. World War I had begun only months before, and the fighting on the Western Front between the Germans and the Allies was very fierce. Hope for a quick war was gone. Both armies knew they would be bitter enemies for years.

A system of trenches separated the two sides, with the area in between regarded as "No Man's Land." But on Christmas Eve, an unofficial truce began. German soldiers began singing "Silent Night" in German, and men on the other side of the great divide joined along in English. Soldiers who hours before had been attempting to kill one another were now singing together about the wonder of Christ's birth.

As the night and the singing continued, the soldiers emerged out of their trenches to join one another in "No Man's Land," where they exchanged gifts, shared in burial services, and played soccer together. An estimated 100,000 soldiers along the Western Front laid down their weapons all that night and the next day. In subsequent years their commanders would demand that they continue fighting on Christmas Day, but in this one sacred interlude in 1914, a reminder of the incarnation caused a cease-fire. Even if for a brief moment, there was peace on earth and good will toward men.

Gospel Continually Forms

Though the believers in Philippi had been brought together only because of the gospel, Paul knew that the gospel must *continually form* community. The Christian faith is and has always been an interdependent grouping of people rescued by Christ. But because of our sinfulness, we tend to drift away from that, toward either dependence or independence.

Some are more likely to move in the direction of *dependence*. This occurs when we find our identity, security, or worth in someone else. Maybe the pastor, a friend we feel we must have, a certain teacher, or a person we don't feel we can do without. Unhealthy dependence is actually a form of idolatry, finding ultimate fulfillment in someone other than God.

Equally destructive and on the other side of the spectrum is *independence*. Some foolishly attempt to live an isolated faith, recklessly believing that the Christian life can be lived in one's own might and merit. Independence shuns community and refuses to lean on others for maturity, growth, sharing, and serving.

The gospel says differently. It pulls us back to *interdependence*.

Paul reminded believers to keep the gospel as the impetus for their community. He challenged them to "[stand] firm in one spirit, with one mind striving side by side for the faith of the gospel" (Phil. 1:27 ESV). He encouraged them because of Christ to have "the same love, being in full accord and of one mind" (2:2 ESV). He pleaded with them to submit to one another as Christ submitted to death, to have the same humble attitude as His (2:5–8). Paul knew that contrary to Jesus-centered community is the thinking that some believers are at a different level of righteousness than other believers, that some believers are "better."

In 1983 an educational commission appointed by President Ronald Reagan released a study that influenced common practice in schools. It chronicled how America was no longer the leader in education, and that one of the reasons was because its smarter students were being held back to accommodate the ones who couldn't keep up. Thus began an emphasis on "gifted" classes—students who were set apart to learn at an accelerated rate apart from the rest of the school population.

If you were in school during that time, you may remember the sting when particular students got pulled out of your class and assigned to special accelerated classes. The thought behind it was this: "The dumb guys are holding down our best and brightest. So we should pull out the smart ones. Let those guys color, and teach these other guys calculus." It was a bit painful and demotivating. Perhaps you thought, *They're gifted and talented, so obviously I'm not.*

Unfortunately, some of this idea has seeped into the Church. Some act as if there are levels of Christianity, and when you hit the gifted level, you don't mingle so much with people who aren't there yet. After all, they're slower than you are, they're not as motivated as you, they don't understand what you understand, and they're not as serious about pursuing the things of the Lord as you are. But the concept of "levels in Christianity" is not a concept built on the gospel of Christ.

Levels are only possible if there are levels of righteousness. And those levels simply do not exist, because we all possess the same amount of righteousness—*none*. The only righteousness any of us have is the righteousness God freely gives to us in Christ.

Some may be more *mature* than others in their understanding of the righteousness that's been freely given, or in how they live in response to it. But no one in the community of faith is more *righteous* than another. Nobody.

Therefore, any attempt to build community on something more than the grace of Christ becomes a subtle move away from grace, a move toward pseudo-community that only puffs up and fails to transform. If something other than the person and work of Jesus becomes the foundation for a group of believers, that "other thing," whatever it is—economic level, social manners, music preferences, common life experiences—becomes what they use to differentiate themselves from others. And it immediately becomes a point of boasting, a way to feel justified.

In the Galatian church, the issue became "circumcision." Those who were circumcised only fellowshipped with others in the same condition. In churches today, perhaps it's "we're the deeper group" or "the homeschool group" or "this zip code group." While there's nothing wrong with people wanting to go deeper, or meet in homeschool groups, or make friends in the same zip code, we must be careful. Because of our sinfulness, these commonalities can become the bond that holds us together instead of the gospel. And worse, these commonalities can become prideful distinctions that repel others from a community that should be open and inclusive.

The commonality of the gospel is something believers share that will never change. Whether we are single or married, with children or no children, hyper-religious or irreligious, young or old, all believers in Jesus-centered community have a common place to stand together. In fact, if your small groups, journey groups, life groups, Sunday school classes, Adult Bible Fellowships, or whatever you call them are not centered on the common need for and common experience of grace, then they are actually doing more harm than good to the gospel movement. If groups are not gospel-centered and gospel-fueled, they are merely a social outlet for people, and they lack the power for transformation.

So what does community centered on Jesus and His work look like . . . practically?

The apostle Paul spent the first eleven chapters of Romans unpacking the fullness and the glory of the gospel. Then in Romans 12, he moved to our responses in light of the gospel, with the back half of the chapter containing some very practical but profound instructions that guide our pursuit of gospel-centered community. After clearly establishing that Christ is the One who forms community and places believers in one body (12:5), Paul issued this challenge:

> Let love be genuine. Abhor what is evil; hold fast to what is good. Love one another with brotherly affection. Outdo one another in showing honor. Do not be slothful in zeal, be fervent in spirit, serve the Lord. Rejoice in hope, be patient in tribulation, be constant in prayer. Contribute to the needs of the saints and seek to show hospitality. Rom. 12:9–13 ESV)

Let's take some of these statements one by one, and see what we can learn.

No Masks Allowed

"Let love be genuine." True, gospel-saturated community is authentic. The original word translated *genuine* means love that is free of "pretending, simulating, or acting." In other words, the community is not surface-only or fake. It's not filled with easy answers that justify the spiritual prowess of those involved. In essence, a sign hangs above the doorway that reads: No Masks Allowed.

The regular confession of sin, struggles, fears, and failures is common in gospel-centered community—which only makes sense, because an essential foundation for this community is the reality that all have fallen woefully short of the glory of God, and that each of us continues to battle our selfish natures daily. The only reason the community exists, in fact, is because Christ has called it into existence, not because any of us earned the right to be in community through our moral strength, family connections, reputation, talent, or anything else.

The word *church* (*ekklesia* in the original language) literally means "the called out ones." The word is plural. Believers, therefore, are placed in community with others for one reason: because God has called them out of their former ways of life. Everyone in the community is deeply sinful. Everyone is called by the same God. And everyone has been mercifully placed in community together.

So why pretend we're more than we are if everything is built on Jesus' righteousness and not our own? Why the need to be fake? The gospel frees us to be authentic, to admit that our struggles and strengths have not been fully sanctified, and to allow others to apply the grace of God to areas of our lives that desperately need it.

When community is honest and authentic, people begin to experience (and lead others to experience) freedom from wearing a mask because Jesus sets people free from the need to be hypocrites. He liberates religious overachievers controlled and dominated by a religious system they can never beat. He emancipates those shackled to their secrets by bringing light to the darkness. He tears off the masks of the seemingly perfect and allows them to walk in the open. That's the nature of authenticity in Jesus-centered community—people constantly emerging from the shadows and finding the sufficiency of grace.

Safe, Not Soft

"Abhor what is evil." A gospel-centered community acknowledges the presence of sin and welcomes the confession of sin. But a truly gospel-centered community never reduces the severity of sin. To "abhor" describes the way a believer should react to sin. The word means to "shiver in horror," the way your body reacts to an unexpectedly freezing cold shower. Believers are to shudder at things that go

against God's revealed purposes, things that harm both ourselves and others.

Yes, gospel-centered community creates a safe environments for people to be honest about where they are, but always with one notable caveat—*without excusing their sin*. Sadly, a tendency exists among Christians to seek authentic environments for the sake of relishing in authenticity. These people get up after a small group meeting or some other accountability structure, slapping each other on the back for their ability to be open and honest about their sin. Yet they never take active steps together in order to combat that sin. True Jesus-centered authenticity lovingly nudges believers toward continual repentance— not just a bunch of "nobody's perfect" confessions but actual, gospel-driven changes in lifestyle.

The apostle Paul challenged the Roman believers: "What shall we say then? Are we to continue in sin that grace may abound? By no means! How can we who died to sin still live in it?" (Rom. 6:1–2 ESV). What he was evidently addressing was a perceived theological loophole some Roman Christians had found that allowed them to live in whatever fashion they wanted—and not only feel OK with it, but feel like they were doing God a big favor. They figured, "If God is going to love and forgive me regardless, then why not do whatever I want so that His grace is made even more obvious by loving me despite how wicked I am?" No way, Paul said, was this the right response to God's incredible grace. When God saves us, our attitude toward sin changes. Sin doesn't become easier to commit; it becomes more despicable to us than ever.

Both personal and communal responsibility is involved in helping us "abhor" sin. Because we are often blind to the areas of our lives that are in the most desperate need of repentance, we need others to encourage us so we will not be hardened by sin's deceit. Because we are masters of self-deception, we often don't even realize these areas of our lives exist. Yet the Lord is gracious to give us the gift of each other— brothers and sisters around us who are willing to engage us and say, "I think this is more of an issue than you realize."

Abhorring what is evil in the context of community requires true love—love that dares to inflict "the wounds of a friend" (Prov. 27:6 ESV). The weakest, saddest, most hypocritical form of pseudo love is the kind that sees someone in danger and simply hopes everything works out in the end. Is it judgmental, ruthless, or wicked to correct your children when they're doing things that are dangerous for them? Normal parents would never watch their kids play in the street and just hope they don't get hurt: "I know it's dangerous, but look how happy they are. They seem to be having so much fun." Our ferocious commitment to their safety and success, along with a heart full of genuine love, drives us to endure the often unhappy experience of disciplining our children. In the same way, gospel-formed believers take responsibility for confronting those who claim to be Christ-followers and yet continue to sin.

Church leaders must strive to create environments that are "safe but not soft," environments that embrace people in their brokenness while guiding them to wholeness in Christ. Gospel-centered community exists with the grace-filled tension of receiving sinners while simultaneously making war on sin.

Furthermore, church leaders must live in community themselves. If possible, staff and spouses should be active participants in one or more groups and fellowships, since they have the same needs to grow and be accountable as others. It's inconsistent and spiritually dangerous for leaders to be pushing and preaching spiritual growth yet not be growing themselves. A leader who is not in community is the epitome of spiritual elitism, living as if he's above the need for encouragement and correction.

One additional way to "abhor" sin in community comes through the biblical practice of church discipline. Most people find even the phrase "church discipline" to be cringe-worthy. They think of church leaders walking around like the Gestapo, constantly snooping into people's business, looking to record any mistake. But the heart of church discipline is an expression of God's kindness, not His wrath. It's

divinely designed to teach people how to live, not to "kick people out of
our church because they're making us look bad." Having clear expectations for membership in the community of faith, as well as guidelines
and steps for church discipline, is a way to communicate God's design
for holiness within community. Church discipline reminds everyone
that the church not only values the commands of God but also the souls
of those who are members. Discipline is an expression of love, the kind
that refuses to allow Christians to deceive themselves into ever thinking
that continual, unrepentant sin is not damaging, both to themselves
and to the community.[3]

Let "Philadelphia" Continue

*"Love one another with brotherly affection."*Jesus-centered community is genuine and abhors evil. It is also filled with "brotherly
affection."

This is much deeper than sitting in a small group, drinking sweet
tea, eating Doritos, and going home, all the while talking about how
great our community is because we've spent a few minutes with each
other. "Brotherly affection" in the original language is composed of
two root words: *philos*, which means "brotherly love," and *adelphos*,
which means "of the same womb." Therefore, because of the gospel,
believers are called to possess a deep brotherly love for each other as if
we were literally born from the same womb . . . which we were.

Think of it in terms of your own home and family. Even though
we might not always be in the same room together, we are fully aware
of each person. We know where they are, what challenges they face,
and what they need most. We would never sit down for a meal with
someone missing from the table and not know their whereabouts.
Why? Because we love them with this kind of familial affection.

Christians throughout the ages have been recognized as a group
who cares deeply for each other. Aristides, a pagan orator, wrote

scornfully of the early Christians, but even he was forced to admit they loved each other deeply: "If these Christians hear that any one of their number is in distress for the sake of Christ's name, they all render aid in his necessity."[4] That's "brotherly love" at work. Hard work.

Paul additionally challenged believers in Romans 12 to "outdo one another in showing honor" (v. 10 ESV). Paul surely doesn't mean merely honoring the pastor or guest speaker with exotic candies in the green room. The giving and receiving of honor is something that should happen between all believers, all the time.

Honor and affection are connected. A husband who honors his wife will also have affection for her. A woman who has affection for her husband will also honor him. Stirred-up affections result in honor. But how do we generate positive feelings for each other if our heart's not really in it, if these other people in our community don't just naturally make us want to "honor" them? The only way to stir up true affection for others is to have a stirred-up realization of God's affection for us in Jesus Christ. Our understanding of God's love for us, despite us, enables us to love others in spite of themselves. Affection for the Lord leads to affection for others, resulting in outdoing one another in honor. It makes us ask ourselves questions like:

- How can I be concerned about you and your needs?
- Why shouldn't I take the farthest parking spot?
- How about if I take the seat that's blocked by a pole?
- What if I lose so you can win?
- How can I disadvantage myself for your advantage?
- What would it mean to consider you more significant than me?

Reminded, Not Instructed

"Rejoice in hope, be patient in tribulation, be constant in prayer." Sometimes we forget the fact that New Testament letters like Paul's to

the Romans were originally meant to be read, studied, and practiced in community. Commands like these from Romans 12, then—to rejoice, to be patient, to be persistent in prayer—are not just for individual Christians. They're for the people of God. We are to rejoice *together*, be patient *together*, pray *together*.

Thankfully, a day is coming on earth when there will be no more memorials, no more remembrances of tragedies, no more cancer, no more sickness, no more sore throats, heartburn, terrorist attacks, anger, or tears. All these things will simply cease to be, and in that truth we rejoice in hope. But for now, we live in the midst of these horrible things, overwhelmed by them, with no human match for them. And though we know we're supposed to rejoice in hope, pray, and be patient, we are "prone to wander." Therefore, God has given us the gift of community to remind us of what we already know we've been given in Christ—a promised reason for enduring. We see this idea expressed beautifully in 1 John 4:10–12 (esv):

> In this is love, not that we have loved God but that
> he loved us and sent his Son to be the propitiation for
> our sins. Beloved, if God so loved us, we also ought to
> love one another. No one has ever seen God; if we love
> one another, God abides in us and his love is perfected
> in us.

That last verse is admittedly a little confusing at first. God's love is "perfected"? Is John saying that God's love isn't perfect otherwise? Has He withheld some element of His love that we only get if we love one another? Absolutely not.

What he's saying is that when we love each other with a love rooted in the gospel, we are able to see an even more tangible expression of God's love for us in Christ. Real-life experiences of loving each other well provide a visceral way of remembering something we so easily forget: the fullness of God's love for us in Christ. When pain makes us forget for a moment about everything God is and everything He's done, we choose to love each other . . . and we remember. Gospel-centered community brings us back to our gospel senses.

Meeting Needs

"*Contribute to the needs of the saints and seek to show hospitality.*" A true mark of a community that's continually being formed in the gospel is the warmth and hospitality that supernaturally flows from within it. Community in which Christ is constantly remembered as the Author of the community is one that is grace-filled and loving.

For the Roman Christians, this was a pretty cut-and-dried issue. There were believers among them without food and clothing. So what was the Church supposed to do for them? Simple: give them food and clothes. The gospel reminds us that we are all needy, every one of us. Since Christ has met our needs, we are motivated to meet the needs of our brothers and sisters.

But while assistance with food, clothing, rent, and utility bills are essential ways churches can meet the needs of believers who are struggling, often the bulk of people's need today is not material but spiritual. How, then, do believers practice Jesus-centered hospitality?

At its core, meeting the needs of others means that those with less are invited to share in the joys and blessings of those who have more. But our tendency is to narrow this definition to money. In a Jesus-centered community, actions of hospitality go beyond those who are rich sharing with those who are poor. Men skilled in plumbing and carpentry share with people who are not. Parents who've raised children share wisdom with new mothers and fathers. Lawyers, doctors, and other professionals utilize their unique skills to serve those in need of those skills at the moment when they are needed. (And those with great tickets share with their pastors.)

The early church instinctively understood meeting each other's needs based on a gospel orientation. They longed for one another, met continually together, provided for each other (Acts 2:44–45). And in God's providence, He has continued to arrange community around each person in order to meet the needs of each individual. He has chosen to use community to ensure His people experience nurture and care.

What Could Be Deeper?

The grand narrative of Scripture features community. In the beginning, our triune God graciously gave community to Adam and Eve. But sin distorted and messed up the perfect community they shared. They lost the beauty of their nativity, and tension existed between them the rest of their days. Yet in His mercy, God pursued and established a new community—Israel. And through Christ, He pursued and established His Church. The end of the story has yet to be realized, but the promise of eternal and everlasting community *will* be fulfilled.

> I heard a loud voice from the throne saying, "Behold, the dwelling place of God is with man. He will dwell with them, and they will be his people, and God himself will be with them as their God. He will wipe away every tear from their eyes, and death shall be no more, neither shall there be mourning, nor crying, nor pain anymore, for the former things have passed away." (Rev. 21:3–4 ESV)

The community that believers will enjoy forever will be perfect. The community we experience now is a reflection of this ultimate and everlasting community; therefore, it must even now be savored, nurtured, fed, invested in. Churches that merely put on Sunday shows and don't preach and practice community grounded in the gospel are a poor reflection of the eternal community promised for believers. Churches that fail to embrace the connection between the gospel and community merely stuff people into rooms around commonalities that can never stand the test of time. Churches that forget the essence of the gospel unintentionally allow false levels of righteousness to prohibit the liberating openness and authenticity that people need.

There is nothing stronger, nothing deeper, than the gospel on which to build community. Is the gospel what your church proclaims and practices as the foundation for community? It must be. Because community is only as strong as what it's built upon.

CHAPTER 4

THE CREATURE SERVES

A Christian man is the most free lord of all,
and subject to none; a Christian man is the most dutiful
servant of all, and subject to every one.
— MARTIN LUTHER[1]

WHEN THE WORLD TRADE CENTER crumbled to the ground on that dreadful day of September 11, 2001, more than three thousand people died. But a few of those who were buried beneath the rubble miraculously survived the toppling of the towers. Two of these individuals were Will Jimeno and John McLoughlin, a pair of Port Authority employees who responded to the attacks and were on the bottom floor when the south tower began to fall. They raced to an elevator shaft and amazingly survived the one-hundred-story collapse around them, but were buried dozens of feet down in the midst of an array of rubble. Trapped without water, breathing smoke-filled air, both Will and John had little hope of survival.

Yet as they lay there, pinned under a mountain of debris, some-thing was stirring inside an accountant in Connecticut they had never met.

Dave Karnes, who had spent twenty-three years active duty in the Marine Corps, was watching the scene play out on television just like the rest of us. But more than allowing it merely to trouble him, he decided to do something about it. He went to his boss and told him he wouldn't be back for a while.

Dave went to a barber shop, asked for a high-and-tight haircut, then stopped by his home to put on his military fatigues, hoping the uniform would allow him access into the blocked-off area surrounding Ground Zero. He drove to Manhattan at speeds of 120 miles an hour and arrived by late afternoon. While rescue workers were being called off the wreckage pile because of danger, Dave was able to stay because of the clout and credential that came with his military uniform. Finding another Marine nearby, the two men walked the pile together, seeking to save the lost.

After an hour of searching, they heard the faint sound of tapping pipes and yelling. Will and John had been trapped for nine hours by that time, completely incapable of working themselves free. Yet in the midst of all the rubble, a Marine who earlier in the morning had been working a spreadsheet in Connecticut found them. Of the twenty people pulled from the heaped-up remains of the World Trade Center, Will Jimeno and John McLoughlin were numbers eighteen and nine-teen. And all because Dave Karnes took off his suit, put on rescue fatigues, and stepped into the despair and darkness of Ground Zero.

In the same way (but to an infinitely greater degree), God took off His royal robes, stepped into our dark and depraved culture, and served us. We were buried in the depths and rubble of our own fool-ishness with zero chance of pulling ourselves out of our own sin. We were without hope until the Holy One clothed Himself in humanity to rescue us, to become sin for us on the cross:

> Have this mind among yourselves, which is yours
> in Christ Jesus, who, though he was in the form of God,
> did not count equality with God a thing to be grasped,
> but emptied himself, by taking the form of a servant,
> being born in the likeness of men. And being found
> in human form, he humbled himself by becoming
> obedient to the point of death, even death on a cross.
> Therefore God has highly exalted him and bestowed on
> him the name that is above every name, so that at the
> name of Jesus every knee should bow, in heaven and
> on earth and under the earth, and every tongue confess
> that Jesus Christ is Lord, to the glory of God the Father.
> (Phil. 2:5–11 ESV)

Our service must be grounded in this truth, in this gospel. The foundation of our service is built upon Christ's birth, life, death, and resurrection for us. It begins and ends with Jesus—*begins* there because He is our original motivation and *ends* there because only in Him are we empowered to serve others.

Foundation for Service

The essence of Christian faith is not that we serve Christ but that He served us. In Matthew 20, the mother of James and John came to Jesus, requesting that her sons be allowed to sit at His side in the kingdom—one on His right, the other on His left. So Jesus turned and asked a question of them: "Are you willing to do what it takes to do that?" Both of them readily, rashly took up the challenge: "You know it!" Then Jesus said, "Oh, you're going to pay the price, all right. But that honor is not Mine to give."

At this point, the other disciples become indignant toward these other two. We would probably have been indignant too, right? "Why is your mom here, bro? You're a grown man." In reality, they were indignant not because James and John asked their mommy to request power and authority, but because they hadn'd taken the chance to ask the favor for themselves.

So Jesus responded by telling them to huddle up:

> "You know that the rulers of the Gentiles lord it over them, and their great ones exercise authority over them. It shall not be so among you. But whoever would be great among you must be your servant, and whoever would be first among you must be your slave, even as the Son of Man came not to be served but to serve, and to give his life as a ransom for many." (Matt. 20:25–28 ESV)

Jesus was doing much more than simply giving out a moral command as a philosopher or a teacher offering a better way to live. He was giving the disciples the essence of the gospel: the Son of Man did not come to be served but to serve, to give His life as a ransom for many. Jesus was saying, "I am here to serve you through My death."

Jesus doesn't need anything. He is self-sufficient. He doesn't need advice, doesn't need gas money, doesn't need your help paying His bills, fixing His house, or making a difficult decision. Yet this all-sufficient, all-knowing, completely holy God stepped out of heaven to serve us through His atoning, sacrificial death.

Jesus was saying that His followers are to serve others not because it's the right thing to do, not because we'd feel guilty if we didn't, not because somebody else suggested it, and not because "causes" are the vogue thing of the day. *We serve because Jesus has served us.* His service should melt our hearts and cause us to serve others out of sheer gratitude to Him. That's the appropriate response to His loving service of us.

Churches centered on Jesus continually remind their people of this.

As humans, we struggle deeply with receiving unconditional love. We want to know why someone loves us and what we've done to deserve it. Unconditional love frustrates our desire to earn and accomplish. It challenges our pride. Sure, we like being loved, but we also like knowing we've proved ourselves worthy of it.

When your girlfriend in tenth grade told you she loved you, you wanted to know why. Was it the cool rims on your truck? The nice way you treated her? Or was it just your overall awesomeness that made her feel so strongly toward you? You had to know what it was so you could continue to do it or be it. If your father told you he was proud of you, you wanted to know what you'd done to earn his favor.

If we're not careful, *serving* can become a way we try to earn the love we've already received from God, to "pay Jesus back" for His generous grace. While churches preaching the grace of God would never suggest that serving or volunteering contributes anything to a person's salvation, a subtle tendency among us leads us to believe that serving is a way to stay "in good" with God. Therefore, unless serving is continually and unapologetically connected to the gospel, it can become a burden, a manipulator, a guilt reliever, or a backhanded method we employ to just keep serving ourselves.

The Burden of Earning

As the movie *Saving Private Ryan* reaches its climax, some of us preachers sit on the edge of our seats looking for an epic illustration. The film seems to be leading to a great comparison of Christ's sacrifice for us. Private Ryan (Matt Damon) has been pursued just as Christ pursues us and has been saved from death just as Christ saves us. The leader of the rescue mission, Captain John Miller (Tom Hanks), is sacrificing his life for Private Ryan. The moment is hanging right there. Wait for it . . .

But then as Miller gasps for his last few breaths, he grabs Ryan's hand and says these final words: "Earn this. Earn it." *I just gave everything for you; now spend the rest of your life earning this moment.*

We sit back in our chairs disappointed, because that one line radically ruins a great illustration. Even in the movie, these words seem to have haunted Private Ryan for the rest of his life. The movie ends by showing him as an elderly man, standing among the tombs of the men who gave their lives for him. And he is hoping he "earned it." Evidently he spent his entire life under the burden of trying to repay the sacrifice that was given for him.

Serving as an attempt to pay God back for His grace is futile—not only because our best efforts would prove woefully inadequate in paying Him back), but because *there is nothing to pay back.* The gospel reminds us that the debt of our sin has already been paid in full. Acts of service, then, must not be unintentionally advertised as a means of restitution for what Christ has done. Believers who live with that burden will serve out of obligation as they drift from the grace of God. Churches who place that burden on believers are peddling a new law that enslaves.

Because of the gospel, we serve because our hearts are overwhelmed with gratitude. Because of the gospel, believers can serve in freedom and joy. If a lack of serving pervades a church culture, the answer is not to crank up the guilt and arm-twisting but rather to instill a new, intense focus and awareness on the gospel.

Motivation for Service

The gospel is not only the *foundation* for our service; it also radically purifies our *motivation* for service. In fact, serving others for reasons other than the gospel actually doesn't make a lot of sense because of the philosophical contradictions beneath the surface.

Take, for example, the predominant worldview of Western culture today—the worldview of evolutionary process. In this thinking, the innate strengths and weaknesses of mankind best dictate what or who survives. So anytime help is extended to someone who is weak, this attacks the premise behind what is naturally best for mankind. Anytime a weak child or helpless person is served, the evolutionary worldview would maintain that humanity is assaulted because the weak are given an illogical, unnatural opportunity for extended survival. If it is really best for the weak to die so the shallow end of the gene pool can be cleared away, as evolutionary theory asserts, then serving others is hypocritical.

The human heart is immensely complex and deceitful. Therefore, a plethora of other motivations can claim to motivate our desire for service. In an altruistic society like ours that values volunteerism, for example, people (even believers) serve others for all kinds of reasons void of gospel motivation.

Some of us are motivated to serve because we value *compassion*. We see the terrible struggle someone else is facing, and it moves us emotionally. We imagine how life would be if we were in the same situation, so we do something out of sympathy, out of empathy. This sounds good at first. After all, Jesus once saw the harassed and helpless crowds and was moved by them (Matt. 9:36).

It is true that compassion often serves as a great starting point for service, but unless compassion is connected with something deeper, it is unsustainable. Because of our sinfulness, causes that appeal to compassion lose their impact as our senses are slowly numbed to the pain around us. Do you remember the first time you saw the commercial with the starving children? Do you still respond with the same sinking feeling in your gut? Compassion that's only connected to human emotion quickly wanes in impact. Only compassion firmly connected to the gospel is sustainable.

Compassion linked to the gospel is compassion that goes beyond merely observing hurting people; it sees hurting people and realizes that Jesus loves them furiously. Ultimately, then, it's not *our* compassion but the compassion of *Jesus* that fuels and sustains our desire to act on others' behalf. When we remember how gracious and compassionate Christ has been to us, our compassion is as sustainable as our remembrance of the gospel. Without Him, compassion will slowly but surely devolve into a weepy moment that we forget as soon as the commercial ends or someone breaks the mood with a funny joke.

Some are motivated to serve because of *guilt*. Many people feel guilty for their over-indulgent lifestyles, so to alleviate the guilt . . . they serve. She thinks, "Buying seven Coach purses is fine as long as I donate my old ones to the homeless shelter downtown." Dropping some clothes in the donation bag numbs a person's self-awareness of his or her materialism.

Sadly, many church leaders unintentionally use guilt as a quick and easy motivator to recruit volunteers "into ministry."

- "Serve one hour a week, and you'll go home feeling awesome."
- "Feeling empty? Well, just help once a month in the preschool area."
- "You've lived for 'you' all week; live just this one hour for our students."

Guilt-driven serving is the antithesis of Jesus-driven serving, because alleviating guilt is ultimately about the person serving rather than the person being served. The person who serves to remove the guilt surrounding his selfish lifestyle is really serving himself.

Guilt-driven serving is also found when someone feels guilty for an action and wants to "make it up to God" through "doing stuff for Him." Gospel motivation is sabotaged when we feel like we're doing God a favor when we serve. The gospel destroys guilt-laden service. The truth of the gospel is that we are *not* guilty, that all condemnation against us has permanently ceased in Christ.

Others serve out of sheer *force*. When we were growing up, we didn't have to perform a certain number of "community service hours" in order to graduate. In many of today's schools, however, students are required to "volunteer" for class credit. In some churches, youth pastors require students to complete a specific number of serving hours, like a judge passing out community service sentences to those charged with a DUI.

Have you ever called a customer service hotline just furious? Consider the poor guy who answers the phone. He has done nothing to you. He is not responsible for what was or was not in the box. He is simply operating under the policies that were set for him by someone higher up on the organizational food chain.

You chew him out about how he ruined your kid's birthday party, and he's making around $8 an hour to listen to you scream at him. He says things like, "Well, that cable can be purchased at our online store," which makes you angrier because you already bought the product. He's getting destroyed by you, and yet he continues to calmly serve you. Because it's his job.

But what's he really thinking? Do you think he's wishing you a Merry Christmas? Do you think his motivation is empathy? "Oh, this poor guy. I'm hearing your story about not being able to pitch the game onto your massive theater wall so your buddies can watch it. I'm tearing up. I'm misty-eyed." Do you think he is motivated by compassion? Do you think he feels guilty that you are not happy? No, he's being forced. He's serving others because he's being forced to serve others.

But when he clocks out, he will not serve you with patience. When he clocks out, he will not wonder how he can help you. Forceful service is very temporary. It melts neither the heart of the person serving nor the person being served.

The gospel crushes force-driven service, reminding us that Christ wants our hearts when we serve, not merely our physical presence. He wants us to delight in Him as we join Him in serving those around us.

Sometimes we serve others out of *pride*. It's a way to elevate ourselves above others who prove their selfishness by sitting on the couch. Prideful service is never private service; it's always public service. Prideful service always results in the serving person feeling the need to give a testimony about their experience—to prove how "humble" they've been. When service is based on flighty compassion, guilt, force, or pride, God doesn't react too kindly. When Israel, the covenant community of faith, was presenting sacrifices to God with hearts far from Him, God rebuked them:

> Hear the word of the LORD, you rulers of Sodom!
> Give ear to the teaching of our God, you people of
> Gomorrah! "What to me is the multitude of your sacri-
> fices? says the LORD; I have had enough of burnt offerings
> of rams and the fat of well-fed beasts; I do not delight in
> the blood of bulls, or of lambs, or of goats. When you
> come to appear before me, who has required of you this
> trampling of my courts? Bring no more vain offerings;
> incense is an abomination to me. New moon and Sab-
> bath and the calling of convocations—I cannot endure
> iniquity and solemn assembly." (Isa. 1:10–13 ESV)

God was saying, "Do you really think I need bulls from you? Do you think this thing is about bulls and goats? If you need to feed Me, we're in trouble here, aren't we? If I need you to serve Me, then how would I ever be capable of serving you?" Service as an attempt to earn God's favor is not only futile, it is repulsive to Him.

In the New Testament, Jesus similarly and aggressively targeted the heart. In the Sermon on the Mount, He said, "You have heard that it was said, 'You shall not commit adultery'" (Matt. 5:27 ESV). One may reason that adultery is an act, right? It's not an idea; it's an act. "But I say to you that everyone who looks at a woman with lustful intent has already committed adultery with her in his heart" (v. 28 ESV).

Jesus was saying, "If you're not committing adultery because of some sort of white-knuckled 'I know it's not right so I shouldn't do it,' then you're not free. I have come to set you *free* from this. I have come to transform your heart so your actions are transformed, not because of self-will but because of a new spirit."

He said the same thing about our temper: "You have heard that it was said to those of old, 'You shall not murder'" (Matt. 5:21 ESV). Now murder is an act. It's not just an idea; it's an act, right. "But I say to you," says Jesus, "that everyone who is angry with his brother will be liable to judgment" (v. 22 ESV). Do you see that Jesus and the Father are very interested in the motives that drive our actions? You can do the right thing with the wrong motive, and God will always call it sin.

But here is the truly remarkable thing: the gospel doesn't just push us outward to serve; it even makes up for what we lack in that very act of service. How many times have you done something for someone else, thinking your motives were pure, only to realize later they were far from it? The really amazing news is that this is yet another situation for you to remember what God has done for you in Christ. God can still use what you did for His honor, all the while forgiving you for your selfish motives and using the realization of your true motives to conform you more and more to the image of Jesus.

Example and Highest End

Jesus is the beginning of service, the foundation and motivation of service, and yet He is also the *end* of our service—because He is both the example for serving and our highest purpose for serving.

Jesus is the most noble of all pursuits, the highest end imaginable. Serving for the sake of service is not the highest end. We must be careful not to teach people that the ultimate goal of Christianity is serving. *Jesus* is the ultimate goal, the highest end. Our serving must ultimately be grounded *in* Him, and *for* Him, our hearts deeply tuned *toward* Him. He is the example and equipper of gospel-centered service. We are incapable of serving for the right reasons, incapable of making any impact on others or on our culture without Him, without His power.

If you want to see Jesus-centered service in action, look to Jesus, who gave an unforgettable picture of authentic service to His disciples just before His death.

In John 13, we pick up on the story:

> Jesus, knowing that the Father had given all things
> into his hands, and that he had come from God and
> was going back to God, rose from supper. He laid aside

his outer garments, and taking a towel, tied it around
his waist. Then he poured water into a basin and began
to wash the disciples' feet and to wipe them with the
towel that was wrapped around him. (vv. 3–5 ESV)

Think of how nasty our feet are today. Now multiply that gross-
ness by about a billion, and you're still not totally feeling the weight
of this moment between Jesus and His disciples. No act was more
demeaning in the first century than the wiping of a man's feet. Dirty.
Smelly. We'll stop with the adjectives, but you know where we're going.
And yet Christ, the Son of God, took off His outer garment, took up
a basin, filled it with water, and began to wipe the muck and mire off
these men's feet.

The equivalent would be to think of someone in power, someone
well beyond you in wealth, status, and fame—the president of the
United States, for example—being over to dinner at your house. After
you get through eating, he quietly gets up, takes off his jacket, goes to
your bathroom, and begins to scrub around your toilet. The next thing
you do is to go in there to say, "Mr. President, what in the world? You
don't have to do this."

But no matter how wildly you protest, he cannot be pulled away.
He's come here to clean the nastiest part of your house.

Jesus, whose power is well beyond any president or superhero in
every possible way, stooped to the lowest rung on the ladder to serve
His disciples. And Peter, who always had something to say, objected:
"Lord, do you wash my feet?" (John 13:6 ESV).

You can't really hold this brashness against Peter. He felt the weight
of what was happening in the moment, and it made him entirely
uncomfortable. Jesus understood, however, and patiently answered
Peter's objection this way: "If I do not wash you, you have no share
with me," which made Peter swing hard in the other direction and say,
"Lord, not my feet only but also my hands and my head!" (You've got

to love this guy. *You shall never wash my feet,* he says. Then Jesus says, "Well, then, you can't have any part of Me." *Wash all of me then!*

Jesus went on to explain the meaning of His service:

> When he had washed their feet and put on his
> outer garments and resumed his place, he said to them,
> "Do you understand what I have done to you? You call
> me Teacher and Lord, and you are right, for so I am. If
> I then, your Lord and Teacher, have washed your feet,
> you also ought to wash one another's feet. For I have
> given you an example, that you also should do just as I
> have done to you. Truly, truly, I say to you, a servant is
> not greater than his master, nor is a messenger greater
> than the one who sent him." (John 13:12–16 ESV)

The culture in Jesus' day (much like our own culture) was built upon the premise of power. The more powerful, wealthy, and talented you were, the less expectation was on you to lower yourself and help other people. Conversely, the less amount of power, wealth, and talent you had, the more you were expected to serve those who were blessed with more.

But Jesus wasn't into this kind of power trip. He swam upstream against cultural views. His kingdom was and is the site of great reverersal. Just as everything in the universe was spun into chaos when sin entered the picture, Jesus reversed things again and put them in their right order. But because we have always lived in the chaos of sin, the kingdom of God feels backward and counterintuitive to us. In the kingdom, the hungry are full. The poor are rich. The mourning are blessed.

And the powerful are servants.

He said to them, "You're right in calling Me Lord and Teacher, because I am." Jesus was addressing Peter's prevailing view that serving would cause Jesus to lose His stature as the Holy One. "I am beyond you. I am the Alpha and the Omega. I have always been, and I will always be. I can tell it to stop raining, and it will. I can tell it to start raining, and it will. I can tell dead people not to be dead, and they'll listen. I can tell sick people they're no longer sick, and any illness will leave them. And yet I do this to set an example for you—that in the kingdom of God, we don't operate this way. We do not use our power or influence selfishly. We do not use our position to keep from serving those under us. Rather, we use that power, position, and ability to actively lower ourselves and serve those under us and around us."

With Christ as our example, we mimic our Savior who turns the power system on its head.

The gospel is our motivation for moving outside ourselves for the sake of others. That's what Jesus did for us, and we are to follow His example. We don't serve others so we can toss an impressive, updated résumé before God. We serve others because we have been greatly served by Jesus. We imitate our Savior as we are being conformed into His image. As Christ emptied Himself of His authority and served us, we are to empty ourselves of any so-called entitlement and serve others.

Jesus washed His disciples' feet. That's a very practical, down-and-dirty means of service. But what does that mean for us today? How do we put this into practice? How do we challenge people in our churches to serve in light of the gospel?

Everyday Serving

A church that challenges its members to live as servants centered on the gospel invites people to serve continually in all the places where they live, for as *long* as they live. Serving is connected to the gospel and is to be encouraged in homes, neighborhoods, workplaces, and the church.

At home. If you're married, your service must begin with your spouse. If you're not married, it's with your roommate. If you don't have a roommate, maybe you should get a roommate—because other believers provide a sanctifying presence in our lives. When we live in close proximity to another person, such as in marriage, our selfishness is exposed on a daily (if not hourly) basis. Those closest to us are used by God to help transform us into the image of His Son.

People wonder why that first year of marriage is so often a train wreck, but here's why: You may have thought beforehand, *I was doing great living in a house by myself. Why should it be any different now?* Well, you actually *weren't* doing awesome before. You just didn't have the luxury of someone pointing out your deficiencies. You were exercising the option to keep your sin private. But now it's gone public. And though you probably didn't see it this way at the time, the tension of that first year was good for you—a relationship with your spouse that was like iron sharpening iron, producing growth amid flashing sparks of sanctifying abrasion.

The gospel frames how our ministry at home should look. The apostle Paul told husbands to "love [their] wives, as Christ loved the Church and gave himself up for her" (Eph. 5:25 ESV). If a husband comes home seeking to be served, he will always be disappointed and the tension will build. But if he stops to remember, before he even gets out of the car, how Christ served him and gave Himself for him, this awe-filled reality will motivate him to serve his wife well. In the same way, wives are to respect and submit to their husbands out of respect for Christ. The service truly goes both ways. The gospel pushes both husbands and wives to place the other's needs above his or her own needs.

In the neighborhood. Serving those around you can be manifested in simple, practical ways: pulling your neighbor's trash cans on trash day when they're out of town; helping them with home and lawn projects; just declaring yourself available if they ever need anything: "Seriously, I'm not just saying that. I mean it."

Church folks who shut the garage door before they even get out of their vehicle do not send a warm servant's message to those living around them. It's hard to serve your neighbors from your living room.

In God's providence, He has placed all the people in your church in their specific neighborhoods, condos, apartment buildings, and college dorms. These people must be shown the connection between the gospel and their mailing address. They were placed in these residences to lovingly represent Christ by serving as He served.

In the workplace. Just as God in His sovereignty placed the people in your church in their respective homes and neighborhoods, He also placed them in their workplaces. A common misconception among Christians is that their work is not spiritual, that a regular 9-to-5 day cannot be sacred. If they're going to do anything spiritual or ministry-oriented, it'll have to happen around these occupied time slots. But this implies that everybody needs to be a full-time pastor of some kind if they're going to be "spiritual" for the better part of the day and week. The misconception that normal work is not spiritual is both inaccurate and damaging.

Work is *very* spiritual. In fact, God invented work. Work was present in the garden of Eden prior to the fall of humanity. Adam and Eve were given responsibility to tend the garden, and their work was enjoyable and honorable to God. When sin entered the world, yes—work became tainted with sweat, difficult bosses, Microsoft Excel, and frustrating situations at the office, but the concept of work is still very spiritual. When we spend forever with God in heaven, we will have work and industry to accomplish.

So don't ever give the impression that work is mundane and insignificant. God desires Christians to bring their best to their profession so the city and culture will benefit and its people will be served well. Martin Luther believed that all professions were sacred, that "God Himself was milking the cows the profession of the milkmaid."[2]

In the workplace, believers are given an opportunity through the gospel to serve in several different directions—upward, downward, and laterally. Serving *upward* means consistently working hard, knowing you ultimately work for the Lord. Believers should be the best employees on the job because they realize their work is truly done for

God's glory. Serving one's supervisor well is a means of serving Christ well. And if a believer works for another believer, he should serve that person even better (1 Tim. 6:1–2).

Believers who are supervising others are given the opportunity to serve *downward*. By treating employees well and fairly, calling out the best of their gifts, the supervisor honors his or her ultimate Boss in heaven, who sees everything that's done on the job . . . and who is not impressed with the lines and boxes on the org chart (Col. 4:1).

Most believers are also given the opportunity to serve *laterally*, assisting the colleagues who work alongside them. Because of the gospel, believers should encourage and serve these who are equal to them in responsibility, without being a burden to them, without being the slouch at the office who must continually be bailed out by others. One of the best ways a believer serves those who work alongside him is just to do his job well (1 Thess. 4:9–12). That alone is more spiritual and gospel-centric than many people realize.

In the Church. Augustine once said, "The church is a whore, but she is still my mother."[3] Throughout history, the Church has pursued other lovers, chasing after control, power, and misplaced agendas instead of pursuing Jesus and His mission. The Church has committed numerous atrocities in the name of God, neglected to influence the world in which God has placed it, and sold out to a myriad of causes other than the gospel.

But as Augustine said, she is still our mother. Despite all the junk, she is beautiful because she is the bride of Christ. God is passionate for His Church, and He has gifted believers to serve His Church. Each time spiritual gifts are mentioned in the Scripture, they are immediately connected to serving others in the Church.

In Romans 12, the apostle Paul built the case that each person belongs to every other person in the Church and that each person should use his gifts according to the grace of God to serve others (v. 7). In 1 Corinthians 12, he devoted an entire chapter to challenging believers to use their gifts for the common good of others in the body

(v. 7). In Ephesians 4, he reminded believers that pastors/teachers are to train believers for ministry so the body of Christ will benefit (vv. 11–12). And in 1 Peter 4, Peter commanded all believers to use whatever gift they have received to serve (v. 10).

After Jesus served His disciples by washing their feet, He told them they should wash one another's feet (John 13:14). Because Christ served *them*, they were to serve each other, and He has placed believers in local churches today so we will serve our brothers and sisters. Wise church leaders will preach the gospel *and* provide opportunities for people to serve in response. Without such opportunities, people will live with all this frustrated, unused spiritual energy balled up inside them, and the Church will not be who she should be.

Jesus, even to this day, continues to wash our dirty feet. Like children who constantly come inside caked with mud, dirt, and filth, we come to Him every day with our sin. And yet He continues, with a towel around His waist, to wash our feet. The painful irony is not that we get dirty again but that many believers fail to put a towel around their own waist to wash dirt off the feet of others. Churches centered on Jesus constantly remind their people how Christ has served and continues to serve them. And this becomes the one, the only, the supreme impetus for serving others.

CHAPTER 5

THE CREATURE MULTIPLIES

Every Christian is either a missionary or an imposter.

~ CHARLES SPURGEON[1]

WE ARE NOT OLD MEN.

We are in our mid to late thirties, but the world has radically changed in our brief years of life. When we were kids, for example, cartoons came on television at specific times of day. You could watch them in the morning, in the afternoons right after school, or on Saturday mornings. That was pretty much it, except for the annual prime-time, holiday showings of things like Charlie Brown, Rudolph, and Frosty the Snowman. Prevailing logic said that cartoons at night made no sense at all because the children would all be in bed. The idea of a twenty-four-hour network that aired only cartoons was about as absurd as a TV show where twenty-five mostly insecure women with loose morals try to make a single man fall in love with them.

Besides having limited cartoons, we also didn't have any such thing as a remote control. If you were fortunate enough to have cable, a box sat on top of your television with a little sliding bar that gave you access to thirty or forty channels, at most. But if you wanted to change the station or adjust the volume, you had to get up out of your seat, walk over to the television set, and make your selections from there. How primitive.

Reach back in your mind and remember some of the simple implications. Commercials were (and still are) broadcast as much as ten times louder than the television shows they were interrupting. So without having a remote at hand, a person could get a stitch in his side running back and forth from the television to the sofa. It wasn't pretty.

We also had no capability of recording something on TV to watch later. That was the stuff of Tomorrowland and futuristic legend. If *Alf* or *Magnum P.I.* happened to come on while we were out doing something else—or at the same time as another program we wanted to watch—well, that was just too bad.

We did have video games. They were in arcades at the mall, and they cost a quarter to play. Imagine how cool it was when Atari came out. Wow, being able to play video games right there in our own homes! There were some drawbacks, though—like, for example, every game on Atari made the same exact noise, and over time the incessant beeping would drive you mad. Today, as one of the signs of my aging, these culture-changing creations are now considered retro and hip.

From the arcade to the theater—on the average weekend only one or two new movies would come out, not ten or twelve, like today. Of those, maybe one or two a year were cartoons. There was no Internet, no smartphones. Sports had their own seasons, and you didn't have pictures to color at restaurants.

So . . . what did we do with ourselves in that apocalyptic setting?

Shocker alert: We played outside.

How crazy is that? "Go outside and play," our parents would tell us, meaning we didn't have to be, nor did they really want us to be, home till dark. And so up until sunset, we ran, we rode our bikes, we made up battles with kids from other blocks. It was anarchy. It is amazing that we're still alive today to tell some of the tales.

Today, we're the most entertained generation the world has ever seen. There's more to do, more to participate in, more to connect with, more to read about, and more information to digest than at any other time in history. And yet having so much access to so much stuff still hasn't filled our need or our desire to be part of something bigger, something grander, something beyond even the wonders that come to us on our phones, laptops, and tablets. Like kids creating and competing in afternoon conquests, we still want to be involved in bigger undertakings, bigger challenges, bigger things that make a bigger difference. We still long for a grand mission.

A conversation once held between colleagues C. S. Lewis and J. R. R. Tolkien speaks to this innate human desire for being part of larger-than-life stories, quests, and victories—the draw of our hearts toward "myths," which Lewis said were "lies and therefore worthless, even though breathed through silver."[2]

"No," Tolkien replied, "they are not lies." Far from being untrue, myths are the best way—sometimes the only way—of conveying truths that would otherwise remain inexpressible. We have come from God, Tolkien argued, and inevitably the myths woven by us, though they do contain error, still reflect a splintered fragment of the true light, the eternal truth that is with God. Myths may be misguided, but they steer however shakily toward the true harbor.[3]

Revisiting some of what we covered in chapter 1 will help bring clarity to what Tolkien was telling Lewis. When sin entered the created order, it fractured everything, from our cells to the very essence of the universe. What was once simply "good" now had the capacity to become perverse, idolatrous, and empty. But God had a rescue plan prepared—a plan to crush the head of the enemy and restore shalom in the universe, to woo home his captured bride and make all things new at great cost. There is no greater battle or love story. And even as you're reading this sentence, the epic is happening all around us.

Tolkien's point to Lewis was this: the reason we're repeatedly drawn into these kinds of mythical stories—the reason we want to be part of a "bigger something"—is because God has imprinted these themes on our souls. And though not everyone knows it, the "bigger something" we long to be part of is the "biggest something" of all, the greatest epic the universe will ever know—God reconciling all things to Himself in Christ.

One of the main reasons mankind is so restless these days, why we so easily and quickly downshift into boredom, is because instead of participating in this one great drama, we're content just to watch and wish we were involved in something this significant. We keep going to movies, watching television shows, and buying video games that give hints of this grand romance and battle. Yet for some reason we fail to see that we are actually caught up in it.

We are in the middle of the love story, the middle of the epic battle. Our real lives are a daring connection point between God and men for the healing of broken lives and a broken culture. By God's grace, we must help the people in our churches see the "epic" in the ordinary details of life? We must challenge them to open their eyes to this grand event happening all around them, in the hearts of every individual they encounter, and then inspire them to play a fearless, tour-de-force role in this gripping drama of the ages. God used believers before us to pull us into the story. Every one of us in the faith was brought into the faith through the influence of others. God has chosen to expand the Creature through multiplication that is centered on Jesus.

For me (Matt), it was my mom. She always had a steadfast faith in the Lord. She loved Him and strove to follow Him. I could see Jesus in her.

There was also a man named Ronnie Hazzard, a Sunday school teacher at First Baptist Church of Texas City. He was a patient, gracious man, and I was moved—even as an unbeliever—by how he loved his wife and daughters and the warmth of their hospitality.

There were others who played key roles in my life: Jerry Hendricks, a youth minister and avid baseball card collector who took an interest in me and welcomed my questions and presence in his office after school. Another was Jeff Faircloth, a fellow high school student who straight-up said to me, "I need to tell you about Jesus. When do you want to do that?" It wasn't, "Hey, read this tract and let me know what you think," or "Hey, do you want to come to church with me on Wednesday night?" It was literally, *"I need to tell you about Jesus. You decide the when and the where, but it's happening—right now before football practice, right afterward, or some other time this week. Whenever you say, we're doing this."* I didn't get saved immediately after he shared the gospel with me, but I did become very intrigued. And over a period of time, God began to break down the walls that were keeping me separated from Him.

Then one day . . . He just saved me. I don't know how to explain it. I was checking things out, studying, finding reasons why I shouldn't believe, reasons why I shouldn't need to buy in and submit to Christ. And yet in the middle of all those questions, doubts, and intellectual barriers, I think Jesus just got tired of playing with me and said, "No, you're Mine." He rescued me and captivated my heart, and I just immediately fell in love. I still had lots of questions, but when God opened up my heart to Him, I truly became, as the Scripture says, a "new creation." The old Matt "passed away." My perspective changed in that moment.

One life. Spotlit on an epic stage. Surrounded by key players who could easily have chosen to be distracted on themselves and their own dreamy interests . . . if they hadn't been aware that a grander story was happening right there in front of them, around a young guy named Matt—a story that brought ultimate suspense and excitement into their lives, a role they were "reborn" to play. What do you bet there's no greater thrill in their lives than seeing their names within this narrative, members of the supporting cast in God's saving work in one person's life? What other weekend entertainment or side hobby could ever fill them with such deep, relentless satisfaction? What's bigger than being part of the biggest story going?

This is the essence of gospel multiplication.

It's how God calls people to Himself, one person at a time, growing His body today in what is becoming an eternal adventure and romance with Him.

And everyone in your church should be invited to join in.

Multiplication Practice

So how does Jesus-centered multiplication work? It works a lot like what we just read in Matt's story: his mom, Ronnie Hazzard, Jerry Hendricks, and Jeff Faircloth talking to him or showing him the gospel, answering his questions about Jesus, pouring into him out of their lives, walking in patience with him, putting up with his ignorance and arrogance. In God's grace, these four influencers were used powerfully by God to multiply the faith into Matt's life, just as each of them had earlier been drawn to Christ themselves through individuals who lived a biblical faith in front of them, proclaimed the excellencies of Jesus where they could hear them, and led them in the direction of the gospel. The "old" passed away, and the "new" came into being (2 Cor. 5:17 ESV). And only the greatest epic, the story to which all stories point, has the power to bring transformation.

But as we move from an individual made new in verse 17, we look directly ahead to the next line: "All this is from God, who through Christ reconciled us to himself and gave us the ministry of reconciliation" (v. 18 ESV). If we follow how gospel-centered multiplication works, we see men and women who have been influenced by others toward faith in Jesus Christ, who have been captured by the gospel, and who have been maturing in their faith through the influence that others have played and are still playing in their lives. Not only have they been reconciled to God, they have also been saved into the covenant community. What next? Now *their* influence starts to multiply—into *others'* lives—as they work from within that community to lead others to faith and maturity in the gospel.

Adding. Multiplying. Exponentially growing.

All the time.

And we all get to be a part of it.

This takes us back to the beginning of the chapter and our assertion for why we're so restless and prone to boredom. We sit here in our modern-day world, demanding that the activities of the moment satisfy us and give us meaning. We order them to meet the yawning lack of significance and purpose that aches in our hearts whenever we turn off our public faces and realize we're getting older without necessarily getting richer, fuller, deeper, better. Whatever we hope to accomplish, achieve, and be known for is bound by the constraints of what remains of our human lifetime. And as the time slips steadily and quickly by, the pulse to find more in each experience intensifies.

But what if our people realized—more each Sunday, more each month, more each year—that their lives are as connected with God's promise to Abraham in Genesis 12 as they are to the business of the day? That God's plan of redeeming and reconciling people from all nations and people groups is as alive and electric today as it was at the dawn of civilization and, indeed, in eternity past? That the work of the apostles and leaders of the early church is as attached to our own work in God's kingdom as their work was attached to God's promises to His people Israel? Today is an opportunity to engage in a centuries-old epic, to splash into an ocean of God's sovereignty, and send out ripples that will continually mount in reach and intensity, stretching eternally in all directions.

This . . . is huge.

Rodney Stark, an expert in the rise of Christianity, estimates that by the year AD 350, an estimated 52.9 percent of the Roman Empire worshipped Jesus as Lord.[4] That's some serious multiplication. Think of it: the reason we are a worshipping, serving, community of faith today is because men and women before us took seriously what they had been given—"the ministry of reconciliation"—and dove headfirst into it by multiplying the work of Christ in them. They were caught up in the great romance, the epic drama.

And now it's our turn. Regardless of where we, or the people we serve, are in spiritual maturity, we are instruments in the hand of God to see all things reconciled to God through Christ.

Whether someone in your church is a young, urban professional, an empty nester, a parent to a young family, or a student, each of them have been uniquely designed and placed here by God for the ministry of reconciliation, multiplying the grace and mercy that has changed them. They are agents of reconciliation.

That's the great, gospel drama you must continually invite them to live. They don't have to watch *Saving Private Ryan* over and over again anymore. They don't have to fantasize about what it would be like to wage some epic battle or to fight for some deep love. They don't have to just imagine what it would be like to be part of something huge and pivotal in history. *They're already in it!* They just need to "go outside and play."

Over the years, we have run into people who think the city in which they live is lame, their job is lame, their church is lame, their neighborhood is lame. Everything . . . lame. How different would they feel if they knew that God had called, equipped, and set them free to be part of His mission of reconciliation in their own workplaces, neighborhoods, cities, and churches—the very things with which they're so very discontent?

Evangelism and More

This mission of multiplication plays out in more diverse ways than simply evangelism. It's never *less* than evangelism, but it can certainly be more. Think of how the apostle Paul painted the gospel in Colossians 1:15–20 (ESV):

> [Jesus] is the image of the invisible God, the firstborn of all creation. For by him all things were created, in heaven and on earth, visible and invisible, whether thrones or dominions or rulers or authorities—all things were created through him and for him. And he is before all things, and in him all things hold together. And he is the head of the body, the church. He is the beginning, the firstborn from the dead, that in everything he might be preeminent. For in him all the fullness of God was pleased to dwell, and through him to reconcile to himself all things, whether on earth or in heaven, making peace by the blood of his cross.

As glorious as the redemption of any one person to Christ is, the majesty of what the gospel accomplishes on a grand, cultural, cosmic scale only adds to its ability to inspire and amaze. So when God calls us to the job description of being "ambassadors for Christ" (2 Cor. 5:20 ESV), He means much more than just repeating a one-time gospel message to those still outside the community of faith.

As church leaders, yes, we must continually encourage people to be bold in sharing their faith. We must not suggest that the potential awkwardness and discomfort involved in challenging people to consider the claims of Christ somehow exempts the squeamish from going there anyway. But at the same time, we must diligently and consistently cast the gospel in larger terms than only evangelism. The gospel consumes the Christian life itself, affecting how our corporate lives play out among the communities where God has placed us, providing us with multiplication potential at every turn.

If someone is a regenerated, Jesus-centered worshipper of God, this change of heart should create a certain ethic in his business style and practices. It should inspire excellence and integrity in his schoolwork.

It should infuse a noticeable joy and genuineness in the way he interacts with those around him. It should make him gracious and kind toward waiters and waitresses and store cashiers. In whatever domain God has place ma believer, a gospel-centered believer is a *faithful presence*,[5] an all-the-time witness of the gospel of Jesus Christ—an ambassador of Jesus Christ.

But as Jesus-centered people, this call to all-around Christian living is not motivated by the desire to be a good person; rather, it is based on the understanding that we are *not* good people, and yet Christ has extended grace to us. Unlike the adherents of other religions, we're not trying to earn anything, nor are we trying to impress anybody. We've been freely given, and so we freely give. We walk uprightly because we've been loved and forgiven, not because we're better than anybody else.

In this way, we are truly ambassadors for Christ—ambassadors of His gospel.

Living and proclaiming the gospel on a daily, ongoing basis, we reach out in love as an implication of this gospel. We're not after converts; we're after disciples—encouraging our neighbors and coworkers in the Lord; speaking life into those we interact with; sharing gospel truth as a matter of course; inviting others into our communities of faith to explore, ask questions, and walk with us; making much of Jesus with those at our kids' sporting events, at the gym, in the dorm halls, and in business relationships.

We're discovering the reality of something bigger, better, and more beautiful than our own desires and comfort. All day every day.

Again, it's all part of being wrapped up in the epic of God's gospel purposes. Do we really see it that way? Do we encourage others to see it that way? He's inviting us to come play our specific parts, maturing others through the power of the Holy Spirit, always multiplying what God has multiplied in us.

The Bigger Story

Whenever people come to a service at your church, they should hear in some way that we are all sinners in need of grace, but that grace has been extended to us in Jesus Christ. His righteousness has been imputed to us, and in His cross God's wrath toward us has been removed if we will hear, submit, and believe. Every week someone should proclaim the gospel, no matter what the topic is. If we're talking about holiness, about manhood, about marriage, parenting, money, or any particular biblical command, we need to teach it and talk about it in view of the gospel, always bringing it back to the epic story of God's redemption.

For this is how we inspire people to see their place in His bigger story. This is how the desire for multiplication keeps being stirred in the hearts of individuals living in community. This is how the seeds of new relationships are stirred into growth, all the way from personal interactions with people down the street to church planting projects with people in other parts of the city, state, region, or world. As people continually embrace and understand the gospel, His love supernaturally compels them to invest their lives in ensuring the gospel is embraced by others. People who own the gospel themselves don't want to be the only ones who own the gospel.

A Creature centered on Jesus multiplies both organically and organizationally. People within the church multiply as they live with a "mission of reconciliation" on the forefront of their minds. Typically church leaders long for a program at this point, a method to help people within the church multiply. And while these ideas are grounded in sincere motivations, the answer is not another program. Organic multiplication simply happens as people are constantly and continually refreshed with the gospel and reminded of their part in the greater story.

In Matthew 16, when Peter answered Jesus' inquiry about who people were saying Jesus was, Peter responded with "You are the

Messiah." Jesus told Peter he was a small stone (*petros*) but that Jesus would build and multiply the Church on the Rock (*petra*), the reality that He was the Christ who came to rescue sinners. The multiplication movement is built on Jesus and His work for us. And each person is a small stone. Each has a part to play in God's redemptive plan for the nations. Multiplication will rise to the level that the people in our churches understand the bigger story and realize they have a part in it,

At the same time, a church consumed with Jesus will be driven to rally people around focused multiplication. A church will be driven to organizational multiplication, a leveraging of resources to ensure other Jesus-centered churches around the world are planted. There will always be a deep relationship between churches embracing the gospel and those churches multiplying and planting new churches. For as a church feasts on Christ's mission, she is driven to multiply. She rallies leaders, leverages resources, and challenges people to participate in the beautiful birth of churches that are grounded in Jesus.

Jesus spoke His Church into existence. She is formed by the Word. When a local church lives as a local Creature of the Word, she is matured as she worships, lives in community, serves, and multiplies. How beautiful the Creature the Lord forms!

CHAPTER 6

JESUS-CENTERED CULTURE

The gospel kingdom is a kingdom of light, life, and love. Opposite to light is ignorance and error. Opposite to life is a religion that consists of shows, dead rites, and empty ceremonies. Opposite to love is uncharitableness, malice, and especially hatred of the power of godliness.

~ THOMAS MANTON[1]

TRAGEDY STRUCK THE MOUNTAIN-CLIMBING COMMUNITY on May 15, 2006. As David Sharp was on his descent from the top of Mount Everest, he sought shelter under a rock in an area known as Green Boots Cave, the site where an individual wearing green hiking boots died in May 1996 and whose body remains there on the mountain. Precisely ten years later, almost to the day, David Sharp sat exhausted and alone in that same exact location, just a few feet away from the man known as "Green Boots."

Dying.

At the same time, a group of forty climbers was ascending the famed Everest, arduously pursuing their lifelong dream of standing on top of the world. Like others before them who've endured this grueling climb, including passage through the "death zone," where lack of oxygen and the extreme cold can cause frostbite to any exposed part of the body, they were intent on fulfilling their quest. Most people pay close to 25,000 US dollars in permit and guide fees for this daring experience. Quitting is hardly in their vocabulary.

And they were close to accomplishing their goal. Very close. Achingly close. But to reach the top of this famed mountain and complete their purpose in coming here, they first had to pass by the legendary Green Boots Cave, where David Sharp lay dying.

What should they do?

What would *you* do? What did *they* do?

Every single climber trudged past David Sharp.

Obviously, there may have been little they could actually have done to help him cling to life. Abandoning their climb at that point in the expedition to pivot into a desperate rescue operation could not have guaranteed success and the survival of this dying man. But the fact remains: when confronted with the choice of either continuing toward the peak or offering help to a dying man, these climbers went on. They left him to die.

Why?

Some blamed the tragedy on a lack of safety messages and strategic systems. They bemoaned the easy access granted to today's climbers regardless of experience level. They pointed to the need for permanent rescue teams, for more formal contingencies and evacuation plans.

However, the first man to reach the summit of Everest, the revered Sir Edmund Hillary, had another reaction. Instead of looking first to blame logistics and procedures, he lamented the mountain-climbing culture: "I think the whole attitude towards climbing Mount Everest has become rather horrifying. People just want to get to the top."

According to him, this tragedy was a result of a cultural dysfunction rather than poor messaging or strategic failures.[2]

As we launch into the second part of this book, we will challenge you to wrestle with the culture of your church. By *culture*, we are not referring to the socioeconomic or ethnic mix of your church. We are referring to the *heart* of your church, the *character* of your church. While messages centered on Jesus are essential in creating a culture shaped by the gospel, your church's culture is broader than a doctrinal statement expressing a commitment to the gospel; it's more comprehensive than teaching the gospel from the platform. Your church needs a culture immersed in the gospel of Jesus, a culture that is centered on and fueled by the reality of His birth, life, death, burial, and resurrection. If your church is to live as a healthy, vibrant Creature of the Word today, you must be concerned with its culture—and willing to change it, if necessary.

Culture 101

Each local church is a small reflection of the larger Church, the called-out ones from every tribe, tongue, and nation purchased with the blood of Christ who will eternally gather to declare the greatness of God. This local body of believers is made up of individuals with specific gifts and personalities who, by the providence of God, have been formed into one body in Christ (Rom. 12:5). And this group has a certain personality, a character, a collective soul, a set of deeply held values, whether openly declared or merely understood, that guides its ongoing actions.

In other words, your church has a distinct and unique culture.

But while every church has a culture, not every church possesses a *healthy* culture. The healthier the culture, the more likely the church will impact the community around her. A healthy gospel-centric culture turns the church from an institution into a movement of truth and grace where people's lives are continually formed in the gospel.

In the 1920s, Alfred Alder, a founder in modern psychology, made some strong assertions about individual personality. He proposed that for a person to have a healthy and strong personality, there must be harmony between how the person sees himself and how others perceive him.[3] If an individual sees himself as loving and benevolent yet is a complete jerk to everyone around him, this clear inconsistency naturally points to an unhealthy personality.

In the same way, a church culture is healthy when there is congruence and consistency between what the church says is important to her and what others know *really is* important to her. If a church declares that the gospel is the most important message the world has ever known, and yet the gospel is not seen as the impetus and motivation for all the church offers, this disconnect is indicative of an unhealthy church personality or culture. If the church leaders say to people, "Living on mission in our city is vital," yet they rarely if ever offer opportunities for people to serve the city, then a chasm exists between how the leaders see the church and how others see her.

You want more? We've got more.

If a pastor teaches on the grace of Christ being bigger than any sin, yet the culture does not allow for openness and confession, an outsider who admits to struggle in his life will be unlikely to experience much mercy in the way people express themselves. Sadly, a culture of law will weed out a doctrine of grace.

If the doctrine of a church is that all believers are priests and ministers, yet the culture is one that is overly dependent on pastoral staff, the culture will initially shrug off a pastor who aims for equipping others rather than hiring the ministry away to "professionals."

If the doctrine of a church is that people outside of Christ will face an eternity in hell, yet the culture is one that does not celebrate conversions or evangelistic witness, the culture of the church will contradict its doctrinal stance by continually focusing inward instead of outward.

If the culture of a church is at odds with the stated beliefs of the church, the culture is typically the overpowering alpha male in the room. The unstated message speaks louder than the stated one.

Harvard business professor John Kotter wrote of organizational culture: "Culture powerfully influences human behavior, can be difficult to change, and its near invisibility makes it hard to address directly."[4] In other words, culture is a powerful yet often unseen force in the life of a church—more powerful than many church leaders estimate. It is what people in the community sense when they think of you. In their minds, your culture is who you really are.

So who *are* you? What *should* they sense from being around you and your people? And how can you accurately assess your church's culture?

We'll spend the balance of this chapter looking at the elements that go into church culture and how to align them so that your core beliefs and your observable reality look the same from both sides. But to get a quick snapshot of your church's culture, organizational theorists and consultants would likely instruct you to look at your heroes. Every organization chooses heroes, people who are the epitome of the culture, the "face" of the group. What would this kind of analysis reveal in terms of your own church climate? How would it help you know if your church is centered on the gospel?

Ask yourself: Is Jesus your hero?

If the pastor's face is the logo of a church, there's a chance that Jesus is not the hero. If programs, creativity, leadership savvy, or innovation is your hero, this is a good indication that the church is not centered on the gospel. Jesus is always the hero of a church centered on the gospel.

And the gospel is what your community needs to experience, not only through your doctrinal or vision statements but also through your church's culture.

Culture typically wins. And only a Jesus-centered culture transforms.

Cultural Frustration

To express love and appreciation to her personal hero, Anna Marie Jarvis founded Mother's Day, then embarked on a campaign to establish it as a national holiday by pushing the right buttons with influencers and politicians. In the early 1900s, Congress passed a law declaring the second Sunday in May—Mother's Day.

But several years later Anna hated what she started, eventually devoting her life (as well as her life savings) to abolishing what she had fought so hard to secure. The commercialization of Mother's Day sickened her, especially the cards too easily chosen by the mother's children and then hastily signed with only their name. "A printed card," she said, "means nothing except that you are too lazy to write to the woman who has done more for you than anyone in the world." The thought of sons and daughters signing cards and buying candy to pacify their mothers and disguise their lack of true affection was deeply disturbing to her.

Mother's Day had started with the highest of ideals, but the Mother's Day *culture* had become something much different than conceived.

In the Old Testament, during Israel's history with the sacrificial system, God often observed the same attitude. He witnessed His people adhering to a system without being filled with gratitude to God for the forgiveness of sin these practices symbolized.

God started the sacrificial system for at least two reasons. *First*, He desired His people to loathe sin. With the constant stream of bloody sacrifices offered by the priests, people were confronted continually with the seriousness of His holiness and their sin. Every time they sinned, something had to die. *Second*, the sacrificial system was intended to help people long for a Savior whose sacrifice would be complete and perfect. The system was elaborate, but it was never intended to be sufficient; instead, it pointed to something much better, something much deeper. It was designed to be a tutor to teach people they could never fulfill the law.

When David was king, many people missed the point. The culture among God's people was filled with empty sacrifices, with no loathing of sin or a longing for the Savior. Much like an ungrateful son quickly signing a Mother's Day card in an empty attempt to pacify his mother, many people mindlessly offered their sacrifices. Into this apathetic and untransformed culture, David wrote the following lines, addressing himself to God:

> In sacrifice and offering you have not delighted, but you have given me an open ear. Burnt offering and sin offering you have not required. Then I said, "Behold, I have come; in the scroll of the book it is written of me: I delight to do your will, O my God; your law is within my heart." (Ps. 40:6–8 ESV)

Surely these words sounded strange to the people of Israel, watching David preside over a nation with the sacrificial system he was lamenting. But David had developed God's distaste for empty sacrifices before he was crowned king. In fact, he was anointed as king after Saul was rejected for attempting to use sacrifices as a way of appeasing God without a heart that longed for Him (1 Sam. 15). David had long been convinced that God was focused on the hearts of His people—their culture—not on the mindless emotions that betrayed their true feelings. So into this culture of meaningless sacrifice, David assured God that his ears were open to Him, that he was ready to listen and obey.

But did David obey perfectly? Were his ears truly open to God to continually do as God instructed?

Of course not. Both his sacrifices and his obedience faltered. But the truth of Psalm 40 lived on, because it ultimately pointed to the King who *would* obey perfectly, whose sacrifice *would* be sufficient. The New Testament confirms that David's psalm was ultimately not

David's psalm; it was the psalm of the King who would suffer for His people.

> For since the law has but a shadow of the good
> things to come instead of the true form of these realities,
> it can never, by the same sacrifices that are continually
> offered every year, make perfect those who draw near.
> Otherwise, would they not have ceased to be offered,
> since the worshipers, having once been cleansed, would
> no longer have any consciousness of sins? But in these
> sacrifices there is a reminder of sins every year. For it is
> impossible for the blood of bulls and goats to take away
> sins. Consequently, when Christ came into the world,
> he said, "Sacrifices and offerings you have not desired,
> but *a body have you prepared for me*; in burnt offerings
> and sin offerings you have taken no pleasure. Then I
> said, 'Behold, I have come to do your will, O God, as
> it is written of me in the scroll of the book.'" When he
> said above, "You have neither desired nor taken pleasure
> in sacrifices and offerings and burnt offerings and sin
> offerings" (these are offered according to the law), then
> he added, "Behold, I have come to do your will." He
> does away with the first in order to establish the second.
> And by that will we have been sanctified through the
> offering of the body of Jesus Christ once for all. (Heb.
> 10:1–10 ESV, italics added)

Under the sacrificial system, the sacrifices never ended, which proved they could not cleanse. The tribe of Levi is an ironic example of the endless nature of the sacrifices. When God divided the land for the twelve tribes, He gave each of them land that would provide for them and meet their needs . . . except for the tribe of Levi. Instead of giving them land, God provided for them by instructing that portions of the sacrifices and offerings be given to them as their provision. In essence, the Levites ate only because the people continued to sin. God knew the sacrifices would be sufficient to feed the Levites because the sacrifices would never end. They were insufficient to take away sin.

Christ came to fulfill, complete, and redeem the system. He stood on the edge of heaven and entered our world in a body so His obedience could become our obedience and His sacrifice would end all other sacrifices. King David offered his ears to God; King Jesus offered His body.

We are not forgiven by our sacrifices but by *His* sacrifice. The earthly priests were always standing, day after day, frantically running around offering sacrifice after sacrifice because the sacrifices were only temporary coverings for sin. But Jesus sat down after He offered Himself because His sacrifice is complete.

We are not forgiven by our obedience but by His obedience. David understood that obedience is better than sacrifice, but none of us obeys perfectly. Our sin has ruined our obedience. But because of the cross, what is true of Him becomes true of us. Because Jesus obeyed perfectly, His obedience is given freely to us.

Cultural Transformation

The sacrificial system was broken because we are broken.

In the same way, church cultures void of the gospel are empty and worthless. Church cultures, apart from the grace of Jesus, are utterly broken. And just because a church talks about grace does not mean its culture is filled with grace. Thankfully Jesus changes everything. Unlike Anna Marie Jarvis, Jesus could change and fulfill the system that was always designed to point to Him. Only Jesus can transform a church culture. But if we refuse to let Him, if we do not embrace a consistent, refreshing, gospel-centered culture, our churches will automatically drift toward a system of mindless and worthless religious feasts that disgust God.

If mission engagement is in the culture of a church *without continual gospel reminders,* the tendency will be to drift toward mission as a way to cleanse the conscience rather than as a response to God's mission for us. If expressive worship is in the culture of a church *without continual gospel awareness,* the tendency will be to focus on what is done for God rather than remembering what He has done. If transparency and honesty are in the culture of a church *without continual gospel encounters,* the tendency will be to discuss the sinfulness without repentance.

Just as Christ stepped into the sacrificial culture of His day to bring transformation, church leaders must realize we need Him to transform the culture in our churches . . . continually.

If forming our culture is a constant endeavor for leaders, then forming a gospel-centric culture is more so. Our tendency to drift away from grace is against us. Our proclivity to wander from the gospel threatens us. Forming culture is not a one-time event—much more than a fresh sermon series or a small group Bible study. It must be a continual priority to infuse the totality of our churches with the beauty and awesomeness of the gospel.

A holy tension is embedded in church ministry. On one hand, Christ clearly declared that He would build His Church (Matt. 16:18). *We* do not build His Church, nor did He promise to build *our* churches. If anything good happens in the church, it is only because God caused the good—in His Church. If any transformation occurs, it is only because God did the transforming—in His Church. He is the author and perfecter of the faith. He is the One who began the good work in the people you shepherd, and He is the One who will complete the transformation.

On the other hand, the apostle Paul laid a foundation for ministry as a skilled builder (1 Cor. 3:10). With great intensity and skill, he planted churches in strategic cities so that the gospel would take root around the world. With intentionality, he invited Timothy along for the journey so he could pour his life into Timothy. With foresight and knowledge, he skillfully addressed the scholars on Mars Hill using their own arguments and poets to dethrone their gods and preach Jesus as God. With time, tears, and love, he instructed people to form their lives on the gospel. In other words, he did not just wing it.

And in this lies the tension. God is the One who is ultimately able to form a culture in your church of deep reliance on the gospel. Yet He has given you responsibility and authority in His Church. He joyfully allows you to steward the Church He is building. Just as spiritual maturation is best characterized as divine-human synergy, so is local church ministry. Spiritual growth is the working out of what God has worked and is working in us (Phil. 2:12–13), and church ministry consists of intentionally forming culture while realizing He is the One who ultimately does the transforming.

As a church leader, you must assume responsibility for the culture of your church. While strategy and structure are essential, culture trumps them both Peter Drucker once remarked that "culture eats strategy for breakfast." If you have strategies and structures inconsistent with your culture, the culture will swallow them. But if you have a healthy gospel-centered culture, the culture will create momentum and carry an impact far greater than any strategy.

A Case Study

Paul wrote the book of Galatians as a scolding letter to the church in that region because the culture in the church had shifted from the gospel. Harmony was broken between what they believed and how they lived.

Despite receiving and believing the gospel, the church culture had been twisted out of shape and marked by disunity as preferential treatment had developed based on circumcision. The Jewish believers were returning to the law as a way of earning God's favor and were reverting to circumcision as a way of setting themselves apart from other believers. Joy in their forgiveness was exchanged for bitter rule-following, and their freedom was traded for careful attention to the religious calendar. Though once alive with thankfulness for the gospel, their hearts were now cold.

If the Galatian church leaders had a doctrinal statement, surely it would have been pure, sound, and gospel-centered. Yet the *practice* of the church was not in harmony with the truth of the gospel. When Paul analyzed the culture of the church, he discovered:

- They were attracted to new teaching, teaching that added to the gospel (1:6).
- They failed to see the gospel's everyday implications, including its impact on how we relate to others (2:14).
- They returned to principles and rules instead of walking in freedom and grace (2:18; 5:1).
- They treated the gospel as essential for their forgiveness but not sufficient for their sanctification (3:3).
- They trusted their formal practices to earn God's approval (4:10).
- Their neglect of grace turned them into a miserable bunch of people (4:15).
- They became preoccupied with externals rather than grace and inward transformation (5:2).
- Their gospel amnesia manifested itself in fighting and disunity (5:15).

This church was attempting to supplement the gospel with other things: circumcision, observing special religious days, adherence to the law. And then, as now, whenever we attempt to supplement the gospel with something else, we unintentionally supplant it.[5] Paul stepped in with a strong rebuke:

> O foolish Galatians! Who has bewitched you? It
> was before your eyes that Jesus Christ was publicly
> portrayed as crucified. Let me ask you only this: Did you
> receive the Spirit by works of the law or by hearing with

faith? Are you so foolish? Having begun by the Spirit, are
you now being perfected by the flesh? (Gal. 3:1–3 ESV)

Paul also confronted Peter during this time because of Peter's failure to apply the gospel to the daily activities of the church (2:14). Peter's
philosophy and practice did not match the theology he preached. Here
was Peter—the man God used to first bring the gospel to the Gentiles,
someone who devoted his life to declaring the gospel. Yet to appease
Jewish believers, he pulled back from eating with Gentile believers
because they were not circumcised. By not eating with other believers
who held to the gospel, Peter gave the impression that circumcision was
important for justification. Paul was livid because he knew that Peter's
practice preached louder than his sermons. In fact, even Barnabas was
led astray by the hypocrisy (2:13).

Terrifying is the reality that inconsistent practice and belief has a
reverse effect on what we believe. Often people will alter their beliefs to
justify their practice. Thus, people involved in a church not centered on
the gospel in practice will likely drift from gospel dependency as well.

Paul begged the church at Galatia for consistency: "You have
embraced the gospel; live fully in the gospel. If it were not enough,
then Christ died for nothing" (see Gal. 2:21). Gospel theology must
translate into gospel practice. For a church culture to be centered on
the gospel, there must be harmony between theology, philosophy, and
practice. The more these three are connected, the stronger a church
culture is. But whenever there is a disconnect among any of these
areas—theology, philosophy, and practice—the culture weakens and
the potential impact of the church suffers. All three must converge to
put the gospel on full display and to keep the gospel paramount.

Gospel-Centered Framework

Some basic definitions will be helpful. *Theology* is your church's
"thinking about God." It is the beliefs to which your church holds

doctrinally, what your church believes. Ministry *philosophy* is your church's "thinking about ministry," the commitments that undergird all your church does. *Practice,* of course, is what your church actually does.

Here is an example. A church believes that God exists as a community of three Persons, that He created a community of people later wrecked by the fall, but that Christ forms a new community of faith through His death and resurrection, commanding His followers to encourage one another. This is important *theology.* So because of that theology, the church holds that believers should meet together in small groups for prayer, study, and support. As part of their *philosophy* of ministry, they are committed to small groups. Their *practice* is the when, where, and how long these groups meet.

Since the Scripture provides language comparing local church ministry to building a house, we will continue with that metaphor.[6] (We tried extending the body metaphor, but it quickly got pretty weird.) *Theology* is the foundation of the house, and the foundation must obviously be laid first. Without a strong foundation, the whole house is weak and in jeopardy of collapse. It matters nothing how the house looks if the foundation is shaky. Everything is added to the house in light of the foundation. Whether the house is custom-built or one of four choices in a cookie-cutter neighborhood, the foundation is still consistent, and its importance cannot be overstated. The foundation must be the timeless and true Word of God. In the Word, we clearly discover the glorious gospel, the metanarrative of Scripture, the grand story to which all Scripture leads us.

Philosophy is the structure of the house, the design. With great planning and intentionality, a wise builder carefully designs and builds on top of the foundation that has been laid. No sane builder would ever advocate for a room to be built apart from the foundation. The number of rooms, their size and shape, their points of access, and the number of windows in each room help give the house its identity. The structure of a house is where the people live.

Look at just these two components for a second: theology and philosophy. The foundation of a church's theology must never change. Ministry philosophy, however, can be changed, just as walls can be moved, but it is a difficult process and often very painful. And even in allowing that certain aspects of philosophy can be adjusted, we must still recognize—just as some of the support beams in a house cannot be moved—there are divine elements (such as preaching, sacraments, church discipline, leadership) that must be present in our ministry philosophy, or else the church ceases to be a church as prescribed in the New Testament.

Practice includes the furnishings and fixtures. The furniture, color schemes, and other decorative touches are important because they give the house its unique character. Two homes with the same foundation, footprint, and floor plan can be very different based on the furniture, lighting, and colors. A savvy designer will choose furniture that is consistent with the vibe of the house's structure, but there is a lot of freedom with furniture. The furnishings are also the easiest to tweak. Walls can be repainted and new furniture purchased and moved around as kids grow up and life changes.

Ministry practice is critical because it's what people in a church interact with on an ongoing basis. At the same time, practice must be held loosely. The furniture exists to serve the family, not the other way around.

A wise homeowner understands the difference between foundation, structure, and furniture. He would never allow someone to change the foundation. If he notices a crack in the concrete next to his house, he inspects it to be sure the crack is not indicative of a shaky foundation. Walls are only moved if it is clear that the change will better serve the family and the guests that visit. No one wants to live in a house where the walls are always shifting. But as far as the color of the walls and the choice of furniture go, he holds much more loosely to these because he knows that every few years his wife will desire a new color in the living room and his kids won't like Spider-Man forever.

The theology, philosophy, and practice together form the house—the culture—in which your church currently lives. To form a Jesus-centered culture, you must ensure that all three are in alignment and immersed in the gospel. Let's dig a little more deeply here into each piece.

Theology Foundation

Your foundation should not be unique. It must be the Word of God and the gospel of Jesus, which is received, not developed or achieved.

In an individualistic Western culture, we tend to want a unique theology, one that is just for us and feels fresh and new. But longing for something "fresh" or "something no one else has said" often leads to bad exegesis. The case study of the church in Galatia proves that any attempt to widen the gospel renders it powerless and useless. Trust the biblical foundation given to us, or you will move on to another gospel (which is really no gospel at all) and find yourself on Paul's castration hit list (Gal. 5:12).

Several texts clearly and powerfully remind us of the foundation on which we must build, the foundation we must receive joyfully:

> Beloved, although I was very eager to write to you about our common salvation, I found it necessary to write appealing to you to contend for the faith that was once for all delivered to the saints. (Jude 3 ESV)

> For no one can lay a foundation other than that which is laid, which is Jesus Christ. (1 Cor. 3:11 ESV)

> So then you are no longer strangers and aliens, but you are fellow citizens with the saints and members of the household of God, built on the foundation of the apostles and prophets, Christ Jesus himself being the

cornerstone, in whom the whole structure, being joined
together, grows into a holy temple in the Lord. (Eph.
2:19–21 ESV)

Ministry Philosophy

Your ministry philosophy, which forms the house that sits on the
foundation, must be anchored in the gospel, informed by the context
in which God has placed you, and in step with the passions that God
has graced you. Many churches possess a solid theology but lack a
ministry philosophy connected to the foundation.

They are like the infamous Chicago Spire building.[7] The Chicago
Spire was heralded as the future of premiere residences for upscale and
discerning buyers. Designed by world-class architects and slated to
contain 150 floors, thus becoming one of the tallest buildings in the
world, the foundation was laid but nothing was ever built on top of it.
In 2010, due to ongoing financial woes, the project was declared dead.
It had a great foundation but nothing else. And what good is a foundation if the house is never built for the people?

If a church has a theology centered on Christ yet the gospel is not
driving the philosophy, then people will be confused and likely uncer-
tain how the gospel applies to their daily lives. After all, the gospel
does not seem to have practical implications for the church; how could
it for them?

How does the foundation of the gospel impact how your church is
designed? How does the gospel impact your church's mission and the
ministries your church offers? If your theology does not impact your
philosophy, your theology is worthless to you. A. W. Tozer lamented
the disconnect:

> There is scarcely anything so dull and meaningless
> as Bible doctrine taught for its own sake. Truth divorced
> from life is not truth in its Biblical sense, but something
> else and something less.[8]

Ministry Practice

A church with contradictory philosophies of ministry suffers from multiple personality disorder. She doesn't know who she is, and the resulting confusion is most clearly exposed in her practice. Many churches practice ministry haphazardly, revealing that competing ministry philosophies are embedded into different segments of the church. By neglecting the practice part of the equation, a church can have a great doctrinal statement in place and philosophical thinkers sitting around discussing intellectually how ministry should be performed without ever actually doing it.

A church that does not carefully attach practice to philosophy and theology is like the infamous Winchester mansion. Sarah Winchester married into the family that designed, built, and sold the Winchester rifle. After her husband died, a psychic convinced her that the spirits of those who were killed by the Winchester rifle would haunt her unless she continuously built her mansion. She actually believed that if construction never ceased on her mansion, she would inherit eternal life. (In case you are wondering, that would be bad theology.)

So every moment of every day for thirty-eight years until she died, hammers pounded on her home. The entire point of the ongoing construction project was not to build anything in particular, but just to keep building. The home is now an attraction because it is so odd. Staircases lead to ceilings. Doors open to the wall. Windows open to the floor. There is an utter lack of purpose to much of the building.

Without a theology and philosophy that are deeply connected to each other, you will just keep tweaking the house with no purpose or direction. Your church will do stuff just to do stuff. Your calendar will be filled with programs, your facility will be used, and you'll distribute an annual budget. But without a coherent theology and philosophy, it will all be meaningless building.

Your church's practice is dictated largely by your context. And as long as your practice flows from a solid theological foundation and ministry philosophy, you should feel released to enjoy an immense amount of freedom.

Bottom line: while practice is important, it is not the starting point. Yet sadly, when ministry leaders connect with each other, *practice* is typically where the discussion begins. Leaders from Church A, for example, hear about the work of the Lord in Church B. So they start observing Church B from a distance, eventually arranging to meet with some of their staff. Immediately they jump to "practice" questions:

> *How long are your services?*
>
> *Are your groups/classes "open" or "closed"?*
>
> *Do you pay your musicians?*
>
> *How far in advance do you plan your sermons?*
>
> *Where did you get this flooring? (as if the answer is simply new flooring)*

These are all valid practice questions, and they are often asked at a relentless pace. But very rarely at any point during such a meeting does anyone ask the deeper questions:

> *What do you believe about "mission" that causes you to set these priorities?*
>
> *Why is _____ so important here?*
>
> *Why have you designed your groups this way?*

The deeper church cultural question is the synergy between theology, philosophy, and practice. When these three come together, formed in the gospel, the impact is tremendous. Here are some practical examples of gospel theology, philosophy, and practice converging together to form the culture in a church:

Theology

God is triune, and the church is plural.

Philosophy

Groups are foundational for transformation.

Practice

We offer groups that _____, move people to groups by
_____, etc.

Theology

Christ is the Word incarnate, and the Scripture is His
special revelation to us.

Philosophy

The text must be heralded in all teaching environments.

Practice

We teach the Word to adults, students, and kids by
_____.

Theology

God became Man (incarnation) to rescue us.

Philosophy

We must step into our local context and serve.

Practice

We serve our local community by _____.

Theology

Christ redeemed us for His own glory. Corporate worship must celebrate what Christ has done.

Philosophy

We sing songs that focus on His character and work, not ours.

Practice

We structure singing in our services by

_____.

Theology

Christ has made all believers priests.

Philosophy

All believers are qualified by God to serve the body of believers.

Practice

We challenge our people to serve in the following ways:

_____.

Cultural Architecture

A church that is a thriving Creature of the Word has deep synergy between theology, philosophy, and practice. But the harmony between the three must be built with godly leaders. In the Old Testament, God shepherded the culture of His people through prophets, priests, and kings. In short, kings provided strong leadership, prophets applied truth to the hearts of people, and priests offered sacrifices for people to assure them of God's readiness to forgive. The imperfect prophets, priests, and kings only foreshadowed the one true Prophet, Priest, and King—Jesus the Christ. John Calvin wrote:

> Therefore, that faith may find in Christ a solid ground of salvation, and so rest in him, we must set out with this principle, that the office which he received from the Father consists of three parts. For he was appointed Prophet, King, and Priest.[9]

Jesus is the perfect *Prophet*, who perfectly pointed people to God through His wisdom and teaching. He is the perfect *King*, who ushered in a new kingdom and displayed His authority over demons, sickness, and nature. And He is the perfect *Priest*, who lovingly and compassionately cared for people and provided healing.

A healthy Creature of the Word is led by Jesus and looks like Jesus.

Jesus is the ultimate Leader of the Church, the only one who completely fulfills the role of Prophet, Priest, and King. At the same time, He has gifted and given authority to those He calls into leadership of His Church. Some leaders are primarily prophets, uniquely gifted to declare truth. Some leaders are primarily priests, uniquely gifted to shepherd people to wholeness and maturity. And some leaders are primarily kings, specifically gifted to provide clear direction.

A church culture that is centered on Jesus is led by prophetic leaders, kingly leaders, and priestly leaders who themselves are each centered on Jesus. All three types of leaders are necessary and essential, and all three types of leaders must be utterly transfixed on the gospel. Without prophetic leadership centered on Jesus, the church will drift theologically either to legalism or to liberalism. Without priestly leadership immersed in the gospel, the people (in practice) will be either pampered with false love or led without grace and mercy. Without a kingly leader saturated in the gospel, the church will philosophically wander without clarity or will be clear on something other than Jesus.

The culture of a church suffers if one of these critical leadership functions is missing *or* if one of them is not immersed in the gospel.

Because there is overlap between theology, philosophy, and practice and between prophetic, priestly, and kingly leadership, it would be a mistake to draw hard and fast lines of separation. In other words, leaders are often a mix of prophet, priest, and king. And a leader whose main task is predominately one of these is not excused to neglect the basic Christian virtues associated with the others. For example, "priestly leaders" are not the only leaders called to love people well, just as "prophetic leaders" are not the only leaders commanded to stand for truth. In the same way that someone without the "gift of evangelism" is still commanded to represent Christ and share the gospel, leaders who are largely defined as being prophetic, kingly, or priestly in their specific role must not neglect the expectations placed on all pastors (see 1 Tim. 3).

At the same time, it is helpful to understand that prophets often direct and guard the *theology* of the church. Kings often oversee and govern the *philosophy* of the church, the high-level structures and systems that enable the vision grounded in theology to be realized. And priests often shepherd people in the daily *practice* of the church. Again, we offer this to be helpful in identifying how a Jesus-centered culture is most often shaped, not to be overly prescriptive.

A healthy Creature of the Word contains gospel-formed prophets, priests, and kings, each harmonizing the theology, philosophy, and practice of the church. Over the next several chapters, we will touch on the key leadership practices related to prophetic, priestly, and kingly leadership. Prophetic leadership roots the teaching of the church deeply in Christ, both from the pulpit and throughout the body (chapters 7 and 8). Kingly leadership develops leaders and systems connected to the gospel (chapters 9 and 10), and priestly leadership nurtures the people within the body while also focusing on people outside the body (chapters 11 and 12). Ultimately, a Jesus-centered church looks like Jesus, the Prophet-King-Priest. Without Him we are hopeless.

Hopeless without Him

Harry Houdini is still considered to be the greatest escape artist of all time. In the early 1900s, he fascinated America with his performances. He would free himself from straitjackets, handcuffs, chains, and ropes. As he grew more popular, his escapes became more daring. He escaped from being buried alive, from being immersed in water inside a coffin, and from a water torture chamber. It seemed Houdini could escape anything, could get himself out of any situation. He was crafty and skilled. Nothing could hold him down.

And as he was nearing death, he told his wife that, if possible, he would communicate to her from the other side. He thought if anyone could escape death, he could.

Houdini died on Halloween 1926. And for ten solid years, his wife held on to the hope that her beloved husband would communicate to her, that he could somehow escape death as he had escaped everything else.

Finally, on the ten-year anniversary of his death, she tried one final séance—to be broadcast all over the world on radio—one final opportunity for Harry to prove he could escape death and communicate with her. After numerous intense appeals to awaken Houdini from his deathly slumber, the host yelled out: "Houdini! Are you here? Are you here, Houdini? Please manifest yourself in any way possible. We have waited, Houdini, oh so long! Never have you been able to present the evidence you promised."

Hearing nothing, like always, the host turned to Houdini's wife and asked for her response. She replied, "Houdini did not come through. My last hope is gone. I do believe he cannot come back to me or to anyone. It is finished. I turn out the light."

Jesus assured His disciples that on the third day after His death, He would rise again. And He delivered on that promise. He suffered on the cross for our sin but overcame sin and death by rising triumphantly.

The same power that conquered the grave is the same power than can transform your church's culture.

Without Jesus, your church culture is useless. But because of Jesus, your church culture can be transformed . . . and become transformational.

If you are frustrated with the lack of gospel-centrality in your current church culture, understand that cultural frustration always precedes cultural transformation. The frustration is good and beautiful if it leads you to long for the grace of Jesus to permeate your theology, philosophy, and practice.

Paul's concluding words to the Galatian believers are poignant: "The grace of our Lord Jesus Christ be with your spirit, brothers" (Gal. 6:18 ESV). Paul believed the only solution to church culture dysfunction is Jesus—the only One who can build a culture of grace in your church. He is the One who brings brokenness and repentance. He is the One we must trust. He is the only One who could remedy the broken sacrificial system among His people, and He is the only One who could repair the shifting church culture in Galatia. Only He can raise a life, and only He can raise a dead culture.

May the grace of the Lord Jesus be with our churches.

CHAPTER 7

PREACHING THE WORD

You do not really preach the gospel if you leave Christ out—
if He is omitted, it is not the gospel! You may invite men
to listen to your message, but you are only inviting them
to gaze upon an empty table unless Christ is the very
center and substance of all that you set before them!
~ CHARLES SPURGEON[1]

EXPECTANT PARENTS KNOW THE THRILL of having a sonogram. There is nothing quite like going to the doctor's office, hearing the assuring rhythms of a little heartbeat, then seeing the image of your baby on the screen. The doctor prints off the black-and-white pictures, and you treasure the opportunity to share them with friends and family. Some parents even take it a step further and get 3D sonogram images. Then as the months pass, one sonogram picture replaces the last as your eager anticipation grows for the baby's birth. You can only imagine what this little one is actually going to look like. You can make out her shape, count her fingers and toes, but your greatest desire is to see her face-to-face.

So . . . you wait.

Sonograms serve as a primer picture; they point toward what is coming. They provide wonderful images, but in their shadings and contrasts we can only see shadows. The substance of that which we so eagerly await is yet to come. But when the baby arrives, then we behold what we could once only infer.

And so it is with the Scriptures. With the birth of Christ, the expectancy of the Old Testament gave way to the flesh and blood of Jesus Christ.

This changes everything . . . especially our preaching and teaching. No longer must we view the Old Testament through the shadows of a sonogram. Jesus fulfills every promise of the Old Testament, bringing light and clarity to the entirety of the canon of Scripture. Our understanding of the promise of Scripture is able to shift from Christ's first coming to the promise of His second coming. No longer are we wondering who will ultimately redeem God's people, for the cross colors our view. The preacher has the privilege of painting with his words the beautiful news of Jesus, through the words of both Old Testament and New.

The clarity afforded to the preacher today is that the Word of God ultimately points to the gospel of Jesus Christ. What was implied in the Old Testament has been made explicit in the New Testament.

The Word, therefore, is Jesus-centered.

Prophets and Preachers[2]

New Testament preaching is rooted in Old Testament prophetic proclamation. The prophets of old were the forerunners of present-day preachers. God has always used His people to herald and proclaim His message both to those within the faith as well as those outside.

Whether this was Jonah, called to preach repentance to the people of Nineveh, or Peter preaching at Pentecost, or Charles Spurgeon relentlessly declaring the gospel to countless thousands over his lifetime, God has consistently used heralds to speak His words. In His ultimate wisdom, God uses foolish men to speak the words of His wondrous salvation.

The nature of preaching begins with an understanding of the words and actions employed in the Scriptures to describe it. According to R. H. Mounce, "The choice of verbs in the Greek NT for the activity of preaching points us back to its original meaning. The most characteristic is *kerysso*,[3] 'to proclaim as a herald.' . . . Preaching is heralding; the message proclaimed is the glad tidings of salvation."[4] Mounce goes on to say, "While *kerysso* tells us something about the activity of preaching, *euangelizomai*,[5] 'to bring good news' . . . emphasizes the quality of the message itself."[6] The preacher is a herald of the good news that salvation has come!

The task of the preacher is to herald the words of God. But how does he go about doing this? The answer may seem obvious—and it is—but we cannot afford to assume such fundamental truths. If the foundation of what the preacher actually preaches is unstable, then the house will not stand.

Preaching: The Foundation

The Jesus-centered preacher preaches the Word of God. He has in his arsenal all sixty-six inspired books of the Bible to expound, exposit, exegete, unpack, and deliver to a people who desperately need to hear. This highlights the inspiration, authority, and sufficiency of Scripture. Many today have a deficient faith in these precious truths. The Church is a "Creature" of this Word.

Gospel-centered preaching and teaching should invade every aspect of teaching in the Church. If the church is a Creature of the

Word, then the Word should be present in every facet of church life, from the Sunday school class to the worship music to small groups.

Martin Luther writes,

> Now, wherever you hear or see the Word preached, believed, professed, and lived, do not doubt that the true *ecclesia sancta catholica* (Christian holy people) must be there. . . . And even if there were no other sign than this alone, it would still suffice to prove that a Christian, holy people must exist there, for God's Word cannot be without God's people and, conversely, God's people cannot be without God's Word.[7]

It is common to see the inspiration and authority of Scripture as a church's stated belief, but the church's normal practice seems to undermine the sufficiency of Scripture. Among other places, this is betrayed in their preaching. A message begins by giving passing platitudes to a text, but what is expounded is another idea altogether or a concoction of worldly wisdom. The underlying current is that Scripture is not sufficient and must be supplemented. This is not to say that ideas and insights cannot be used to round out a message, but the sermon or teaching must be based on what the text says. The role of the preacher is to dive into the text, mine the depths, and reveal the truth that is there in the Scripture.

John Stott writes:

> It is my contention that all true Christian preaching is expository preaching. Of course if by an "expository" sermon is meant a verse-by-verse explanation of a lengthy passage of Scripture, then indeed it is only one possible way of preaching, but this would be a misuse of the word. Properly speaking, "exposition" has a much broader meaning. It refers to the content of the sermon (biblical truth) rather than its style (a running commentary). To expound Scripture is to bring out of the

text what is there and expose it to view. The expositor
pries open what appears to be closed, makes plain what
is obscure, unravels what is knotted and unfolds what is
tightly packed. . . . Whether long or short, our responsibility as expositors is to open it up in such a way that it
speaks its message clearly, plainly, accurately, relevantly,
without addition, subtraction or falsification.[8]

The preacher must courageously and ferociously believe that transformation occurs through the interplay of God's Word and Spirit. He
is simply a vessel, a broken jar of clay, spilling out before the people the
water of life. The Holy Spirit always uses the revealed Word of God
to open the eyes of both the unbeliever and believer to the wonders of
the gospel. The preacher should not feel as if he is carrying the burden
of life change; he merely carries the burden of faithful exposition and
the robust proclamation of the text at hand, trusting that God's Word
will never return void (Isa. 55:10–11). This is the wonder and weight
of preaching.

One Message, Multiple Audiences, and a Myriad of Needs

On any given Sunday, the preacher is faced with a diverse audience. There are those who are lost and doubting and those who are
saved and trusting. Some are maturing; others are sliding. The room
is a kaleidoscope of hurts, habits, and hang-ups. You preach to the
desperate and humiliated prodigal as well as his entitled and prideful
older brother—all in the same sermon. Thankfully, the message is the
same for anyone and everyone.

The gospel of Jesus Christ saves us, and the gospel of Jesus Christ
sanctifies us. Grace ushers us into salvation, and grace sustains us
through it. The gospel is for the world as well as for the Church. The
gospel is always the point of application.

James Boice writes,

> It is by the preaching of the Word that God moves in the hearts and lives of people to turn them from sin to Jesus Christ. . . . Preaching is important as a means of grace not merely because it is used of God to bring about conversions, but also because it is used for our sanctification, that is, our growth in holiness once we are born again. . . . Preaching is also the primary means of growth for the local church. There is a great deal of debate about this in our day, but it is the preaching of the Word that God most uses to build up a church, not only numerically but above all (and far more importantly) in the spiritual depth and understanding of the people who make up the congregation.[9]

The content of the preacher's message is the Word of God. It has the unique ability, by the power of the Holy Spirit, to rightly divide the soul. The Word can heal the broken and break the proud. The Word can assure the weak and weaken the strong. It brings wisdom to the foolish and makes fools out of the wise. The Word of God bears the uncanny ability to do what you and I cannot: transcend human limitations. So the preacher must preach the Word, confident that the Word ultimately points to the gospel.

The Emmaus Road

On a lonely road to Emmaus just days after the crucifixion of Jesus, two disciples walked and talked together. Their conversation was filled with the talk of the town. Confusion and sadness flooded their hearts as they tried to make sense of what had transpired. Jesus, who they thought to be the Messiah, had come to Jerusalem. The people sang hosannas as they welcomed Him by laying cloaks and branches on the road He travelled. They were ushering in the One they believed would redeem Israel and establish the nation again to prominence. But the song of praise soon gave way to shouts of condemnation. Jesus was crucified, and the hopes of a nation were dashed in despair. There would be no redemption for Israel. Another prophet lay dead in a tomb.

As the two disciples talked and talked, trying to make sense of their circumstances, a stranger joined them. At first He seemed oblivious to all that had occurred over the weekend. The disciples, shocked at how He could be so unaware of these things, recounted the events and even shared that some women said Jesus' tomb was now empty. The course of the conversation then took a sharp turn when the stranger declared, "'How unwise and slow you are to believe in your hearts all that the prophets have spoken! Didn't the Messiah have to suffer these things and enter into His glory?' Then beginning with Moses and all the Prophets, He interpreted for them the things concerning Himself in all the Scriptures" (Luke 24:25–27 HCSB). Eventually their eyes were opened—first to understand the Scriptures, and then to the Savior who dined with them.

Jesus showed the two disciples that all Scripture, which at this point included only the Old Testament, pointed to Him. He is the common thread. He is the fulfillment of every prophecy and promise. He is the greater Moses and the Lamb to which the sacrificial system pointed. He establishes the eternal throne of David. Jesus is the perfect Prophet, Priest, and King.

The Story above the Stories: Metanarrative

We don't have to guess what Jesus shared with the disciples on the road to Emmaus. The writers of the New Testament essentially let us in on that conversation as they show how Jesus fulfills a variety of prophecies as the Son of God, conquering King and Savior of the world. All of this was in accordance with the will of the Father who sent Him to accomplish redemption and then sent His Spirit to apply it to His people.

Now that the canon is closed, we can read the Scriptures as a complete story. Although we don't have every answer and haven't experienced everything contained within its pages, we do have a clear picture. In short, the Bible is about God. He has given us sixty-six books (thirty-nine in the Old Testament, twenty-seven in the New Testament) written in three languages (Hebrew, Greek, and a bit of Aramaic) over a period of more than a thousand years, written by more than forty authors on three continents (Asia, Africa, and Europe). Authors included kings, peasants, philosophers, fishermen, poets, statesmen, and scholars among them. These books cover history, sermons, letters, hymns, and even a love song. There are geographical surveys, architectural specifications, travel diaries, family trees, and numerous legal documents. It covers hundreds of controversial subjects, yet with amazing unity. And all of it reveals to us the triune God and His plan for a people.

The big story above the individual stories is often referred to as the *metanarrative*, or grand story. As previously stated, the Word is gospel-centered. This is the grand story we want to tell while weaving for our people a complete, biblical theology of the Word of God. In short, the Bible is God's Word about His creation, which He created by His word. But when humanity—the pinnacle of His creation—rebelled and failed to trust in God's Word, He worked to restore what was fractured by sending the divine Word, His Son, to accomplish redemption. The story then resolves with God keeping His Word in the consummation of all things.

It's helpful, we believe, to capture this metanarrative in the following outline, which (while always a refresher of things we know by heart, as well as something we've touched on previously in the book) must never grow old and out-of-date in our minds. The imperative of keeping this story rushing and reverberating throughout our thinking, prayer, and meditations keeps us perpetually drawn to the only reason for our hope. Maintaining a fresh familiarity with the truths of this epic story ensures that it more naturally informs and flows from our preaching, our conversation, our priorities, and our witness. We as proclaimers of this message must anchor it front and center in our lives, so that we may continually do the same for those who hear us proclaim His Word.

In repeating it again in this space, it's also a visual reminder of how frequently, incessantly, and unapologetically we should keep this note sounding throughout our church culture. The gospel is all. It is complete. It is what has made us, makes us, and even today is remaking us, from glory to glory, now and forever.

Here now . . . the story.

The Beginning of the Story: Creation

God creates through His Word: "Let there be . . ." Light floods the dark, formless void, and the heavens and the earth are established and filled with vibrant life. Ultimately, the pinnacle of God's creation—the ones uniquely created in God's image—appear at His Word. Adam and Eve are set apart as image-bearers and given charge by God's Word to reign and rule over the rest of creation. Humanity is to serve as God's vice-regents who faithfully represent Him on the earth while enjoying a special relationship with both their God and one another in a sinless existence. The only boundary put on Adam and Eve is not to eat from the tree of the knowledge of good and evil.

The Problem of the Story: Fall

All of creation is fractured in the fall of humanity, as we see our first parents failing to trust in God's Word. The rhythms established in the created order are now broken and perverted. Sin enters the picture when Adam and Eve doubt God's Word and trust their own inclinations. They reject God's command and go their own way through the temptation of Satan. As they partake of the apple, a collapse occurs in creation.

Their eyes are now opened to a new reality. The foreign emotions of fear, guilt, and shame engulf their hearts as they hide from God. No longer do they run to Him in relationship but instead retreat from Him in hiding. Yet God graciously calls out to them, and a conversation ensues. We not only see that humanity's vertical relationship with God has been altered, but the horizontal relationship between one another is marred as well. The man blames the woman directly and God indirectly: "The woman You gave to be with me—she gave me some fruit from the tree, and I ate" (Gen. 3:12 HCSB). The woman responds with a similar lack of responsibility: "It was the serpent. He deceived me, and I ate" (v. 13 HCSB).

God justly responds to the rebellion of Adam and Eve by cursing them, along with all of creation. The curse is comprehensive as its consequences include the physical, spiritual, relational, and emotional. Eve, the mother of all the living (Gen. 3:20), will suffer through childbirth and have an unhealthy desire to usurp her husband. Adam, who was formed from the dirt of the earth, will endure ongoing frustration in his efforts to live upon it. In the end, both physical and spiritual death results. In every direction imaginable, Adam, Eve, and the rest of humanity suffer the strife of utter brokenness: before God, before one another, and before nature.

But even in the midst of this crushing curse, a flicker of hope dawns. There is a promise. A word given. In God's cursing of the serpent, we see through the keyhole of His redemptive plan. Genesis 3:15 is referred to as the *protoevangelium*, Latin for "first gospel." Here we see the foreshadowing of what is to come: "I will put hostility between you and the woman, and between your seed and her seed. He will strike your head, and you will strike his heel" (HCSB). God will bring forth one born of woman who will suffer but ultimately crush the head of the serpent.

The Plot of the Story: Redemption

God does not abandon His creation. In fact, He goes to great lengths to call out a people to Himself. The rest of Genesis depicts the story of God making a promise to Abraham to bless him and establish a people through him. Through these people God will restore all things.

The Bible introduces us to the key figures in redemptive history—people like Abraham, Isaac, Jacob, Joseph, Moses, and David. We learn of God's gracious power in the exodus event, pointing to a greater exodus from a more insidious master. We see the beauty of the law and the simultaneous inability of humanity to keep it. The sacrificial system foreshadows a greater sacrifice and eternal atonement. The story unfolds with bold prophets, passionate psalms, a fickle nation, and the increased longing for the promised Messiah who would rule and reign.

Then, God goes silent for four hundred years.

The silence is broken with the cries of a newborn lying in a Bethlehem manger—the baby of promise. God has not abandoned His creation; in fact, He has become flesh and has dwelled among us. God has sent His Word, personified in Jesus Christ.

Luke tells us, "The boy grew up and became strong, filled with wisdom, and God's grace was on Him" (Luke 2:40 HCSB). Then eventually, John the Baptist heralds to the crowds, "Here is the Lamb of God, who takes away the sin of the world!" (John 1:29 HCSB). Jesus is baptized, and the Spirit of God descends upon Him, punctuated by the Father's declaration: "You are My beloved Son. I take delight in You" (Luke 3:22 HCSB). God's plan is unfolding before the world.

Jesus' public ministry includes a variety of miracles, signs, and wonders. He teaches as One having authority, speaking audaciously about the good news of the kingdom of God. Most of the religious establishment abhors Him, while the tax collectors and sinners tend to gravitate toward Him. Through all of this, Jesus' face is set like flint toward Jerusalem.

God's Son moves toward the cross in concert with God's heart to reconcile a lost and broken world. Along the way He is betrayed by a friend and taken into custody, suffering unjust trials and false accusations. A mob mentality permeates the courts as the people are filled with an insatiable desire to see Jesus crucified. Those He desires to give life are calling for His death.

Eventually soldiers drive nails through His hands and feet, then lift Him up to hang and die on a cross, while His own followers scatter. Jesus breathes His last, declaring, "It is finished!" (John 19:30 HCSB). He hangs on the cross as the last sacrifice necessary for sin, an eternal one. But all of this is contingent on Jesus defeating one last enemy: death.

On the third day after His death, Jesus rises victoriously over sin, death, and hell. News of His resurrection spreads from the testimony of the women who visit the tomb, to the other disciples, to hundreds of eyewitness accounts. Jesus allows people to touch Him. He dines with them. He reiterates His teaching and gives His disciples the Great Commission, instructing them to go and make disciples. Then shortly before He ascends into heaven, He tells His disciples to start sharing the good news of the gospel with those in Jerusalem, and then spread the message to the ends of the earth. According to His Word, they eagerly wait in expectant prayer for the promised Holy Spirit to come and empower them in the work, for the Spirit will apply the divine Word to human hearts to grow the Church.

The Resolution of the Story: Consummation

What began as a whisper in Genesis 3:15 culminates with a shout in Revelation 21: "Look! God's dwelling is with humanity, and He will live with them. They will be His people, and God Himself will be with them and be their God. He will wipe away every tear from their eyes. Death will no longer exist; grief, crying and pain will exist no

longer, because the previous things have passed away" (vv. 3–4 HCSB).
The story resolves with God keeping His Word to His people, proving
Himself trustworthy and sure.

God will fulfill and complete our redemption when the Son
returns for His people. This time, however, He will come with the
sword, eliminating the wicked and all their ways, casting them away
forever from God and His redeemed. Those who love and trust in Jesus
will live and reign with Him for all eternity in the new heavens and the
new earth, enjoying the glory of a new, resurrected body. The mood of
the consummation will be festive and alive with joy. Death will have
been defeated and all things made new. Better than Eden.

The Story and the Gospel

Understanding the metanarrative of Scripture means that we can
preach the gospel from all of Scripture. In fact, the gospel *must* be
preached from all of Scripture. It not only provides the hearer with a
better understanding of the continuity of the Bible, it also enlightens
them to the wonder of God's redemptive plan from the beginning.

Mike Bullmore writes:

> While the substance of the apostolic preaching
> was the good news of reconciliation with God through
> Christ Jesus, that message was delivered and explained
> almost invariably by means of an exposition of Old
> Testament Scripture. So preaching in New Testament
> times involved the preaching of "the word of God,"
> and an essential component of such preaching was the
> exposition of the Old Testament. This in turn leads us
> to the conclusion that the Old Testament Scriptures
> must be included in our conception of "the word" to
> be preached, a conclusion confirmed by both the direct
> and indirect claims of the New Testament.[10]

The preacher has the ability, given the testimony and authority of the full biblical witness, to preach the text and to preach *above* the text. This does not give him license to preach *outside* of the text. Preaching above the text means lifting the eyes of the hearers to see how a particular text fits into the overall arc of the grand story of the Bible. It means preaching a passage in both its immediate context and its canonical (or big-picture) context. It means we can exegete a passage and show how it fits into the wider reality of God's redemptive plan for His creation. In many ways it allows us to be a type of helicopter pilot who can freely navigate from the ground to the air and back down again. Our perspectives are widened, our vision is increased, and our hearts are humbled as we see the same text from a variety of angles. It is truly astounding to consider how intentional God's plan for His people really is.

Michael Lawrence, in his helpful work on biblical theology, highlights the importance of such an understanding:

> Biblical theology . . . allows us to preach Christ from both the Levitical food laws and the Gospel of Mark. It allows us to recognize and preach the whole Bible for what it is, Christian Scripture. It prevents us from moralizing the Old Testament, while at the same time giving due weight to the meaning of every Old Testament text in its original context. It encourages us to constantly connect every passage we preach to what God has done in the past and what he has promised to do in the future. It provides us with a worldview, a storyline that challenges the reigning stories of our culture. It prevents us from preaching narrowly on our own hobbyhorses. And most important, it focuses the main point of every passage within the grand storyline of Scripture, the story of God's actions to redeem a people for himself, through the judgment of his Son, to the praise of his glorious grace.[11]

The preacher/teacher should be flooded with a joy that gives him seriousness, as well as a burden that gives him freedom for the opportunity to elucidate a message that saves, redeems, and transforms. He is given charge, whether to adults or children, to preach the Word and hold out the treasure of the gospel for all who would believe.

The Preacher: Preach to Yourself First

We have talked about the power of the preached Word to transform those who hear, but the first person transformed by the Word should be the preacher himself. A common adage is that one cannot impart what one doesn't first possess. The idea is that the preacher needs to be like a sponge, soaking in the truths of the gospel himself first, and then being squeezed so that gospel realities can be allowed to spill over. The sad reality is that many are gifted enough to entertain or creative enough to produce clever smoke screens. We can coast on talent alone or employ a variety of elements in the message that provide a buffer between the Word and our own hearts. We can easily replace our time of study and saturation with less important matters. The effects of this may not be noticed initially, but the impact will be severe over time. A hollow soul can only survive for so long. The church will invariably shrink back and follow the shallowness of its pastors, or the church will rise up and oust them. The charge then is to preach the Word . . . and to start with your own heart.

The gospel must first become a treasure to the one expounding it. This does not mean the preacher is perfect. In fact, this would actually be contrary to an authentic representation of the gospel in the life of the preacher. The gospel assumes we are *not* perfect. In fact, it shouts from the rooftop that we are completely despicable apart from Christ. So the preacher should first and foremost understand his own shortcomings, deficiencies, and sinful inclinations. Failure to understand this is a failure to understand the gospel. It is a shameful act for the preacher/pastor to pretend to wear a cape. There is only one Hero in the Church, and it is *not* the preacher.

The Preacher: Jesus-Centered Culture Creator

The primary objective of preaching is to herald the good news of the gospel. A *secondary* by-product of preaching and teaching is the establishment of a pervasive Jesus-centered church culture. A church will not be Jesus-centered without "prophets" faithfully heralding the gospel and applying it to the direction of the church. The culture of any given church—as defined in the previous chapter as the harmonious synthesis of doctrine, philosophy, and practice—is primarily established and reinforced, both deliberately and unintentionally, through the pulpit.

It would be foolish to pretend that the pulpit does not impact church culture. Everything from the content of the sermons, the style of delivery, the clothes one chooses to wear, and the presence or absence of a pulpit both reinforce and create culture. Our hope in this book is to unashamedly promote a certain type of church culture: *an all-pervasive, Jesus-saturated culture.* All other church cultures are left wanting. The beauty of a gospel culture is that it can take shape in a myriad of ways.

A common trend in many churches is a deliberate and stated push to be "relevant," which often translates to being "cool" or "hip." What is missed in the relevance discussion is the heart behind Paul's plea to become "all things to all people," which we see displayed in his ministry over and over. There is a way to walk in genuine concern for those who are outside of the faith so that they feel comfortable and welcomed. There is also a way to try making Jesus cool enough for the world to like Him. The former flows from a gospel-oriented view of hospitality and compassion; the latter reeks of a poor understanding of the divisive nature of the gospel as it relates to the world. The Church should spend less time trying to be relevant (which can actually come across as disingenuous) and more time trying to align their hearts to the authentic gospel message.

Authentic gospel-centered preaching is intensely relevant. The barrier for salvation and sanctification is not whether the preacher is in jeans or a suit; the barrier is the sinful condition of the human heart. Address their hearts with the gospel first, and worry about what to wear later.

The preacher should also consider his own authenticity from the pulpit. As we said above, he should not preach as if he wears a spiritual cape. The impact of a preacher who shares all of his triumphs and never his struggles will be an anxious congregation who hears one thing espoused week after week, being left to wallow alone in the reality of their own shortcomings. The congregant can go one of two ways at this point. First, she can pretend that everything is great in her own life, expending all her energies in propping up a self-righteous, self-supporting image. Or, on the other hand, she can snap under the pressure of living up to what she knows is unattainable. The preacher owns the opportunity to assure the congregation that it is OK not to be OK—*but* that the gospel will not leave us there. What good news! In this case, you can create a culture in a church that understands the hope of grace.

Flimsy sermons will create a flimsy flock. Consider the words of John Stott:

> This is the age of the sermonette; and sermonettes make Christianettes. Much of the current uncertainty about the gospel and the mission of the church must be due to a generation of preaching which has lost confidence in the Word of God, and no longer takes the trouble to study it in depth and to proclaim it without fear or favor.[12]

The pastor should not underestimate the impact of his preaching. No, we do not want to make too much of preaching, taking it beyond its helpful scope of importance. The preacher should not read about the weight of his impact and become inflated with importance and thoughts of grandeur. Rather, he should retreat in humble prayer when considering the significance of such a charge.

The preacher has the opportunity to create in the culture of a church the importance of the Word of God. If the Word is central in preaching, teaching, music, and the ordinances, then the church culture will flow from this. Similar to buttoning a shirt, the first button is essential. If this one is off line, then all the other buttons will be misaligned as well. The church must hear from the pulpit the gospel of God from the Word of God preached week after week. This is primary.

CHAPTER 8

PULPIT TO PRESCHOOL (AND PUBERTY TOO)

The gospel is not a doctrine of the tongue, but of life.
It cannot be grasped by reason and memory only,
but it is fully understood when it possesses the whole soul
and penetrates to the inner recesses of the heart.

~ JOHN CALVIN[1]

ONE OF THE MOST UNIQUE sporting events in the world did not begin as a sporting event. Each year riders and their dogs race more than 1,000 miles for several days through the Alaskan snow from Anchorage to Nome for Iditarod, the famous dogsled race. While an intriguing event that even allows fans to track the teams online, the genesis of Iditarod was something very serious.

In 1925, hundreds of children in Nome had been exposed to diphtheria. At this point in history, children around the world died from the highly contagious disease because widespread vaccinations had not yet been introduced. The only serum to combat the disease was far away in Anchorage. To get the serum to Nome quickly, it was first carried by train to Nenana. Then teams of riders (known as mushers) and their dogs, strategically placed along the path, carried the serum to Nome via a relay.

More than 150 dogs and 20 mushers were involved in the heroic efforts, which became called "The Great Race of Mercy." With passion and intensity, the mushers hurtled the 300,000 units of life-saving serum across the Alaskan countryside, arriving in Nome in only 127 hours—a record that has yet to be broken. By combining the right medicine with radical effort, an entire generation was rescued, and the riders and their dogs became heroes.

The children in our churches find themselves in an even deadlier situation. Although churches exert massive amounts of energy for the sake of their children and students, oftentimes the medicine—message—does not save.

Sadly, even in churches where the gospel is heralded as the essential message of the Christian faith from the pulpit, children and students are often pummeled with curriculum designed for behavioral modification rather than gospel transformation. It is foolish to feast on the life-giving gospel in one area of the church while using a placebo in another. Quite frankly, children and student ministries are often a wasteland for well-intentioned morality training.

If the gospel is taught from the platform to adults, but "character building" is the theme of the kids' ministry, what are parents to discuss with their children? If the gospel is the focus of the teaching ministry, but law masquerading as "morals while in high school" is the vibe of the ministry to students, what are the students to believe is of first importance?

To form a church centered on the gospel, the church must strategically and seamlessly pass the message of the gospel on from generation to generation. The church must be united from the preschool ministry to the pulpit around one central understanding: *the gospel transforms*. Yes, the gospel must be the foundational truth on which each of these ministries takes their stand. The church must not only be concerned with the messages that are proclaimed from the pulpit, as we discussed in the previous chapter, but also with the teaching that forms the children and students. Jesus-centered "prophets" value the teaching that takes place in all environments within a church.

The Gospel for Kids

The gospel is only for children.

According to Jesus, only those who receive the kingdom of heaven with the faith of a child will ever enter (Matt. 18:3). He continually welcomed children, despite the insistence of others that they not be allowed to bother Him (19:14). When He purified the temple in Jerusalem, children gathered around Him and cried out to Him. The religious leaders were frustrated with the kids and asked Jesus if He heard the noise, as if to say, "Are You not going to stop this madness?" Jesus replied with a quote from a messianic psalm that ultimately pointed to Him (21:16):

> Out of the mouth of babies and infants, you have
> established strength because of your foes, to still the
> enemy and the avenger. (Ps. 8:2 ESV)

Jesus reminded the religious leaders that God has chosen to manifest His power through weakness, through children. He is the great and magnificent God who does not need anyone or anything to conquer an enemy; yet, He has chosen to work through those who are frail and feeble. He is attracted to childlike faith and dependence on Him. The message of the Christian faith is not "God helps those who help themselves" but "God helps the helpless." All of us are like helpless children before Him. And His grace is for those who realize and embrace the beauty of weakness.

Since Jesus referred to children as an object lesson for true faith, should we as leaders not fully embrace the sacredness of childhood and the opportunity to form their hearts on the gospel? Because children already have a realization of their weakness, is this not the best opportunity to apply the gospel to their hearts?

Or do we believe they need something other than the gospel?

Perhaps many churches fail to teach the gospel to children because *law* is more attractive. Law provides children's ministry leaders and parents with the false assurance that we are doing the right things, that we can check boxes off a spiritual checklist. Some would rather children walk away with lessons on being a better child to Mommy and Daddy. After all, the handout about being a better kid appeals to the mother who desperately wants someone else to tell her child to behave. But that handout—unless it's connected to faith in Jesus—reveals our lack of confidence in both the gospel to transform and the sufficiency of Scripture to accomplish what it says it will accomplish.

Some children's ministries are simply viewed as child care, which is most tragic when we understand the blessed vulnerability of children. Why would we be content to provide child care while Mom and Dad, who are far less likely to realize their own weakness, are somewhere else being taught the Christian faith? No, this is the time to lovingly melt the hearts of children with the good news of Jesus. With children especially, we must help them see that the goal of the Commandments was much deeper than tweaked behavior.

The Heart of the Commandments

In the book of Exodus, God rescued His people from Egyptian slavery. After the miraculous rescue, inaugurated with the blood of lambs on doorposts and then powerfully displayed with the parting of the Red Sea, the Israelites were free. The *Jesus Storybook Bible* picks up the story well:

> So God led them to a tall mountain. God wanted to talk to his people and show them what he was like. "I have chosen you—you are my special family. I want you to live in a way that shows everyone else what I'm like— so they can know me, too."
>
> God called Moses up the mountain. The great mountain shook. A thick cloud fell. Thunder roared. Lightning crackled. And God gave Moses Ten Rules, called "Commandments."
>
> "I want you to love me more than anything else in all the world—and know that I love you, too," God told them. "That's the most important thing of all."
>
> God gave them other rules, like don't make yourselves pretend gods; don't kill people; or steal; or lie. The rules showed God's people how to live, and how to be close to him, and how to be happy. They showed how life worked best.
>
> "God promises to always look after you," Moses said. "Will you love him and keep these rules?"
>
> "We can do it! Yes! We promise!" But they were wrong. They couldn't do it. No matter how hard they tried, they could never keep God's rules all the time. God knew they couldn't. And he wanted them to know it, too.
>
> Only one Person could keep all the rules. And many years later God would send him—to stand in their place and be perfect for them. Because the rules couldn't save them. Only God could save them.[2]

The Ten Commandments were given in *response* to God's salvation, while simultaneously *pointing ahead* to God's salvation. He gave His people commands to help frame their appropriate response to the salvation He had graciously and freely given them from Egypt. Their obedience was to be the heart's answer to God's grace. At the same time, the Ten Commandments point to Jesus because we realize we can never obey God as we should. The Commandments show us we cannot keep them. We need a Savior, someone to obey *for* us.

In Deuteronomy 6, Moses reminds the people of the Commandments and then speaks strongly to families:

> "Hear, O Israel: The LORD our God, the LORD is
> one. You shall love the LORD your God with all your
> heart and with all your soul and with all your might.
> And these words that I command you today shall be on
> your heart. You shall teach them diligently to your chil-
> dren, and shall talk of them when you sit in your house,
> and when you walk by the way, and when you lie down,
> and when you rise." (vv. 4–7 ESV)

Amazon.com advertises more than 60,000 books in stock on rais- ing children. That means if you were to read one parenting book a day, you would need 165 years to read all the parenting books currently available. And the majority of the books, even the Christian ones, pri- marily focus on behavior: how to get a child to act a certain way, to be nice, to be polite, to control his temper, to respect others.

Moses took a very different approach; he went for the heart.

We are not articulating that behavior is unimportant. We each have kids, and we would love our sin-babies to behave well for their mothers. What we are saying and what we feel strongly that every church must believe—not only in doctrine but also in practice—is that a transformed heart is infinitely more important than behavior. A changed heart will result in obedience.

Churches centered on the gospel aggressively go for the heart, not for behavior. Morality, or good behavior, is not the goal of godly parenting nor the goal of sound children's ministry. *A changed heart is.* Obedience or morals may be the result, but a changed heart must be the goal. A change in behavior that does not stem from a change in heart is not commendable; it is condemnable.[3] A church that goes after a child's behavior and not the child's heart is shepherding that child in opposition to the gospel. Children can be taught how to behave without hearts impacted by Jesus, but the "good behavior" that results will only last for a season because it lacks the power of inner transformation.

A church's practice in their ministry to children reveals their foundational theology about the human heart. There is a massive difference between defensive and offensive children's ministry as well as defensive and offensive parenting. In football, teams who are winning will often play "prevent defense." Fans hate it because teams blow big leads. With prevent defense, the team assumes they will win. They don't need to score any more points; they just need to protect what they already have. They have stopped playing to win and are now basically playing not to lose.

Defensive children's ministry and defensive parenting play "not to lose" the heart of the child to the world. The focus is primarily on protecting children from influences in the world and pulling out great character traits that must already be within the child. The theology beneath the practice is the assumption that the hearts of children are pure and in need of protection.

Theologically, this is deeply flawed. We are not pure from birth but are terribly sinful—sinful from the time our mothers conceived us. So the hearts of children ultimately do not need *protection* but *transformation*. Puritan pastor Richard Baxter instructed parents:

> Understand and lament the corrupted and miserable state of your children, which they have derived from you, and thankfully accept the offers of a Savior for yourselves and them, and absolutely resign, and dedicate them to God in Christ in the sacred covenant.[4]

While the message that children are depraved sounds very harsh, it is actually gracious because it prepares them (and their parents) for the mercy of God. Much more harsh would be the lie that unacceptable behavior is solely the result of unfit role models, challenging circumstances, or a difficult environment. Much *more* harsh would be the insurmountable burden placed on someone whose futile and vain attempts to earn God's blessing and favor leave nothing but despair.

Children's ministry and parenting that choose *offensive* strategies are different. They seek primarily not to protect a child from the world but to help a child overcome the world as the child's heart is changed by the gospel. Offensive ministry understands the power of the gospel, trusts the power of new birth, and knows that if the child will encounter the truth of Jesus, then obedience will be the joyful result.[5]

So how does a church aggressively go after the hearts of children? From Moses' words, we are challenged to *impress the gospel* and *instruct the gospel*.

Impress the Gospel

Moses emphasized the heart because he knew that faith is more caught than taught, more effectively learned by seeing it than by hearing about it alone. Before he gave instructions about teaching the next generation, he told the people that these words "shall be on your heart." If we want children in our churches to overcome the world because their hearts have been transformed, then they must be around people whose hearts have likewise been transformed. Thomas Chalmers wrote:

> The best way to overcome the world is not with morality or self-discipline. Christians overcome the world by seeing the beauty and excellence of Christ. They overcome the world by seeing something more attractive than the world: Christ.[6]

Children must be impressed with the awesomeness of Christ, with His nature and character. They must see in their leaders a sense of awe for the beauty and attractiveness of Christ. They must see what it means to treasure Christ more than anything else. Children are perceptive, and if they see leaders and parents talk with boredom and apathy about faith yet become overtly passionate about sports teams or shopping malls, they will think the sport or the mall is more attractive than Jesus.

The solution is not to muster a false passion for the attractiveness of Jesus but to apply the gospel to parents while simultaneously placing leaders in front of children who are overwhelmed with the excellency of Christ. The solution is to give children incarnational leaders who stoop down to invest in them as Christ stooped down to us, leaders who have discovered that nothing is as attractive as Christ, leaders whose hearts have been melted by the goodness of God. As Jonathan Edwards declared, nothing is as excellent as Christ, and children need leaders who know and live as if this is true:

> Before Christ is found, there is nothing that is truly
> lovely that is ever found or seen. Those things that they
> had been conversant with before and had set their hearts
> upon had no true excellency. They only deceived them
> with a false, empty show. But now they have found
> Christ, they have found one that is excellent indeed.
> They see in him a real and substantial excellency.[7]

The gospel is impressed on children by what they see in parents and leaders; thus, those who lovingly live a godly life in front of children are heroes. If children see husbands who love their wives and treat them with respect, they learn that Christ, the Bridegroom, pursues and loves His bride unconditionally. If they see leaders and parents hungrily devouring the Scripture, they learn that adults need Jesus for strength each day. If they see leaders forgive someone else, they will learn that their heavenly Father is eager to forgive. If they see service from a thankful heart, they will see that God the perfect Father humbly bowed and served us. When they see the church disadvantage herself to help someone in need, they will more likely understand that God, who is eternally rich, became poor for us.

Instruct the Gospel

While the evidence of a changed heart is incredibly influential in helping children see Jesus with greater clarity and authenticity, active instruction is also a key part of their training in the gospel. Moses challenged parents both to teach the faith diligently and to maximize normal encounters for ongoing discussion: "when you sit at your home, when you walk, when you go to bed, and when you wake." He challenged parents to make the most of everyday opportunities to instruct their children.

This same intensity and intentionality must be applied to the community of faith in regard to its children. Churches must make the most of opportunities to apply the gospel to the hearts of children through diligent teaching and conversations.

There is actually a bit of danger in some of the ways we teach Scripture to children. If leaders are not careful, they will emphasize the *stories* of the sacred text without teaching the *story*. As Ed Clowney warned:

> There are great stories in the Bible . . . but it is possible to know Bible stories, yet miss the Bible story. . . .
> The Bible has a story line. It traces an unfolding drama.
> The story follows the history of Israel, but it does not begin there, nor does it contain what you would expect in a national history. . . . If we forget the story line, we cut the heart out of the Bible. Sunday school stories are then told as tamer versions of the Sunday comics, where

> Samson substitutes for Superman; David becomes a
> Hebrew version of Jack the Giant Killer. No, David
> is not a brave little boy who isn't afraid of the big bad
> giant. He is the Lord's anointed. . . . God chose David
> as a king after his own heart in order to prepare the way
> for David's great Son, our Deliverer and Champion.[8]

If children are taught from the historical narrative of David and Goliath to be brave like David, to grab five stones to tackle the giant in their lives, they will inevitably be set up for failure. When *they* toss the stones, they may not land on the giant's forehead. To the contrary, some children will lose parents and siblings to tragedy. They will get cut from the baseball team despite their many nights of praying. They will have their hearts broken. Whatever the "giant" represents in their minds will continually destroy them.

Unless . . .

Unless they realize the bigger story—that another King comes to destroy sin and death once and for all on their behalf. And that no matter what struggles come, He is with them and will be with them through all eternity.

No matter what your *practice* regarding children's ministry (Sunday school, kid's worship, family worship, large group/small group, etc.), ensure that your *philosophy* of ministry impresses children with the gospel through living examples of grace, while also instructing their hearts with the grand story of Scripture. Don't teach grace from the pulpit to adults while viewing your kid's ministry as necessary child care. Otherwise, you will squander many opportunities to love these children to Jesus. In the same manner, don't boldly proclaim the gospel to parents while burdening their children with virtues apart from the Vine (John 15:5).

Impress and Instruct . . .

Transforming Teenagers

All three of us served in student ministry at one point in our ministries; therefore, we know that many churches put pressure on student leaders and ministries to "keep the kids busy" with a myriad of programs, events, and activities. The motivation is to provide constant alternatives for students so they are helped in avoiding the trappings of the world. But busyness is not next to godliness. Students don't need their social calendars planned; they need their hearts continually transformed.

The "next big thing" mind-set regarding a student-ministry calendar fosters an unhealthy dependence on programs. When students believe that God only engages them at big events, they unconsciously accept that God will only speak to them in those places. Thus, they struggle to see their daily lives as opportunities to walk with God. Like an addict, they crave their next connection to God via a big event with louder speakers and more pizza. Meanwhile, the available time and energy of leaders is swallowed up chaperoning events instead of pouring themselves out in incarnational ministry that invests in a teenager over coffee or lunch.

We applaud Wayne Rice for his transparency on the successes and failures of Youth Specialties, the highly influential organization he helped start. For years, Youth Specialties provided volumes of books on games and other fresh ideas to assist youth-ministry leaders in their programming. Rice has revealed that Youth Specialties initially was designed for three purposes: resources, respect, and relevance. They wanted to provide resources for leaders, make the role of youth pastor a respectable and professional role in the church, and instigate churches to provide relevant ministry to teenagers. And they got what they wanted:

> We got what we wanted. We turned youth ministry into the toy department of the church. Churches

now hire professionals to lead youth ministry. We got relevance but we created a generation of teenagers who are a mile wide and are an inch deep.[9]

Thankfully, Rice now encourages youth-ministry leaders to offer nothing more than the gospel because there is nothing better to offer than the gospel of Jesus. Yet in many churches the gospel remains buried amidst the numerous events. Lock-ins, skating parties, and games of chubby bunny will not transform a teenager. Only the gospel has the power to do so. Activities for students are not sinful; they are often helpful in building relationships. But when the focus becomes the events or the activities rather than Jesus, the only thing that is changed is the calendar.

Morals for Middle School?

A plethora of programming is not the only false indicator of life in many student ministries. Similar to some moralistic messages common in children's ministry is the tendency to continually address teenagers' behavior rather than their hearts. While children's ministry can drift toward teaching *for* behaviors people *want* to see in children, student ministries tend to drift toward teaching *against* behaviors people *don't* want to see in teenagers.

The irony is painful in many churches: teach kids how to behave until they hit puberty, and then teach them how not to behave until they graduate. Is it any wonder that researchers and consultants continually tell us that the majority of students leave the church after high school graduation? If they've grown up under the burden of attempting to live by a list of dos and don'ts apart from a changed heart, we send them out with a surplus of repressed behavior bottled up inside.

In many student ministries, Leo Tolstoy would be viewed as a hero, a model for moral discipline and Christian virtue. Tolstoy was a famous Russian philosopher and author in the mid-1800s, best known for his novel *War and Peace*. But what many may not know is that he pursued moralistic perfection in his faith, a task that many viewed as noble. He set up lengthy and complex lists of rules for himself and trusted those lists to guide his life. He even had a list of rules for controlling his emotions. Several times he publicly vowed to be celibate, even though he was married. He lived in a separate bedroom from his wife.

But Tolstoy could never live up to his own expectations and standards. His wife's sixteen pregnancies, for example, were a reminder of his inability to keep his own self-prescribed vow of celibacy. A. N. Wilson, a Tolstoy biographer, wrote:

> Tolstoy suffered from a fundamental theological
> inability to understand the Incarnation. His religion was
> a thing of Law rather than a thing of Grace, a scheme
> for human betterment rather than a vision for God
> penetrating a fallen world.[10]

Tolstoy pursued perfection in his own strength and energy apart from the grace of God. He constantly lived under guilt and shame, and he died an unhappy vagrant. He never enjoyed the Christian life because he missed the essence of Christianity.

The essence of sin is our attempt to take the place of God; the essence of the Christian faith is God taking our place. He lives the Christian life for us. We simply surrender to Him and follow Him with all we are. Tolstoy, because he missed grace, actually lived the antithesis of the Christian faith.

Students, indeed all of us, are incapable of living the Christian life in our own merit. We are utterly unable to transform ourselves. Because of this simple truth, transformation is not about trying; it's about dying. The apostle Paul knew that transformation occurs when we continually die to ourselves and trust the grace of Christ fully:

> For we who live are always being given over to
> death for Jesus' sake, so that the life of Jesus also may be
> manifested in our mortal flesh. (2 Cor. 4:11 ESV)

Students must be taught to live in His grace and then return to His grace when failure and the humiliation of sin come. Because it will. Students will choke spiritually, and they must learn from us that God's grace is bigger. When a student struggles, he must find grace and forgiveness from leaders. The grace and mercy he finds, though not soft, will teach him to run to God—not away from God—as he continues to struggle with sin throughout his life.

Choking and Grace

Sports psychologists have developed theories about what causes an athlete to choke under pressure. Some believe the pressure of the moment causes them to think about every move and every play, and that the over-thinking causes them to revert to their earlier playing days. They lose the fluidity and second nature they've developed. They become less of a player than they truly are. They revert to their old nature.

During the most important moment in the life of Jesus, one of His followers completely choked spiritually. Peter reverted to his old ways and experienced a spiritual meltdown. He acted contrary to the new life Jesus had given him. Jesus warned this would happen:

> "Simon, Simon, behold, Satan demanded to have
> you, that he might sift you like wheat, but I have prayed
> for you that your faith may not fail. And when you
> have turned again, strengthen your brothers." (Luke
> 22:31–32 ESV)

Notice Jesus calls him Simon. Earlier in the Gospels, Jesus gave him the new name Peter, which means "small rock." But in this instance, Jesus calls him Simon, as if to say, "You're not living as Peter but as Simon." Jesus assured Peter that despite the attempts of Satan, He had secured Peter's faith, and Peter *would* turn back to Him.

Peter's failure to live up to his promise points to our incompetence to live the Christian life in the flesh, in our own ability. Peter placed confidence in the flesh. Matthew's account of Jesus' warning to Peter reveals Peter's thinking about his own ability to follow Jesus:

> Then Jesus said to them, "You will all fall away because of me this night. For it is written, 'I will strike the shepherd, and the sheep of the flock will be scattered.' But after I am raised up, I will go before you to Galilee." Peter answered him, "Though they all fall away because of you, *I will never fall away*." Jesus said to him, "Truly, I tell you, this very night, before the rooster crows, you will deny me three times." Peter said to him, "Even if I must die with you, *I will not deny you!*" And all the disciples said the same. (Matt. 26:31–35 ESV, italics added)

Pride led Peter to believe he was better than the other disciples and that he could win an argument with Jesus. Several verses later, Jesus found the disciples sleeping after He asked them to pray. Jesus said to Peter:

> "So, could you not watch with me one hour? Watch and pray that you may not enter into temptation. The spirit indeed is willing, but the flesh is weak." (Matt. 26:40–41 ESV)

The flesh is truly weak, and we are foolish to attempt to live in it. And we are cruel if we teach students they can.

According to Luke's Gospel, Jesus stared into the eyes of Peter after his third denial of Jesus. Peter also looked into the eyes of his holy and pure God and was overwhelmed with his sinfulness. He rushed out of the courtyard and wept bitterly. Why? Because he had placed his faith in Jesus, and his sin had crushed him. He experienced a godly sorrow that leads to repentance. Thus, the story of Peter does not end with the bitter weeping.

At the end of the Gospel of John, Jesus approached the disciples while they were fishing. He initiated a conversation with Peter and restored him. Jesus told Peter that he would feed His sheep. In other words, what Jesus had said the night Peter denied Him ("when you have turned again, strengthen your brothers") was still true. Jesus was not finished with Peter; He had fully forgiven him and had big plans for him. At the moment of Peter's denial, Jesus was suffering for the sin of Peter's denial.

Peter found the unlimited forgiveness of Jesus, and it marked him significantly. Jesus would utilize Peter as a significant person in the spread of Christianity, as Peter preached Christ till his death. Church history tells us that he was crucified, but in humility he pleaded to be crucified upside down because he was not worthy to be crucified in the same manner as Christ was.

Some fifty years after his denial of Jesus, Peter wrote the letter known as 1 Peter. The words within reveal the lessons Peter learned from both placing confidence in the flesh and in the tender mercy of Jesus. For some examples, see 1 Peter 5:6–10 (ESV) (with a few of our comments interspersed that might have been on Peter's mind as he wrote):

> Humble yourselves, therefore, under the mighty hand of God so that at the proper time he may exalt you, casting all your anxieties on him, because he cares for you. [Don't claim you can follow Him in your own strength. Trust His strength.]
>
> Be sober-minded; be watchful. [Don't fall asleep in the garden.]
>
> Your adversary the devil prowls around like a roaring lion, seeking someone to devour. [The Enemy does indeed want to sift us like wheat.]

> Resist him, firm in your faith, knowing that the
> same kinds of suffering are being experienced by your
> brotherhood throughout the world. And after you have
> suffered a little while, the God of all grace, who has
> called you to his eternal glory in Christ, will himself
> restore, confirm, strengthen, and establish you. [He
> does restore. I know.]

If the only thing teenagers learn in student ministry is to "bring a friend and don't have sex," they will not weep bitterly when they falter because their hearts will not be in awe of God. If they are pounded with a new version of law in their youth group, they won't return to Jesus when the sting of sin comes because they won't think of Him as the God who restores. They will think of Him solely as the God who gives rules. Students must be taught the gospel and the new identity—the new name—the gospel provides them.

Gospel Identity

In the 1960s, a social psychologist named Erik Erikson developed a theory of human development. While he was not a biblical scholar or a theologian, he did study one aspect of God's general revelation: humanity, God's crowning work of creation.

In Erikson's model, teenagers reach a point of developmental crisis called "role confusion versus identity."[11] Teenagers search intently for an identity. They want to be known for something, anything. Those who serve teenagers know that Erikson's model has some credence. Teenagers are searching for an identity, a reputation. They experiment with their dress, music, friends, and hobbies to help form the version of who they are, the person they want to be.

And often the question of "Who am I?" should be answered with "Whose am I?"[12]

The gospel provides the greatest identity one can ever find. Because of the gospel, students can understand that they are His. Because of the gospel, students can walk in confidence. They are His child, His bride, His ambassador, His servant.

Erikson believed that if teenagers did not leave adolescence without a deep sense of their identity, they would struggle throughout adulthood with issues related to their identity. His research and theory only confirm the conviction that a student's identity must be grounded in the gospel. Belonging to God because of the all-sufficient sacrifice of Jesus is the only identity that is secure. All the other identities discovered in middle school (athlete, honor student, boyfriend, in-crowd, etc.) will quickly fade. No other identity, other than the identity found in Christ, will last.

Ministry practice to students will vary from church to church and context to context. Some will offer separate student services. Some will tout intergenerational community groups. Regardless of where you land, your student-ministry practice (programs, strategy, etc.) must be built on a solid theology and coherent philosophy of ministry. If you believe that keeping students busy is a noble student ministry goal, you will offer excessive programming. If you believe that morals transform, you will emphasize right behavior and persuade students to sign covenants. But if you believe the gospel is sufficient for students, you will ensure they know the gospel and the identity that comes from it.

Stakes Are Higher

While the Iditarod had an amazing origin, it is now just another sporting event. What was once a life-saving mission is now a sport, a game. The teams race a similar path, but the motivation is different. They still tie sleds behind dogs, but they are not racing to save lives anymore.

The same is often true of our churches. What was once a life-saving mission can become something perceived as much less. If we are not careful, we will gather children and teenagers and go through the motions of Christian discipleship without a sense of the life-giving message and mission we have been given.

The race is on, and the stakes are high. Instill the grace of God into the entire church, from the pulpit to preschool and through puberty too. And as you race, understand that your seamless relay strategy is not the magic cure that can bring about transformation. The serum—the gospel—is the only thing that saves.

CHAPTER 9

THE JESUS-CENTERED LEADER

Were we able to know exactly what our most influential religious leaders think of God today, we might be able with some precision to foretell where the Church will stand tomorrow.

~ A. W. Tozer[1]

EASY COMPANY WAS A GROUP of unlikely heroes.

This group of men, along with countless thousands of others, sacrificed their lives for a cause greater than themselves. The Axis Powers of Germany, Italy, and Japan had aligned with hopes of creating a new world under the auspices of their warped ideologies. Their militaries ransacked the globe, instilling fear and concern. The global response to these threats by the Allied Powers is what is known as World War II.

Stephen Ambrose's book *Band of Brothers*, later made into a TV miniseries, followed the journey of one group of men through their trials and triumphs in the European theatre of war. This group was known as Easy Company, an ensemble of paratroopers in the 101st Airborne Division of the United States Army.

The miniseries paints a picture of everyday men displaying extraordinary courage in the midst of harrowing fear. It can be dissected from a variety of angles, but one that stands out is the necessity of *leadership*. Easy Company experienced and was shaped by both poor leadership and exemplary leadership.

The series begins with Easy Company in Camp Toccoa, Georgia, training under the leadership of First Lieutenant Herbert Sobel (later Captain). He is dictatorial, unreasonable, and inept. Although the men honor his rank, they disdain his character. The implications are disastrous. Imagine preparing a group of men for a mission that would likely cost them their lives, yet asking them to follow a man they don't trust or respect. Grumbling ensues. His orders are begrudgingly followed, but he has not won the affection of his men. The *esprit de corps* is glaringly absent from a group of soldiers who would most definitely perish without it.

From within the ranks of Easy Company is another leader. Although he does not have the rank or title, he does have the respect of the men. He leads by example and proves to be the glue that holds Easy Company together through their tumultuous season with First Lieutenant Sobel. Second Lieutenant Richard Winters (later Major) proves to have the character, competency, and chemistry to lead this group.

Sobel is reassigned, and Winters is given the charge to officially lead Easy Company into Normandy. The change within the men is nearly immediate. The *esprit de corps* that was absent begins to form as the men unify around one another, their leader, and the mission before them. Why?

Because culture depends on leadership.

This is true in any organization, group, or family. Culture and ethos is a reflection of leadership. Your church culture—over time, at least—is a reflection of the leadership of the church. The kingly function of leadership is as vital to the health of a local church as is the prophetic function of teaching.

So in many ways, the culture serves as a diagnostic mirror that reveals the implications of our leadership. If you want an honest evaluation of your leadership, then look at the ethos of your church. It's time we stopped complaining about the culture of our churches and started leading within them. We can only complain about the church culture for a few years; after that, it's a reflection of how we are leading. It is a mirror reflecting leadership, and sometimes what we see can be painful.

Given the importance of leadership within the church, we want to take a substantial look at how the gospel should impact our leadership.

A gospel-centered church is infused with gospel-centered leadership. If a local church corporately bears the fruit of the Spirit, then you can be confident individuals who have been marked by the gospel of Jesus Christ lead it. There is a direct correlation between the personal impact of the gospel on a leader's heart and the way he leads. The gospel is not good advice simply to be taken into consideration in certain situations; rather, the gospel is good news of sweeping transformation. A gospel-centered leader will lead differently.

A Brief Biblical Theology of Leadership[2]

Leadership is a hot topic. Myriads of books dissect it from every angle, universities offer doctoral degrees on it, and leadership gurus debate over the exact combination of personality types and attributes that make the perfect leader. While much of this conversation is profitable, perhaps the attempt to produce a formula for making the ultimate leader has caused us to lose the wonder of God's providence in choosing and using leaders. Throughout history, God has raised up men and women, some weak and some strong, some smart and some slow, in certain seasons and certain situations, to accomplish His overarching purposes in the world. A distinctly Christian understanding of leadership must be biblically rooted and theologically formed. Even a cursory study of the biblical witness provides several prominent elements necessary for our understanding of leadership.

First, our leadership is a derivative leadership sourced in God Himself. He establishes nations and governments and directs the course of the king's heart (Rom. 13:1; Prov. 21:1). He dresses the lilies of the field and watches over the sparrow (Matt. 6:26–31; 10:29). This becomes even more explicit when talking about God's sovereign leadership over His church. Jesus is the Head of the Church and has been given authority over all (Eph. 1:20; 5:23). He is the preeminent One and the "chief Shepherd" of the Church (Col. 1:18; 1 Pet. 5:4 HCSB). Every joint and ligament in the body of Christ is held together and fits together in Him (Eph. 4:16; Col. 2:19). God's sovereign leadership over all is foundational for understanding human leadership.

In short, because our leadership is ultimately derived from God's, it is always subservient, always secondary. In no way does this demean the role and responsibility of human leaders; rather, it defines the scope of human leadership. It puts it in its proper place and provides the right limitations. The apostle Paul discusses this in 2 Corinthians 5 when he describes the role and responsibility of the believer in ambassadorial terms (v. 20). We are sent to the world as agents on behalf of another. We are representatives carrying the message of one greater than ourselves.

Second, God raises up leaders. They are born under His auspices. They are elected under His watch. They rise to the occasion under His reign. They are given a voice by His decree. He builds up platforms and dismantles platforms. He gives some of them long seasons of influence, while others have shorter windows in which to serve.

Yet in all of this, there is mystery. God's sovereign reign over leaders does not diminish the freedom for humanity to seize opportunities. Consider, for example, Mordecai's wisdom to Queen Esther: "If you keep silent at this time, liberation and deliverance will come to the Jewish people from another place, but you and your father's house will be destroyed. Who knows, perhaps you have come to your royal position for such a time as this" (Esth. 4:14 HCSB). In this passage we see that God's purposes cannot be thwarted (namely, that deliverance will come to His people), but Esther still had the opportunity to act, to lead. God's sovereignty doesn't diminish our responsibility or opportunity.

God doesn't call the qualified; He qualifies the called. How often we see Him in Scripture calling the unexpected and the average into significant roles of leadership. In some sense, there is no concrete mold or predictable pattern for the person God raises up to lead. Consider the calling of Moses to lead the Israelites out of slavery. Moses was filled with reluctance and anxiety. He was slow and hesitant in speech. How was he to be God's mouthpiece?

> But Moses replied to the LORD, "Please, Lord, I have never been eloquent—either in the past or recently or since You have been speaking to Your servant— because I am slow and hesitant in speech."
> Yahweh said to him, "Who made the human mouth? Who makes him mute or deaf, seeing or blind? Is it not I, Yahweh? Now go! I will help you speak and I will teach you what to say." (Exod. 4:10–12 HCSB)

Samuel was called to anoint the new king of Israel, knowing it would be one of Jesse's sons. However, even this godly judge of Israel forgot that God qualifies those He calls. Samuel was looking for certain outward indicators of who this next king would be, but God shows us through the calling of David that a certain age, appearance, or pecking order is not God's criteria for leadership:

> "In peace," he replied. "I've come to sacrifice to the LORD. Consecrate yourselves and come with me to the sacrifice." Then he consecrated Jesse and his sons and invited them to the sacrifice. When they arrived, Samuel saw Eliab and said, "Certainly the LORD's anointed one is here before Him."

But the Lord said to Samuel, "Do not look at his appearance or his stature, because I have rejected him. Man does not see what the Lord sees, for man sees what is visible, but the Lord sees the heart."

Jesse called Abinadab and presented him to Samuel. "The Lord hasn't chosen this one either," Samuel said. Then Jesse presented Shammah, but Samuel said, "The Lord hasn't chosen this one either." After Jesse presented seven of his sons to him, Samuel told Jesse, "The Lord hasn't chosen any of these." Samuel asked him, "Are these all the sons you have?"

"There is still the youngest," he answered, "but right now he's tending the sheep." Samuel told Jesse, "Send for him. We won't sit down to eat until he gets here." So Jesse sent for him. He had beautiful eyes and a healthy, handsome appearance.

Then the Lord said, "Anoint him, for he is the one." So Samuel took the horn of oil, anointed him in the presence of his brothers, and the Spirit of the Lord took control of David from that day forward. Then Samuel set out and went to Ramah." (1 Sam. 16:5–13 HCSB)

The testimony of God calling the ordinary and unexpected continues in the New Testament. Jesus' calling of the first disciples is a wonderful example of God choosing the ordinary, uneducated, and common to engage in a work that is extraordinary, brilliant, and supernatural. The apostle Paul reminds the Corinthian church to consider their calling. They were not wise. They lacked power and influence and a good pedigree (1 Cor. 1:26–31). Yet, He chose them to be His ambassadors to carry the most important message in the world.

Third, leadership is a gift of the Holy Spirit. The Old Testament bears the story of how God called and anointed a specific group of people for specific functions. Prophets, priests, and kings each fulfilled distinct roles and responsibilities in the leading of God's people. In the New Testament, leadership is listed in one of the apostle Paul's list of spiritual gifts, found in Romans 12:6–8 (HCSB): "According to the grace given to us, we have different gifts . . . if exhorting, in exhortation; giving with generosity; *leading, with diligence"* (italics added). Obviously, a common grace of leadership is extended to men and women who are not endowed with the gift of the Holy Spirit and are not believers in Jesus Christ. But the Scriptures make a specific point that there is a unique "gift" of leadership, sovereignly doled out to some for the edification of the Church and the building up of the saints. And it is to be stewarded with diligence. The primary implication for leaders is that there is no room for boasting. God graciously gives gifts, leaving no room for haughty and prideful leadership.

Finally, godly leaders are concerned with God's agenda. Godly leadership is stewardship. It is the recognition that personal agendas, entitlements, vainglory, and selfish ambition must be put to death. A leader who is transformed by the gospel seeks not to make a name for himself but to lift high the name of Jesus. His obsession is not with building his own empire but living for the kingdom of God.

We see this example in Abraham, Moses, Joshua, Caleb, David, Isaiah, Daniel, the apostles, and in the Lord Jesus Himself. The primary declaration of the godly leader is, "Yes, Yahweh, we wait for You in the path of Your judgments. Our desire is for Your name and renown" (Isa. 26:8 HCSB).

The Scriptures are replete with examples of leadership, both godly and wicked, giving us several key theological points to extrapolate and ponder when considering leadership—its source, its purpose, its requirements upon those who lead. But what takes us from here to the place where we can view the distinguishing marks of gospel-centered, Jesus-centered leadership?

What Is Gospel-Centered Leadership?

Most Christian approaches to leadership simply find good and bad examples of leaders in the Bible and say, "Be like this," or "Don't be like that." Although the Bible certainly provides great examples of leadership, these approaches often assume the Bible is a book primarily about you and what you are to do, rather than primarily about God and what He has done in Christ. Gospel-centered leadership does not begin with the command to *imitate*, but with the good news that God is gracious and has sent His Son to take our sins and give us life.

So, yes, gospel-centered leadership may end up looking like Nehemiah or Moses, but that's because it's grounded in being united to the One toward whom they point: Jesus. When you're united to the One who died on the cross and rose from the grave, then your life (and your leadership) is shaped by dying to self and allowing Christ to live in you.

In light of all of this, how can we best understand and define leadership, specifically gospel-centered leadership? *Jesus-centered leadership is God-focused, Christ-exalting, and Spirit-led influence toward a kingdom agenda.* Gospel-centered leadership is inextricably linked to the work of the triune God in redemption. The gospel is Trinitarian. The Father sends, the Son accomplishes, and the Spirit applies. Thus, gospel-centered leadership is marked by its redemptive influence and kingdom initiatives.

This definition is in accord with the theological grid distilled from the Scriptures. Gospel-centered leadership focuses on the glory of God and is grounded in God's reign and rule. Gospel-centered leadership aims to exalt Christ Jesus in all things and is sourced in His Person and work. He is the Chief Shepherd, the Senior Pastor, and Head of the body. Gospel-centered leadership recognizes that we cannot afford to be self-directed in our influence; rather we must be Spirit-led. All of our influence and inertia is toward advancing the kingdom of God by pushing back the darkness.

Who Does God Use: Who Is a Jesus-Centered Leader?

A gospel-centered leader is characterized less by the exemplification of certain personality traits and more by being united to the Person of Jesus. Our brief look at the Scriptures showed that God uses a variety of people from an assortment of backgrounds with differing skills and shortcomings to accomplish His work. He isn't looking for a certain skill-set to employ; rather, He is looking for people who are united to the Son through His death and resurrection. Our gifting and skills are secondary to our union with Christ.

The gospel also redefines leadership in terms of leaders being born or leaders being created over time. All gospel-centered leaders are both *reborn* and *re-created*. This is their primary mark. They are not the same people as they were prior to the regenerative work of the Spirit in their hearts.

The work of the Holy Spirit in regeneration necessarily starts the work of the Holy Spirit in sanctification. A leader's life is consistently being shaped, molded, and formed into the image of Christ. This is often a slow, but always consistent, work of the Spirit. Because of the indwelling presence of the Holy Spirit, a gospel-centered leader should not be the same person in his leadership, his character, or his life today that he was years ago. The Spirit uses our experiences, our natural maturing, and the Word of God to supernaturally etch our souls and enliven our hearts. The leader who does not have a pliable heart lacks one of the distinctive marks of the gospel. We are constantly changing and being changed from one degree of glory to the next (2 Cor. 3:18).

We become what we behold. If we obsess over food, then we ultimately become gluttonous. If we obsess over certain material items or possessions, then we become covetous. But if we behold the glory of Christ, then we will ultimately become like Him. This truth cannot be overstated for the leader in the church. There are a myriad of responsibilities facing the church leader, but the one thing that cannot be forsaken is the simple beholding of Jesus (Luke 10:39–42).

The fact that gospel-centered leaders are both reborn and re-created is evidenced in the lists of qualifications found in 1 Timothy 3 and Titus 1.[3] The overarching qualification is that the leader (specifically here dealing with elders and deacons) must be above reproach, having integrity and character. Our tendency in reading this is to think that the elder or deacon has perfect behavior and doesn't face the struggles common to the rest of us. But nothing can be further from the truth.

The gospel declares that we are not a perfect people; this is foundational to our understanding. In fact, the gospel unashamedly pronounces our lack of perfection and affirms that our hearts have been soiled with sin. But Christ has died for this and has given us a new heart. We are not the same people. Morality and integrity are the by-products—not of our own effort, but of the work of the Spirit. A man who is above reproach, then, is a man who is united to Christ. Yes, he still sins. Yes, he still struggles. But he runs *to* the Savior instead of *away from* Him. He is quick to confess and repent before others and before the Lord. Repentance is the continual ethic of the gospel-centered leader. The leader who is above reproach lives a life that is free of accusation; his struggles are known and covered by the blood of Jesus.[4]

Far too often we have looked at these lists and simply seen them as actions divorced from the heart and separate from the work of the gospel. For instance, "hospitality" is listed as a qualification for leadership. This certainly involves more than having people over to our homes for punch and cookies. It is a response of the heart to the work of the gospel in our lives. Jesus has invited us to His table. He has set a place for us and brought us near. We who were once strangers and aliens have been ushered into the palace of the King and called His sons (Eph. 2:12–13; John 14:1–3). Certainly the gospel impacts our understanding of hospitality.

Scripture also says the leader is not a "lover of money." How does the gospel inform our understanding of this? The gospel-centered leader has already given everything needed to buy the field that gains him the treasure of the gospel (Matt. 13:44). Treasures, therefore, have been redefined for him. Jesus is the treasure. He is the prize. As a result, money and possessions have lost, and are losing, their grip on the heart.

This is how the gospel brings weight, meaning, and perspective to all of the leadership qualifications listed.

Consider how our churches might be different if our leadership reflected a gospel-centered understanding and application of these qualifications. The gospel would become the grid by which we understand our calling and our qualification. Not only would it inform us but also sustain us in those qualifications. We would not need to manufacture behaviors; rather, this would simply be the type of people we're becoming as we behold the glory of God in the face of Jesus Christ (2 Cor. 4:6).

As we are changed more and more into the image of Christ, we begin to be moved by the things that moved our Lord. Our union with Christ manifests itself by having the heart of Christ. And all of this produces a deep angst and burden in the soul of a leader. This combination presses on the heart of the leader and produces a confident vision. Beholding Jesus ultimately moves us to action.

Vision that is birthed in the heart of the leader is sourced in the heart of the triune God. In this case, the gospel becomes the primary driver for a particular vision or cause, rather than a certain vision or cause being the primary driver. Gospel-driven vision leads our church to be sustaining and persevering, while cause-driven vision can be temporary and faddish. Gospel-driven vision will undoubtedly lead you and your church to tackle weighty causes, but not all cause-driven vision will lead you and your people to the gospel. What drives your vision is essential.

The church cannot afford to settle for merely "good leadership." There is nothing distinctively Christian about leadership in general. What the church desperately needs are men and women who are marked by the distinctiveness of the gospel in their leadership.

Leaders, more than anyone, should be acutely aware that their gifting, qualification, and competence are not of their own doing; rather, they give ongoing evidence of the grace of God in their lives (2 Cor. 3:4–6; 1 Tim. 1:12).

Leading by Following: How a Jesus-Centered Leader Leads

We have done a brief biblical theology of leadership, defined gospel-centered leadership, and looked at who a gospel-centered leader is. We now want to look at how a gospel-centered leader leads.

In short, gospel-centered leadership is essentially leading by following.

We love stories of pioneers blazing new trails, adventurists tackling new feats, and explorers making new discoveries. The rugged individualism of Western culture has been celebrated and esteemed. There is definitely room in the Church for entrepreneurialism, ingenuity, and innovation. In fact, we need more leaders who possess these gifts and this level of drive. But gospel-centered leaders are always tempered by the fact that they are ultimately not leading the charge.

We do not need mavericks who think they get to fly solo. These types of leaders are far too common and can be potentially dangerous to the Church. Instead, Scripture demands that we are vice-regents who act in the name of Another. We are first *followers* before we are ever *leaders*. And our leadership is always subjected to following Jesus.

This cannot be overstated. We are a people under authority, and authority is a blessing. We are under the authority of the Spirit, for example. We are under the authority of the laws of the land. There are shadows of authority all around us, reminding us of the greater Authority that we are all subject to. If we see this as a leash on our leadership or a needless restriction on our abilities, then we have gross error in our understanding of our relationship with the Lord. We must recognize that our hearts have a proclivity toward the things of the world and the flesh (Jer. 17:9). Proverbs 14:12 says, "There is a way that seems right to a man, but its end is the way to death" (HCSB). If we begin to lead in our own fleshly wisdom, strength, and direction, we will surely lead others and ourselves toward death and decay. This is not a shock-value statement; it's an inevitable implication of flesh-led leadership. The Spirit leads to life. Nothing and no one else does.

A leader who understands that he is under the authority of God also understands that he is *accountable* to God. The way he leads matters. The directions, decisions, and actions he makes have both a significant and subtle impact. Far too often we've seen a leader, engulfed in ego-driven power, who believes he answers to no one. He may say the right things and know the right answers, but his actions betray him. He lives as if he's the king. This is a failure to understand the gospel and a failure to apply the gospel to leadership.

We have also seen leaders with a messiah complex. Such people have obviously lost sight of the fact that there is one Savior and one sacrifice that is sufficient—and that neither of those realities have anything to do with us. We are role players in the unfolding kingdom agenda, being called to faithfulness, and we can easily be replaced. It is actually freeing to know this and to lead with this—to know that we are not essential. It engenders a heart of gratitude for the role we've been given and also for the fact that it doesn't depend on us. We will all give an account for our leadership, but we will not be held accountable for being a savior. That job belongs to Another, who has already done it perfectly.

None of us ever graduate from the gospel to move on to something else; rather, we continue to grow into the fullness of the gospel more and more. A gospel-centered leader continues to trust wholeheartedly in the provision and sufficiency of the gospel, leading others to do the same. The natural pipeline for leadership is first learning to be led by Christ ourselves, then leading others, then leading other leaders, and finally learning to lead *with* other leaders.

But learning to be led by Christ—the first order of business—can be one of the more challenging aspects to all of leadership. It requires submission, self-awareness, honesty, and the ability to discern our own clever self-justifications. Perhaps the most important note about learning to be led by Christ ourselves is discovering we cannot do it alone. We need other voices and others speaking into us, helping us to see. The Holy Spirit uses gospel-centered community to be that voice and those eyes for us.

Obviously, if we as leaders do not have a community of trusted believers to walk closely with, then our leadership will be stunted. We will continue to lead with blinders on and will fail to see our weaknesses in their proper light. We will stall our growth in the Lord. Learning to be led ourselves means our lives are marked by a growing obedience before Him. We first trust in the promises of God personally before expecting others to do the same.

As our leadership extends beyond learning to be led, we are entrusted with more and more responsibility. But even in all of this, the way we lead does not change. *We lead by following, and we lead with the gospel.* There should never be a time when these two points are not present in our leadership.

One other valuable note here to church leaders: Most of us will have the privilege of learning to lead others. This can come in the form of leading a new believer in his or her faith, or leading a small group or Sunday school class. But often overlooked is our calling to lead our families. This is our primary place of learning to lead others. Husbands are called to lead their wives, and parents are called to lead their children. Despite the nobility of our call to serve the body as a leader, we must champion our role as a leader in our home. Ineffectiveness and inattentiveness in this area will eventually lead to a lack of trusting, confident leadership in other areas.

Again, the environment may change and the responsibility of influence may be more widespread, but the manner in which we lead does not change. We are anchored by the truth that we are a people under authority, given charge to faithfully lead others in the provision and sufficiency of the gospel.

Motivations Matter: Why One Leads

The end does not justify the means. The means matter.

Jesus put a spotlight on our motivations in the Sermon on the Mount when He decried those who merely possessed a cleaned-up outward behavior yet harbored faulty motivations in the heart. The religious leaders of the day lived as if outward actions alone were sufficient. Murder and adultery were seen only as physical acts, but Jesus declared them first to be postures of the heart—a heart filled with anger and lust before the actions are ever demonstrated. In fact, He was bold enough in His teaching to say that a person who burns with anger or lust is called a murderer and adulterer. Jesus was moving the pervasive paradigm away from outward morality to see that the problem lies inside. The problem lurks within. *Our motivations matter to Jesus.* The heart of a gospel-centered leader is compelled by the love of Christ and constrained by the fear of the Lord.

In a society enamored with results, we would be foolish to pretend that this same outward mind-set has not bled into the culture of the Church as well. Results, yes, are a good thing. The Church should maintain goals and metrics and plans for achieving certain benchmarks. But what are empty results if we lose our soul along the way? One result each leader should be striving for is a heart that is right before the Lord in its ambitions and motivations.

In 2 Corinthians 5 we gain a picture of righteous gospel motivations. The chapter begins by stating that a right desire for the future leads to right ambitions in the present. Our confidence in Christ's promises of the future should be a key motivator for us—a gospel motivation.

Paul paints a picture of the permanence of our eternal home in the heavens, a home that God Himself is constructing. All of our earthly groaning will finally subside when we receive our newly glorified body. The Holy Spirit guarantees this will be accomplished for those who love and trust in Jesus (2 Cor. 5:1–5). This is the believer's view of heaven, and this view impacts (or motivates) our lives in the present. Since our present actions contain eternal implications, we make it our aim, Paul says, to please Christ in all things (5:6–10).

But that's not all. The next section begins with Paul stating, "Therefore, because we know the fear of the Lord, we seek to persuade people" (v. 11 HCSB). The fear of the Lord should be a motivating factor for the gospel-centered leader. Unfortunately, we are often confused by the fear of the Lord. We tend to think of cowering away from a vindictive God who is ready to strike us. But a biblical understanding of the fear of the Lord actually draws us closer to the Father:

> The true fear of God is a child-like fear. Some of the Puritans used to call it a "filial fear." It is a combination of holy respect and glowing love. To fear God is to have a heart that is sensitive to both His God-ness and His graciousness. It means to experience great awe and a deep joy simultaneously when one begins to understand who God really is and what He has done for us. Therefore the true fear of God is not a fear that makes a person run away and flee from God. It is a fear that drives him to God. Love for God and fear of Him are, therefore, not at all incompatible. To think that they are is to fail to see the richness of the character of the God we worship. It is to ignore the way in which knowing Him in all of His attributes, and responding appropriately to Him, stretches our emotional capacities to their limit. Scripture portrays the fear of the Lord and the love of the Lord as companion emotions.[5]

Paul's fear of the Lord and his sensitivity to the character and nature of God ultimately led him to persuade people. He knew that he was a man under authority commissioned by the Father to be His ambassador. And what was Paul trying to persuade people toward? He was persuading them to be reconciled to the God who loves them and has made a way for them through Jesus Christ.

So the *fear* of God was not the only motivating factor in Paul's life, nor should it be in ours. The *love* of God accompanies healthy fear.

Second Corinthians 5:14 says, "For Christ's love compels us . . ." The Greek verb translated "compels" in this verse is *synecho*, which carries with it the idea of being held together, hemmed in, sustained, and pressed. The word picture is of two walls closing around you, causing you to go in a certain direction or a particular way. Paul is saying here that the love of Christ *motivated* him to move in a certain way. He was hemmed in by Christ's love and compelled to act. Why? Because . . . "if One died for all, then all died. And He died for all so that those who live should no longer live for themselves, but for the One who died for them and was raised" (vv. 14–15 HCSB)—the One who loves them. Paul's motivations, both the fear of the Lord and the love of Christ, lie squarely in the gospel.

The challenge for the leader, as with any believer, is the understanding that our motivations are always a mixed bag. There is never a time when we are entirely pure in our ambitions and motivations. So we place ourselves in danger when we mask our motivations. We must always remember—and never be surprised by the fact—that our hearts creatively generate justifications for why we do what we do. There is undoubtedly a dark side to leadership. We can be praised for our achievements while knowing full well that what motivated our hearts was a fear of failure, fear of man, or fear of rejection. Yet because we apparently achieved praiseworthy results, we easily become inoculated to our false motivations. This is like building a house of cards; it may look impressive at a glance, but the structure is weak and flimsy. If we lead in order to garner the approval of others or to substantiate our identity or worth, then people become a means to our end. They become either objects or obstacles to us. Whenever this happens, we are not loving them and desiring their greatest good in the gospel; rather, we are seeking our own perceived good or meeting our own needs. And ironically, what we are pursuing has already been accomplished for us in the gospel. Leading from false motives is not gospel-centered leadership; it is self-focused and self-protective leadership.

Yet thankfully, God provides grace even for this. His antidote for discovering the places where we're masking our motivations, uncovering the dark side of leadership that we all struggle with, is found in the work of the Holy Spirit in the community of faith. Leaders of all people should be the first to move from the shadows to the light, making repentance a continual ethic in their lives. Our hearts, of course, will craft a myriad of reasons and rationales for why we cannot possibly be honest about our weaknesses, shortcomings, and sins. But recognize this as a scheme of the enemy to continue isolating you and leaving you content to lead from the shadows. The problem with living in the shadows is that there is just enough light for you to justify staying there.

The author of Hebrews writes, "Watch out brothers, so that there won't be in any of you an evil, unbelieving heart that departs from the living God. But encourage each other daily, while it is still called today, so that none of you is hardened by sin's deception" (Heb. 3:12–13 HCSB). These verses bear a sense of urgency to them. The call is for the believer to be on close watch, not only for himself but for those around him as well. While standing guard, we are commissioned to encourage one another in the gospel promises, day in and day out, remaining disciplined in both introspection and inspection.

The word from Scripture to the leader desiring to be gospel-centered is: *first, look within your own heart* and allow the Holy Spirit to speak to you concerning issues of sanctification. You are a work in progress, and to live any differently is to live deceived. There is too much at stake for your life personally and for those you have been called to lead. But coupled with honest introspection is the need for outside inspection. *So, second, look to others for help in exposing impure motivations.* A leader, just like all believers, needs his gospel-centered community to inspect his heart. We have blind spots, strongholds that won't die easily. The author of Hebrews assumes a level of transparency, forthright communication, and nearness in the community of faith.

Far too often the leader has made the decision to create distance between himself and community. But the text gives no credence to such a decision. In fact, the text would say this decision is actually further evidence of one's need for community. It cannot be said loudly enough or with too much emphasis: gaining leadership prestige or accomplishment and losing your soul is a worthless trade. Leaders have the unique opportunity to demonstrate before the ones they are given charge to lead, whether it be their family or their flock, that no healing is available in the shadows. There is no victory in the darkness. Jesus-centered leaders lead from the light of honesty and openness, trusting fully in Christ's provision—and Christ's provision alone—to make up for what is faulty in their leadership.

Leading With the End in Mind: The Goal of Jesus-Centered Leadership

In this chapter we have looked at the biblical testimony on leadership in order to gain a theological perspective on the subject. The ministry of the new covenant in the death and resurrection of Jesus Christ further shapes and informs our perspective of leadership. Gospel-centered leadership, again, is God-focused, Christ-exalting, and Spirit-led influence toward a kingdom agenda. A gospel-centered leader is characterized less by the exemplification of certain personality traits and more by being united to the Person of Jesus Christ. When a leader is impacted by the gospel, it changes everything, every day. In short, gospel-centered leadership is essentially leading by following. The leader understands that he cannot afford to be flesh-directed in his leadership, but that he is to be led by the Holy Spirit in the context of community. And the way in which he leads matters as much as what his leadership produces. Gospel-centered leaders are compelled by the love of Christ and constrained by the fear of the Lord. We are challenged by the Scriptures to leave the shadows and lead from the light, unmasking false motivations.

In the end, therefore, the goal or aim of gospel-centered leadership is the formation of Christ in people who long to see the formation of Christ in other people. We are called to make disciples who make disciples. It should be clear from what we know about our own sanctification process that this is a slow, arduous calling requiring patience and perseverance. The question we need to keep asking in our leadership is, "Who or what are we leading them to?" In the end, our calling is to pursue faithful action before results. We will discuss this in greater detail in the following chapter.

God ultimately raises up leaders for one primary reason: His glory. He shows His power in our weakness. He demonstrates His wisdom in our folly. We are all like a turtle on a fence post. If you walk by a fence post and see a turtle on top of it, then you know someone came by and put it there. In the same way, God gives leadership according to His good pleasure.

Major Richard Winters of Easy Company was raised up in a unique and pivotal time in history. He supplanted a man, Hebert Sobel, who had the same opportunity to lead with heart, courage, and strength, but forfeited his occasion by his insecure and inept leadership. Sobel seemed to fear the success of others and stifled any leadership that bubbled up within the ranks. Winters, however, was just the opposite. His security and character allowed him to lead from a posture of humility.

The *Band of Brothers* miniseries ends by playing an interview with Winters as an elderly man, in which he quotes one of his men, Sergeant Mike Ranney: "I treasure my remark to my grandson who asked, 'Grandpa, were you a hero in the war?' The man answered, 'No, but I served in a company of heroes.'" Which type of leader will you be?

CHAPTER 10

JESUS-CENTERED FLOWER COMMITTEE

The Church exists for nothing else but to draw men into Christ, to make them little Christs. If we are not doing that, all the cathedrals, clergy, missions, sermons, even the Bible itself, are simply a waste of time.

~ C. S. Lewis[1]

IT WAS AN ORDINARY FLAG football game for the Sigma Nu's of Oklahoma State University. As they stretched out on the chilly October evening, they expected an hour of good competition with another frat on campus. But then everything changed as an imposing figure walked out of the crowd and asked for a set of flags.

It was Kevin Durant, star player for the Oklahoma City Thunder. One of the Sigma Nu brothers had sent a random Twitter message to Durant offhandedly asking him to accept an invitation to come to

Stillwater and play on their team. Durant showed up, and word spread quickly on campus that the NBA superstar was on the field in a pair of sweatpants playing quarterback and defensive back for the Sigma Nu's.[2]

Surely the move caused basketball executives to shudder as Durant put his multi-million-dollar knees on the line, but based on the grins on everyone's faces, the evening was a success, even though the Sigma's had to forfeit the game for bringing a ringer.

But they did not mind. They got to play ball with Kevin Durant: former NBA Rookie of the Year, the youngest player ever to lead the league in scoring, and the hoop daddy who lit up the famed Rucker Park in his free time. This was the guy playing flag football on that October evening. That's what made it special. It was the fact that someone so great was willing to come and play a game with a bunch of random guys on a random field in the middle of Oklahoma. Those random young men were blown away with the goodness of Kevin Durant because they were already in awe of his greatness. In their minds, someone great descended into the details. He came from the stratosphere of athletic greatness to mingle with the never-will-be's (no offense to the Sigma's).

Rarely do we see greatness and goodness combined. Typically the more famous or popular someone becomes, the less expectation there is for the person to interact with his fans. Rarely does the great choose to be good, the big choose to be small.

While Durant's basketball prowess is great now, his glory will fade. In a few years, his athletic ability will quickly wane. Another player will rise to take his place. His goodness, as touching as it was, was also very temporary. He spent a few hours on an intramural field.

God is infinitely greater. His glory will never fade; it will never be shared with another. And His goodness is far deeper than a quick appearance on an athletic field. In Psalm 8 (ESV), David stands in awe of God's willing condescension:

O LORD, our Lord, how majestic is your name in
all the earth! You have set your glory above the heavens.
Out of the mouth of babies and infants, you have established strength because of your foes, to still the enemy
and the avenger. When I look at your heavens, the work
of your fingers, the moon and the stars, which you have
set in place, what is man that you are mindful of him,
and the son of man that you care for him? Yet you have
made him a little lower than the heavenly beings and
crowned him with glory and honor. You have given him
dominion over the works of your hands; you have put
all things under his feet, all sheep and oxen, and also the
beasts of the field, the birds of the heavens, and the fish
of the sea, whatever passes along the paths of the seas.
O LORD, our Lord, how majestic is your name in all the
earth!

This psalm is a beautiful blend of the greatness and goodness of
God, His transcendence and immanence, demonstrated in crafting the
cosmos *and* being involved in the details of humanity. Because David
was awed by God's greatness, he was melted by His goodness. And
David only had a taste of what we now know in full.

Jesus is the culmination of both the greatness and the goodness of
God. The gospel is the showplace of His eternal and everlasting plan
and His willing condescension to suffer death—even death on a cross!
Jonathan Edwards wrote:

In Christ infinite greatness, and infinite goodness
meet together, and receive luster and glory one from
another. His greatness is rendered lovely by his goodness. The greater anyone is without goodness, so much
the greater evil; but when infinite goodness is joined
with greatness, it renders it a glorious and adorable
greatness.[3]

The wonder of Psalm 8 is pushed to its full extent by the knowledge of the gospel. Awe of the gospel inspired the writer of Hebrews, centuries later, to reflect on the same passage. After quoting the psalm of David, he declared:

> Now in putting everything in subjection to him, he left nothing outside his control. At present, we do not yet see everything in subjection to him. But we see him who for a little while was made lower than the angels, namely Jesus, crowned with glory and honor because of the suffering of death, so that by the grace of God he might taste death for everyone. (Heb. 2:8–9 ESV)

The birth, life, death, and resurrection of Jesus and the wholeness that it entails demonstrates that there is no area of the universe—great or small—that is untouched by the gospel. Therefore, there is no area of church life that should remain untouched by the gospel.

Yet for many church leaders, "gospel centrality" is a theological term that dwells in the arena of theory or sporadic "salvation appeals" from the platform. Tragically, confining the gospel to the "big" aspects of church life unwittingly teaches people that the ramifications of the gospel end, that there are moments in their days and sections of their lives that can remain unaffected by Christ. If a church member does not see how the details of church ministry are impacted by the gospel, how would he ever see how the gospel applies to the mundane aspects of his day?

There is an immense amount of important details related to church ministry, and because of their narrow focus, there is a temptation to view them as outside the reach of the gospel. Perhaps some have wondered, "What are these details that the Son of Man is mindful of them?" But He is mindful of them, and how we treat these elements of church ministry reveals a lot about our hearts.

Churches centered on the gospel and those anemic of the gospel live with these details, but gospel-centered churches see them with a different vision. They have embraced both the bigness and the small-ness of the gospel, realizing that no area of church life is untouched.

The gospel is for the counseling ministry, the deacon nomination process, the budget planning, the custodial checklist, the equipment purchases, the hiring process, the church calendar, the facilities, the greeters . . . everything.

Not everything is the gospel, but the gospel is for everything.

One way to know how deeply the gospel is being woven into the culture of your church is to continually check the small details for gospel proof. If there is gospel absence in practice, you will know what areas of your theological foundation and ministry philosophy need to be addressed. Instead of people finding "the devil in the details," lead in such a way that they find "grace in the details."

Check the Details

If you've ever hosted a speaking event or concert, you may be familiar with what's known as the "rider," a detailed list of requests or demands that an artist expects from a venue. The rock band Van Halen, for example, was notorious for their rider that specified that a bowl of M&Ms always be placed in their dressing room before a concert . . . oh, and one more thing: make sure all the brown ones are removed.

Most people would hear a demand like that and consider it further evidence of Van Halen's prima-donna mentality, or perhaps write it off as some kind of superstitious eccentricity common to creative types. But despite how we might interpret away the nitpicky nature of this request, the group actually—believe it or not—had a reasonable, foun-dational reason behind it. Goes like this . . .

Van Halen's management group had begun cautioning them on the ever-increasing size of their production, a rock show that had steadily grown into an entertainment extravaganza. During Van Halen's rise to fame in the 1970s and '80s, rock bands typically traveled with three semitrucks to handle all their stage gear. Van Halen, however, traveled with *nine* semitrucks. The weight of their equipment and the electric load it required were much greater than a lot of arenas were set up to handle. So when they and their entourage showed up at a certain place, they needed to know for sure that the venue was able to manage the size of the production. A careless, incapable entertainment site could lead not only to a glitchy performance but even a dangerous scenario for the performers as well as the audience. So to determine if the venue possessed a culture of preparation, this statement was subtly placed in their rider: absolutely no brown M&Ms.[4]

David Lee Roth of Van Halen wrote in his autobiography that if he walked into their dressing room before a show and noticed brown M&Ms in the bowl, he would immediately order a line check. And guess what? It very often revealed that the venue was not adequately prepared for the group's performance. The existence of the brown M&Ms, though a small matter by itself, revealed a greater cultural problem—a lack of attention to details.

What are the "brown M&Ms" in your church, the important practice issues that speak loudly about your overall church culture? Not only are the following elements of church life essential for the church's mission in the world, but they are also a helpful gauge for evaluating how deeply the gospel has been driven into the church. The gospel must be continually surfaced as the reason for each ministry's existence and the pursuit of each ministry. For a culture to be continually immersed in the gospel, kingly leaders must ensure that the systems and direction of the church are grounded in the truth of Jesus. In this chapter, we will surface many details church leaders face on a weekly or daily basis and show how they may be connected to the gospel for the sake of the people.

Gospel and Polity

While many seminary students avoid the lectures on church polity because of the renowned boredom associated with them, and while many church members associate "church polity" with a negative experience of authoritarian dictatorships or a plethora of committees slowing down ministry, the gospel radically impacts the way we view the leadership structure of the Church and how it affects other areas within the body. Ephesians 4 highlights, in a broad sense, Paul's vision for church polity:

> And he gave the apostles, the prophets, the evan-
> gelists, the shepherds and teachers, to equip the saints
> for the work of ministry, for building up the body of
> Christ, until we all attain to the unity of the faith and of
> the knowledge of the Son of God, to mature manhood,
> to the measure of the stature of the fullness of Christ.
> (vv. 11–13 ESV)

Paul affirms that some are appointed as the leaders in the Church. And yet the calling of these leaders (as discussed in the last chapter) is built on the foundation of the gospel:

> But grace was given to each one of us according to
> the measure of Christ's gift. Therefore it says, "When
> he ascended on high he led a host of captives, and he
> gave gifts to men." (In saying, "He ascended," what does
> it mean but that he had also descended into the lower
> regions, the earth? He who descended is the one who
> also ascended far above all the heavens, that he might
> fill all things.) (vv. 7–10 ESV)

In these verses, Paul draws on the language and context of Psalm 68, a psalm originally written about a military victor who had earned the right to receive gifts from the people he had conquered. We, like those in the psalm, were the enemies of God, but Jesus has conquered our hearts and we have become His subjects through His grace. Jesus, however, is a very different kind of conquering King. Instead of demanding gifts from His new subjects, He *gives* gifts. And included in His gifts to His Church are leaders.

But notice that the goal of these leaders is the *preparing of God's people* for building up the body of Christ. Authority in the Church is not meant to be wielded as a weapon. It's meant to be another expression of the gospel; therefore, leaders must think of themselves as servants. They are the equippers whose goal is not to expand their territory but to build up the body of Christ. The goal of a leadership team should not be to rule over people, because the gospel sets us free from the need for control. Rather, the goal of the leadership team must be to release people for ministry. The leaders should not "do ministry" but prepare others for ministry and release them to serve.

There is often deep lamenting and bemoaning from pastors and staff teams about the lack of volunteer engagement in their churches. Often the problem is not with the people but with a faulty ministry culture that fosters low levels of volunteerism and perpetuates an unhealthy dependence on clergy. The typical approach to ministry in most churches stands in stark contrast to Paul's admonishment.

The approach to ministry in many churches looks like this:

(Pastors) >> minister >> (people)

Typically pastors or staff persons are hired to minister to people. The number of children increases, so the solution is another staff person. The number of sick people is on the rise; therefore, someone is hired to visit people in the hospitals, and on and on. This far-too-common approach is both illogical and unbiblical: *illogical* because a church will never be able to afford hiring the entire ministry away, and *unbiblical* because it violates the essential doctrines of the priesthood of believers and spiritual gifting.

Paul's challenge looks like this:

(Pastors) >> prepare >> (people) >> to minister >> (each other)

In other words, pastors and staff equip and prepare people to do ministry. Churches that have effectively created a volunteer culture possess a deep-seated biblical conviction that all believers are gifted for ministry, not just the "professional" ministers. The gospel reminds us that all believers have been brought into the family of God, and in this family we are all priests (1 Pet. 2:9). Thus, the leaders invite all believers to engage in ministry, and the leaders view themselves as equippers/trainers of the ministers within their church.

It is easy to drift from the biblical view toward the typical view. Every savvy staff person or department can articulate the need for more staff. And as the church grows, money is often available to hire more people. But the consequences of drifting toward typical ways of doing things are damaging. Here are two:

First, the typical approach hampers spiritual growth. When following a clergy-heavy mentality, people who are gifted by God and called to serve Him are put on the bench as they watch the professionals make the ministry happen. And as their spiritual gifts go underutilized, their spiritual growth is hampered. They miss the joy of experiencing Christ serve others through them. Instead of fostering a serving posture among believers because of the gospel, the typical approach to ministry helps develop consumers. By keeping ministry from the majority of the people, people are actually taught to be moochers and consumers of the faith rather than participators and contributors.

Second, the typical approach hampers the movement of the church. In Exodus 18, Moses' father-in-law confronted him because of his unhealthy approach to ministry. Moses was attempting to meet all the needs himself, which was ineffective on many levels. Not only was he overwhelmed but the people were going home unsatisfied. Their needs were not met. How *could* they be when Moses was in the way? Jethro told Moses to build a leadership system to distribute the care for all the people through other leaders. He asked Moses to stop doing ministry (except for the difficult cases) and to prepare others to do ministry. He asked Moses to repent of his control and to release others to serve.

Jethro was right. Sometimes fathers-in-law are. As a church leader, don't settle for a typical view of ministry. The gospel has made all the people in your church ministers. Stop doing ministry. Prepare others to do so.

Jesus-centered ministry needs to happen in this very way—through people who are drawn out from among the community to take their places as ministers of the gospel in a wide variety of avenues.

Gospel and Hospitality

Every church sends a message through their strategy for hospitality. Those with no system for greeting new people, welcoming them, and pursuing them in a loving way send the loudest message: "Our theology has not impacted how we treat you."

Clear signage and friendly people really do go a long way in expressing God's welcoming heart in a tangible way. Your context, of course, will dictate a lot about your hospitality: whether you train greeters to shake, hug, nod, or fist bump. But by all means, put some type of plan in place to express hospitality. Some of our Reformed brothers need to understand that a sign and friendly greeters directing a new family to the kids' area is not doctrinal compromise. To the contrary, it can be an expression of doctrine beyond the pulpit.

The real issue, as we've said in previous chapters, is both the *theology* and *philosophy* that drive the *practice* of hospitality. Hospitality is the combination of two words: *stranger* and *love*. Hospitality at its core is the love of strangers, and it's one of the characteristics mentioned in

Scripture that should embody those called to the highest office in the Church:

> Therefore an overseer must be above reproach, the
> husband of one wife, sober-minded, self-controlled,
> respectable, *hospitable*, able to teach. (1 Tim. 3:2 ESV,
> italics added)

Hospitality is included in the necessary qualifications for an overseer because hospitality is a direct and tangible link to the gospel. What has God done in the gospel if not welcome strangers? We were all strangers to the family of God and the household of faith. We were enemies, in fact, but God in His great mercy welcomed us. He has practiced hospitality toward us. Therefore, we must accept one another as Christ has accepted us (Rom. 15:7).

Hospitality, when seen in light of the gospel, becomes more than just parking cars and pointing people to the kids' area. Hospitality is the means by which the church, from the ground level, models the gospel to others. And by God's grace, the teams of people investing in hospitality will set the tone for the entire church so that everyone who has experienced the hospitality of God practices hospitality in the church.

Gospel and Programming

All churches have programs. Even churches that meet in people's homes still schedule meetings, outreach opportunities, and dinners together. Because programs are embedded into church life, there should be a theology of programming. Or you can divorce your theology from your programming and just do stuff that has always been done.

The church programming spectrum ranges from churches with bulletins stuffed like a Sunday paper with dozens of events each week, to churches with a very minimalistic and streamlined approach. The bigger question is: What is driving the programming? Unfortunately, many churches simply haven't wrestled with the question.

Every single thing the Church does teaches. Culture is continually being reinforced as leaders are always teaching and people are always learning. Much of this teaching and learning comes through implicit messages rather than explicit ones: the songs selected, the way Scripture is read, the attitude of the children's leaders, and the programs that are offered. If the *implicit* message communicated via the programs contradicts the *explicit* message communicated in the teaching environments, then people are left confused and frustrated. For example, if a pastor preaches about investing in the lives of neighbors and coworkers, all while announcing a dozen events on the church calendar this week—things that everyone feels at least a little pressure to attend—the people in the church will have a difficult time applying the message. Which message are the people more likely to believe?

Because church programs communicate, we must consciously bring the gospel to bear on them. Perhaps in analyzing your programs, you'll discover that you schedule activities or programs because of guilty obligation. The gospel, on the other hand, frees us from feverish attempts to appease God with religious activities. The gospel frees us to say no and to rest from our work because we trust His finished work.

What stops a church from saying no to endless or mindless programming? Is it the leaders' insecurity? Is it the need to compete with other church calendars? Is it the desire for people in the congregation to feel they're getting a good return on their giving?

Christ's great love frees us from needing validation or approval through programming. When we live in freedom, we can honestly look at every program and ask the hard questions, like:

- What are we implicitly teaching through the giving of resources to this program?
- Is this program furthering the gospel in the hearts and minds of our people and the community?

- Could the time we are asking of people be better utilized for the sake of the gospel in a different way than this?
- Would the removal of this program serve to diminish or rather increase the capacity of our people to love and treasure Jesus and make Him known?
- If we were starting from scratch with only the foundation of the gospel, would we do this program in this manner?
- Why do we do this?

Gospel and Operations

No matter what the size of the church, leaders must provide direction to important issues, such as facilities, security, office administration, policies, and a host of other details. As with programming, the spectrum of approach is wide. Some churches choose an intentionally minimalistic approach to operations, thinking that there is something inherently worldly about owning a sound system or having a policy. The pendulum swings to the other side of the spectrum, too, with churches that see themselves as competing with the world for the attention of those in the audience, and therefore feel they must have the best of everything.

While the gospel does not address the color scheme in your foyer, it does address the attitude with which we view the operations of the church. There is an obvious tension.

On one hand is the truth that our great and good God deserves worship in all things because of who He is and His great acts:

> Praise the LORD! Praise God in his sanctuary; praise him in his mighty heavens! Praise him for his mighty deeds; praise him according to his excellent greatness! Praise him with trumpet sound; praise him with lute and harp! Praise him with tambourine and dance; praise him with strings and pipe! Praise him with sounding

cymbals; praise him with loud clashing cymbals! Let everything that has breath praise the LORD! Praise the LORD! (Ps. 150 ESV)

Our God, who is so extravagant in His mercy and grace, truly does deserve the best we can offer. And everything should be used to praise Him, including the operations of a church. It was Jesus, in fact, who commended the extravagant and expensive act of washing His feet with perfume; it was Judas who questioned whether such excellence should be better spent elsewhere (John 12:3–7). A disgusting bathroom or a dirty facility is inconsistent with pleas for worship to be extravagant because of Christ.

On the other hand, "excellence" can also be used to justify materialism, and "innovation" can be used to justify compromise. Painfully ironic are sermon illustrations that challenge people to live on mission, yet the props and staging cost more money to produce than the church invests supporting local mission efforts. The New Testament frequently warns of the love of money and the dangers that wealth can bring into the heart of a person, much less an entire church.

The gospel allows us to live with the tension while focusing on the true issue: the motivation of the heart. We must recognize the inherent dangers, because of our sinfulness, of each side of the spectrum. If improving the facilities or insisting we remain mobile becomes a way to justify ourselves before God or man, we have drifted from the gospel. Both approaches can be right, and both can be wrong, depending on the motivation of the heart. The gospel frees us to honestly evaluate ourselves, as church leaders, at the level of the heart.

Gospel and Church Finances

Challenges for people to give generously to the work of Christ occur in every church, as they should. While giving is only one aspect of church finances, the giving challenges are a good barometer of gospel centrality. If an outsider could hear only your church's giving challenges and nothing else over a period of time, what would they conclude your church believes?

Some churches build their giving philosophy on blessing: "Give, and God will give back to you." And there is much truth in this challenge. The only area in which God invites us to test Him is in the realm of giving (Mal. 3:10). But this text must be held in light of the overall narrative of Scripture. Paul gave sacrificially, and he ended his life without his head. Peter gave generously, and he died upside down on a cross. Stephen gave boldly and cheerfully, and he was beaten to death by stoning. Yes, he received a standing ovation from the Lord as he died, and yes, they are each enjoying ultimate paradise right now. But none of them lived large with an ocean view.

Other churches build their giving philosophy on need, continually begging people to support the church. Wiser leaders move to vision, correctly believing that people give to vision more than need. But how often does a leader need to deliver a new vision? And is vision always enough? How many teary-eyed videos will it take?

Paul's giving philosophy and practice were built firmly on a theology of grace. When he challenged the Corinthians to give, he wrote:

> But as you excel in everything—in faith, in speech, in knowledge, in all earnestness, and in our love for you—see that you excel in this act of grace also. I say this not as a command, but to prove by the earnestness of others that your love also is genuine. For you know the grace of our Lord Jesus Christ, that though he was rich, yet for your sake he became poor, so that you by his poverty might become rich. (2 Cor. 8:7–9 ESV)

The gospel pushes us deeper into our pockets by reminding us of how deeply God went into His. To incite the generosity of the Corinthians to help the impoverished church in Jerusalem, Paul simply reminded them of the gospel: "You know the grace of the Lord. Let the grace of the Lord compel you to give."

The church budget is a doctrinal statement. The budget clearly reveals your practice, which reveals your theology and philosophy. It is hypocritical to espouse a church culture that values mission in the city yet budgets more for landscaping. There is a deep disconnect if the vision statement articulates a passion to take the gospel to the nations yet the budget reveals a miniscule commitment.

A budget grounded in the gospel will reflect gospel priorities. As you budget, simply consider the question: "What does the gospel say we are called to do and be for our members and in this community?" Perhaps you should start with a blank sheet of paper and the biblical text.

Gospel and Communication

Communication in the church is becoming an increasingly complex issue, what with the ever-expanding breadth of technology. Thankfully, the gospel has much to say about it. The only reason we can know God, for instance, is because He graciously stooped low to speak to us. He accommodated Himself to us and yet retained the essence of Himself. The gospel principle is one of accommodation without compromise.

Every church communicates the gospel in a specific context. Some contexts are predominately "blue collar" workers, while others are filled with "white collar" professionals. Some are more technologically proficient than others; some serve more senior adults than young families. The context should drive the means of communication, but always with the goal of helping people encounter the gospel. The means of communication itself must not become the focal point. Once again, the apostle Paul is helpful:

> And I, when I came to you, brothers, did not come
> proclaiming to you the testimony of God with lofty
> speech or wisdom. For I decided to know nothing among
> you except Jesus Christ and him crucified. And I was
> with you in weakness and in fear and much trembling,
> and my speech and my message were not in plausible
> words of wisdom, but in demonstration of the Spirit and
> of power, that your faith might not rest in the wisdom of
> men but in the power of God. (1 Cor. 2:1–5 ESV)

The primacy of the message was what dominated the methodology of the apostle. The problem with attracting people with bells and whistles is that they'll only come back for bells and whistles. Leaders might fall in love with a particular piece of technology or communication technique without considering whether or not the gospel is actually served well by it. Sadly, the medium becomes louder than the message. And while the medium might impress, only the message can transform. Communication is meant to serve the gospel, not the other way around. When we keep the gospel central in the message, people's confidence can rest firmly on that message rather than on the show accompanying it.

While the message was of primary importance to Paul, he also used any means possible to point people to the gospel. So for Paul, the issue of communication was simple: *let the medium serve the message.* The whole New Testament was written, after all, in koine Greek rather than classical. It was written in the street language—the vernacular of the day—because the biblical writers wanted the undiluted message of Jesus accessible to as many people as possible.

Paul reminded Titus that "to the pure, all things are pure, but to the defiled and unbelieving, nothing is pure" (Titus 1:15 ESV). To the pure church leader, technology and communication can be pure vessels to deliver the gospel. The Reformation wouldn't have happened without the printing press, and Billy Graham's crusades wouldn't have happened without the microphone. To the impure church leader, technology becomes a bloodthirsty god that must constantly be fed with new resources. Thankfully, Christ continually purifies our motives and allows us to steward the opportunity to expose more people to the gospel through all means possible.

Gospel and Benevolence

Regardless of the economic outlook of the region in which a church resides, every church will be faced with the opportunity to serve those who are struggling and under-resourced. And while church leaders often strategize on how to reach upper-middle-class professionals, historically His Church has thrived through the fringes of society. God loves and uses wealthy people in His kingdom, but the wealthy have a tendency to feel sufficient in their own goodness, hard work, or their own fulfillment of the American dream. Thus, the wealthy are less likely to call out to God for grace and mercy. Because of this, the faith throughout history has been made up primarily of common people (1 Cor. 1:26).

In reality, the gospel is only for the poor.

The gospel is only for those who realize they are poor and desolate before our holy God. In comparison to Him, all of us were poor. No one was worthy. Yet God in His great love pursued us—not because we showed promise, not because we impressed Him as good recruits for His team. To the contrary, He pursued us when we had nothing to offer Him at all.

Church leaders must remind people that God rescued us in our spiritual poverty; therefore, we must be concerned for the poor because we are poor alongside them. When the early church pillars (Peter, James, and John) realized that Paul was teaching the same gospel as Peter, they agreed that Paul should focus on the Gentiles; Peter, the Jews. They had only one request for Paul: "remember the poor" (Gal. 2:10 ESV), which was the very thing Paul was eager to do.

Jonathan Edwards wrote of the connection between the gospel and benevolence:

> It [caring for the poor] is especially reasonable, considering our circumstances, under such a dispensation of grace as that of the gospel. Consider how much God hath done for us, how greatly he hath loved us, what he hath given us, when we were so unworthy, and when he could have no addition to his happiness by us.[5]

Paul and Edwards agree—the gospel must impact how you care for the poor among you.

Whether your church's strategy for benevolent ministry to the poor is partnering with local ministries, offering direct services, or providing a niche service to the community, allow the gospel to drive you toward a developed strategy. And remind others that the gospel is what informs this approach, not merely the opportunity to be better people. Don't allow social activism to replace the gospel of Jesus in ministering to the needs of the hurting and under-resourced.

Furthermore, those who are served must be confronted with the truth of the gospel. Like us, what they need most is Jesus. We must not offer people the short-term help they're looking for without also offering them the eternal One they may not be looking for. Just as Jesus does not dismiss us with a quick fix, just as He is with us for the long haul, churches must take the longer road with people. More is involved than slipping a tract alongside a $20 bill for groceries. Much more. People must be loved and invited into the family of faith.

Gospel and the Flower Committee

We aren't going to write about the flower committee . . .

We would not know what to say as none of us has worked with one directly. But we are confident that the gospel in all its fullness has implications for everything in your church. It should really go that deep.

But again, as you seek to infuse your church culture with the gospel, don't confuse the implications of the gospel with the gospel itself. The gospel impacts all the aforementioned, but the aforementioned are not the gospel. D. A. Carson wisely warned:

> One must distinguish between, on the one hand, the gospel as what God has done and what is the message to be announced and, on the other hand, what is demanded by God or effected by the gospel in assorted human responses. . . . The Bible can exhort those who trust the living God to be concerned with issues of social justice (Isa 2; Amos); it can tell new covenant believers to do good to all human beings, especially to those of the household of faith (Gal 6); it exhorts us to remember the poor and to ask, not "Who is my neighbor?" but "Whom am I serving as neighbor?" We may even argue that some such list of moral commitment is a necessary consequence of the gospel. But it is not the gospel. . . . Failure to distinguish between the gospel and all the effects of the gospel tends, on the long haul, to replace the good news as to what God has done with a moralism that is finally without the power and the glory of Christ crucified, resurrected, ascended, and reigning.[6]

Not only must we guard against confusing the implications of the gospel with the gospel, but also be careful that in our sinfulness we don't use the lingo of "gospel centrality" to craft a new badge of spiritual superiority, as if those who do not use the term are lesser brothers. Let's not forget that Jesus is the gospel. Let's not forget that the gospel must impact our attitudes. It would be a sad betrayal of gospel centrality if we abuse its truths, allowing us to rise up as superstars of the faith enlightened with a new doctrine. There is nothing new and innovative about the gospel. It is the foundation of the faith, and it is received by faith—nothing we could or would create. It is also possible, in our foolishness, to haphazardly attach the label to anything in our church as if attaching the label breathes new life into something. We must repent of both errors.

Van Halen learned that the presence of brown M&Ms pointed to a bigger cultural issue with a host venue. Similarly, if you want to know how centered your church really is on the gospel, don't just examine your messages for gospel-centered content. Check and see if people leave the budget meeting room with the gospel in their hearts. Check and see if the hospitality team is dripping with the kindness shown to us in Christ. Examine the motivation for facility and communication decisions. Check the bowl for "brown M&Ms"—continually.

C. S. Lewis quoted Samuel Johnson who said, "People need to be reminded more than instructed."[7] Charles Spurgeon said, "The most important daily habit we can possess is to remind ourselves of the gospel."[8]

Remind the people you serve of the gospel. Continually.

CHAPTER 11

JESUS-CENTERED CONTEXTUALIZATION

One living sermon is worth a hundred explanations.
~ ROBERT COLEMAN[1]

IT IS HARD TO OVERSTATE the popularity that the show *24* experienced throughout the first decade of the 2000s in America. For a few years there was consistent chatter in offices, living rooms, and at dinner tables about how the show was unfolding. Each episode ended with a ridiculous cliffhanger that made waiting a week to find out how the most precarious of situations would be resolved seem insufferable. Jack Bauer, the lead character, played by Keiffer Sutherland, a seemingly unstoppable force who could squeeze more productivity out of one hour than most people could in a year, always seemed to find a way to save the country while tiptoeing on the line of ethics. The end often justified the means, and his behavior was easier to explain away given what was at stake.

During the third season, Jack finds himself in another somewhat typical, impossible situation when he learns about the existence of the deadly "Cordilla" virus, which kills anything it comes into contact with. Of course, this becomes an issue of national security and requires that the virus is found and disposed of before it is used against the nation. Bauer learns that Roman Salazar, a narco-terrorist who leads one of the largest drug cartels in Mexico, has access to the virus.

Jack has to do what Jack always does: he sets a plan in place to save the day in a few hours. No big deal. He goes undercover in an effort to get close to Salazar, find the virus, and dispose of the threat. Going undercover means that Bauer faces a myriad of ethical dilemmas. How much should he affirm of the culture of a drug cartel to get close enough to the boss to dismantle the cartel? Should he kill like they kill? Should he use the drugs that are placed before him? How far does he go for the sake of the mission? As fans of the show already know, Jack often pushes the ethical envelope and affirms many aspects of the culture for the sake of the mission. He identifies with his context in order to be effective in that context. In season 3 he chooses to use heroin, which eventually leads to an addiction that he has to wrestle with in later days. But, he also thwarts the plans of Salazar, alleviates the threat, and continues to reinforce the enigma that is Jack Bauer. All in a day's work.

Most church leaders don't struggle with the question of whether or not they should shoot up heroin to reach their cities for Christ, but they do wrestle with the questions of cultural contextualization and identification. The Church has been given a mission, not to save the world, but to announce the saving work of Christ for the salvation of the world. And in order to achieve this mission, the Church must make decisions about what it will affirm from its surrounding culture and what it will not. Most churches, of course, don't struggle with whether or not to shoot up heroin (if this is a struggle, then we have another book to recommend). But church leaders do struggle with how to deliver the message of Christ in a culturally meaningful way. After all, churches don't minister to people in general. Instead, they reach particular people with particular values, idols, aspirations, dreams, gifts, strongholds, and sins.

This means that churches need to understand how their church should look and minister in relation to their particular church's surrounding culture and context. What kind of cultural practices and beliefs should be strategically affirmed and which should not? How will church practice, not theology, look differently in the South than in the North? How does a rural cultural context like those in small county-seat churches impact ministry decisions in a way that makes it distinct from churches serving in more urban areas like Manhattan, San Francisco, or Hong Kong? How will a church that is near a thriving college campus approach ministry different from a church nestled in a quiet suburban neighborhood of young families? Or, what about the church in Sudan, Dubai, or London? Praise the Lord that the Church finds herself within countless nations, tribes, languages, and contexts. These questions and others reveal the type of challenges that the Church faces. She is a Creature of the Word, created to exist within a contextual system. These are all questions that uncover the type of contextualization your church is doing.

And listen, everybody contextualizes. We have all heard it said, "Everybody is a theologian; the question is what kind of theologian." Similarly, we should say, "Everybody contextualizes; the question is how well." When you use the language of a culture, you are contextualizing. When you deliver age-appropriate messages from the pulpit and the children's ministry, you are contextualizing. When you wear a suit rather than a tunic, you are contextualizing. These are very basic levels of contextualization, but they still illustrate the point: *everybody makes contextual decisions.*

In some aspects, contextualization is like breathing: it just comes naturally and doesn't require any forethought or planning. Other contextualization issues necessitate investigation, understanding, and intentionality. Like we saw with Jack Bauer, there are potential pitfalls and dilemmas that leaders must navigate with godly wisdom and insight. For the Church, the end does not justify the means. The means matters.

And in order for the Creature of the Word to thrive in any particular environment, it needs to understand Jesus' method of contextualization.

Incarnation as Contextualization

We are all surrounded by a culture filled with people who have plans for Jesus. They place priorities on Jesus' to-do list. Or to put it another way, the culture wants Jesus to affirm their ways. Of course, this isn't new. When Jesus stepped onto the dusty roads of Israel, He stepped into a culture filled with ideas about how Jesus could best carry out His mission. Peter, for example, wanted to take Rome by force, cutting off the ear of the soldier in the garden, but Jesus had other plans. The crowds wanted to make Jesus king immediately, but Jesus didn't let them. The rich man wanted Jesus to justify his religious performance, but he didn't get the verdict he wanted. The Jewish leaders wanted Jesus to put a stop to His healing-on-the-Sabbath ways, but He refused to be confined to their thinly sliced way of thinking. Jesus faced pressures to accommodate to His surrounding culture at the expense of His mission at almost every point along the way . . . but He didn't.

Yet, although Jesus rejected much of the culture around Him, He didn't reject it all. He did—(brace yourself)—"affirm" certain cultural practices. He didn't come to earth as an American who spoke English to reach the English-speaking world. Instead, He came as a Jewish man who spoke Aramaic (and Hebrew) to reach Israel. That was His context. He dressed like Jewish men dressed. He talked like Jewish men talked. He could be hidden in a crowd because He looked like the people He came to reach. Jesus' mission was a contextualized mission. And He didn't just *look* like His culture; He also understood their struggles. The writer of Hebrews tells us, "For we do not have a high priest who is unable to sympathize with our weaknesses, but One who has been tested in every way as we are, yet without sin" (Heb. 4:15 HCSB).

There are two points we want to introduce here. First, the contextual challenge is a directional challenge: either over-contextualizing or under-contextualizing (we will expand on this in the section on common errors of contextualization). If we affirm too much of the surrounding culture, our ministry would lose the distinction of the message. This is the slippery slope of over-contextualization. We can drift into identifying so much with the culture that we are a part of that we lose any semblance of healthy biblical separation and substance. All cultures are broken, marred with sin, and in need of transformation (Eph. 2:1–4). The gospel message is clearly countercultural in any given context and must always contain a clear edge of distinction. But on the other hand, if we affirm too little of the surrounding culture, our ministry loses its clarity and connection. This is the danger of under-contextualization. We can contend for the purity of the gospel of Jesus but lose the very opportunity to clearly present this message if we fail to speak and contend for it in a way that is meaningful to the culture at hand. Jesus contextualized by affirming the culture without compromising the message. By affirming cultural characteristics, He made the message connect to the culture. By holding uncompromisingly onto the message, He bore a message that critiqued the culture and offered a countercultural understanding of life. This is the essence of the second point: there is need to both contend for the message and contextualize the mission.

The Creature of the Word is formed within a culture, from a culture, in order to be the organism that is used to redeem the culture. The church is called to contend for the faith. God has established leaders and overseers in the Church to protect and guard the precious truths that mark biblical Christianity. In this sense, the Church takes on a defensive posture of protection and covering over the doctrines of the faith. This is right and good and biblical. The Church also has an offensive posture of movement. She is a people moving forward and pushing back what is dark. As the Church defensively contends for the faith, she offensively contextualizes it in such a way that it becomes accessible. The balance of contending and contextualizing is the tension a faithful leader must consistently consider. Fear will lead toward under-contextualizing and over-contending. Foolishness will lead to over-contextualizing and under-contending. The fear of the Lord produces godly wisdom that will lead to a healthy balance of contending and contextualization.

The way in which Jesus came to earth shapes the way the Church goes to the world. The more that a Jesus-centered church looks to Jesus, the more it becomes like Him. And the more it becomes like Him, the more wisdom the Church will display in navigating the contextual challenge.

As we look through the rest of the New Testament, we see that Jesus' method of contextualization continues. The apostles led the churches to affirm cultural practices without compromising the message so the world would receive the gospel. The apostle Paul significantly wrote,

> Although I am a free man and not anyone's slave,
> I have made myself a slave to everyone, in order to
> win more people. To the Jews I became like a Jew, to
> win Jews; to those under the law, like one under the
> law—though I myself am not under the law—to win
> those under the law. To those who are without that law,
> like one without the law—not being without God's law
> but within Christ's law—to win those without the law.
> To the weak I became weak, in order to win the weak.
> I have become all things to all people, so that I may
> by every possible means save some. Now I do all this
> because of the gospel, so I may become a partner in its
> benefits. (1 Cor. 9:19–23 HCSB)

Paul also affirmed certain cultural distinctives in order to deliver a meaningful message. The message drove the mission and the mission necessitated that the message be delivered by accessible means. It is important to emphasize that the message drives the mission. Scattered throughout the New Testament is the reality that the wonder and grace of the gospel message fuels and motivates the heart for mission. There is a direct correlation between our understanding of God's heart for us in Christ and our heart for the lost world. To distort this order is to distort our motivation, which ultimately leads to unhealthy mission and contextualization.

This is why we can say that Paul's heart for the lost, which was driven by the message of the gospel, fueled his missional methods. He had a diverse arsenal of approaches from quoting secular poets in Acts 17, showing up to preach in synagogues, requiring that Timothy be circumcised for the sake of the Jews in Acts 16, but saying that Titus did not need to be circumcised for the sake of the Gentiles in Galatians 2. All of these decisions were contextual decisions made for the sake of the gospel mission.

Paul may have varied in his approach and practice but never in his theology. Again, we see him both contending for and contextualizing the message. Paul was not motivated to become all things to all people so that he might be popular or liked. This goes back to the reality that the message has to drive the mission. Paul became all things so that he might point others to Christ in a meaningful way. His desire for them to become like Jesus ensured that he would become like them.

The true impetus for meaningful contextualization is biblical love. This love recognizes an opportunity to serve those around us, and in this case, we are trying to consider how we might best serve their greatest need. Consider the story of the Good Samaritan. Jesus flips the question of, "who is my neighbor?" to, "who can I be a neighbor to?" The idea is that we are looking for ways to be neighborly, ways to serve and help those in distress. Although the story of the Good Samaritan is not a story about contextualization per se, it does provoke our hearts to consider the vantage point of our orientations. Are we primarily considering how we might best serve others or are we finding reasons, even using religion as a cloak, to pass by those in need. Unfortunately, some churches have failed to be neighborly to those around them by not considering helpful ways they might deliver the gospel message.

Unfortunately, the idea of contextualization has been misunderstood and misapplied. Some have been wary of the potential pitfalls of it, while others have wandered outside the biblical boundaries of what is wise and permissible. As with anything, the extremes are unhelpful. We want to explore in greater detail some common errors in contextualization in hopes that we might walk in wisdom.

Common Errors in Contextualization

The Jesus-centered church is a church that affirms certain characteristics from its surrounding culture while still holding faithfully to the gospel. The purpose of contextualization is to glorify God by reaching sinners with the gospel of Christ. And every church executes some type of contextualization to this end.

But as we all know, good efforts and intentions are not enough. If there were ever any question about the sufficiency or insufficiency of good intentions, a cursory reading of church history reveals the truth. While it's hard to detail all of the errors the Church has committed in its attempts to contextualize, the mistakes can rightfully be placed into two categories: over-contextualizing churches and under-contextualizing churches.

Over-contextualizing takes place when a church affirms so much of the culture around them that they compromise the message, thus losing the distinctive edge of the gospel of Jesus Christ. So, for instance, a church that over-contextualizes will blend with the culture in a way that causes them to wander outside biblical boundaries. Gailyn Van Rheenen rightly describes this as syncretism:

> Syncretism occurs when Christian leaders accommodate, either consciously or unconsciously, to the prevailing plausibility structures or worldviews of their culture. Syncretism, then, is the conscious or unconscious reshaping of Christian plausibility structures, beliefs, and practices through cultural accommodation so that they reflect those of the dominant culture. Or, stated in other terms, syncretism is the blending of Christian beliefs and practices with those of the dominant culture so that Christianity loses it distinctiveness and speaks with a voice reflective of its culture.[2]

It could be argued that this is what has happened, by and large, in liberal churches. In these instances, enlightenment thinking eroded the biblical witness, and many churches said that it is unreasonable to believe in the supernatural. But when a culture rejects the supernatural, it rejects such things as the divine inspiration of Scripture, the miracles of Jesus, the resurrection, and more. When liberal churches adhere to these beliefs, they are over-contextualizing and falling victim to syncretism. They are compromising the truth to placate a people and thus losing the very power of the gospel. A right view of contextualization holds that the message is central, not the culture. Interestingly enough, the church often drifts into this compromise. Their heart to serve and love people is misguided by a failure to understand the scriptural reality of biblical love. In the end, however, their failure to hold on to certain biblical beliefs leads to the disappearance of the message. And without the message of Christ, there is no good news. If there is no good news, then the Creature of the Word is not formed.

Other examples of the Church over-contextualizing abound. For example, the recent cultural shift regarding homosexuality and marriage is making headway into the Church. Rather than maintaining biblical faithfulness and speaking lovingly into the culture in hopes of seeing the message of Jesus Christ redeem and transform, many churches have allowed the culture to hijack and define the biblical message. Again, this is a clear example of syncretism and over-contextualization. Certainly this is a delicate issue and one that will require humility and courage for the people of God, and thankfully, there are many faithful pastors who are not shirking their responsibility to engage with the grace and truth of Jesus.

To name another common example, we can look at contemporary American evangelicalism. Most Americans do not worship the gods of other religions. Instead, we worship comfort, control, power, or approval. We have an imbedded sense of entitlement. The culture goes to great lengths to build self-esteem and fuel an idolatrous look within to find strength, peace, and control. As you might imagine, the doctrine of original sin is offensive to this popular notion of self-esteem and the inherent goodness of people. So, some churches do not mention sin for fear it will turn off those they are trying to reach. The culture also says that we should get what we want when we want it. So, some churches proclaim a God who is akin to a genie in a bottle, simply waiting to grant our every wish and desire. In each of these instances, the church has forsaken their light and drifted into the shadows of compromise, thus losing the opportunity to rightly live out the command to be in the world, but not of it. When a church over-contextualizes, it isn't merely "getting it wrong" (although it is definitely doing this). The over-contextualized church is altering the message of Jesus, thus perverting the Creator/Creature relationship. This deadly mistake has little to do with one's intentions. Sadly, liberal theologians denied the divinity of Christ and the substitutionary atonement for the sake of their "evangelistic" and "missional" goals. These efforts, of course, denied the gospel and destroyed the evangelistic message. The Creature of the Word takes on the character and nature of her Creator and, subsequently, represents Him rightly.

The other major contextual error that churches make is *under-contextualizing*. These churches affirm so little of their surrounding culture's practices that they fail to create meaningful opportunities and pathways to reach the lost. Contrary to the missional example of the apostle Paul, walls are built rather than bridges. There is no effort to understand the culture. There is no empathy or compassion. There is no desire to incarnate and become like them to win them. The heart has shriveled toward the plight of a lost and dying world, and no prayerful discernment is given to how the Church might, by God's grace, gain an opportunity to speak words of life into dead hearts.

But this does not mean contextualization is absent. Churches *must* contextualize. The question is only to which culture they contextualize.

This error has been seen most obviously, perhaps, in some of the well-intentioned missionary efforts in Africa in the twentieth century. Missionaries have entered into the African bush and planted churches. But instead of planting churches that meet in culturally appropriate settings, the missionaries have built church buildings for them. The problem here is that the use of church buildings is a Western practice. Africans did not use church buildings until Westerners built them. These missionaries "under-contextualized" to the African culture around them, injecting their Western ways—doing church from buildings, dress codes, styles of music—into African culture. This had the result of hindering the mission there because Africans believed to a certain degree that they must become Western to become Christians. They were unwittingly taught that what made them culturally unique could not be redeemed; rather, it had to be disregarded. Wrong.

Another example of under-contextualizing to a surrounding culture is typically found in America. Here, churches fail to change their church practices with the culture around them. (Remember, they should not change their *theology*; they should change their *practices* in order to better fit with their changing surrounding culture.) Oftentimes, "traditional" churches will fail to change to their nontraditional surrounding culture, even though their immediate surrounding culture has drastically changed. They continue doing things the way they always have simply because it is the way they have always done it. In this case, the love of tradition, which can be a beautiful thing, is misplaced above their love for their neighbors. The mission suffers because the church under-contextualizes to its surrounding culture.

It's important to note we are not saying that all "traditional" churches should change or that they have failed to change. We are saying that in some contexts the mission has been hindered because people are led to believe they must convert to an older culture (the 1950s) in order to be a Christian. Instead of simply coming to Christ, they must come to the Christ and community of years past.

Every church has a tendency toward one of these two errors. If you aren't aware of the spots where your church ministry rubs against the culture, then you are probably missing the contextualization mark by a long shot. The Jesus-centered church is a church that holds firm to the message of the gospel while strategically affirming cultural practices. Like Jesus, these churches become like those they want to reach. And like Jesus, they hold fast to the truth so that they have something with which to reach the surrounding culture.

Contextualization and The Village

God has extended grace upon grace to The Village Church. And one of the greatest evidences of God's grace has been the opportunity He has given us to be involved in church planting all around the globe. As we have strategized, planted, and cultivated partnerships with other churches, along with our own, we have observed some practical things about contextualization that we had only known in theory. Perhaps by hearing a few of our stories and struggles, you will be in a better place to evaluate your own efforts.

Contextualization, we've learned, is about much more than wearing the same clothes as the surrounding culture; it's about entering their stories. Chuck Colson writes:

> We must enter into the stories of the surrounding
> culture, which takes real listening. We connect with the

> literature, music, theater, arts, and issues that express
> the existing culture's hopes, dreams, and fears. This
> builds a bridge by which we can show how the Gospel
> can enter and transform those stories.[3]

Through a relationship with a partner church in New York we realized a great difference in the stories from those we were accustomed to in Dallas. As we listened to New Yorkers, we began to realize that the "normal" way of life in Dallas was not the "normal" way of life in New York. New Yorkers have a hunger for power that isn't nearly as pronounced in Dallas. On the other hand, Dallas natives have a hunger and expectation of comfort that is not present in the New Yorkers' stories. Dallas natives have pools; New Yorkers have influence.

Both cultures come with significant expectations and aspirations, yet they are very different from each other, and churches in each of these contexts must understand their respective culture's ethos. No, they should not allow these cultural priorities to blunt their message. But when they communicate their messages, they need to show an awareness of these unique cultural tensions, which will shape the way their messages are heard.

In New York, for instance, as the preacher talks about pursuing servanthood instead of the halls of power, he must know how foreign this thinking will sound. This might lead him to interact with the prevailing notions of power, showing its bankruptcy. Or in Dallas, when the preacher talks about costly sacrifice, he needs to understand how absurd this sounds. This awareness might lead him to talk about the fleeting comfort this world offers and the eternal comfort found in Christ. Whatever the context, the church must understand the nature of its surrounding context in order to both faithfully and effectively "win some." The prevailing current of culture should affect the church's approach to loving its neighbors.

Another area at The Village where we have grown in our understanding of contextualization is in our next-generation ministries (preschool, children, and youth). This area of ministry is often over-looked in the contextual conversation, but we have seen great fruit in doing the hard work of considering how we might best communicate the precious truths of the gospel to little hearts and minds. The language is crafted in such a way that young children can understand the rich doctrines of the triune God, original sin, justification by faith, substitutionary atonement, propitiation, adoption, and a host of others.

The result is a growing number of children who are gaining an understanding of the character and nature of God. In fact, the essence of what is being taught to the children is not fundamentally different from what is being taught to their parents. There is no compromise or dumbing down of the message; rather, there is recognition that the contexts necessitate a different approach. If we over-contextualize this example, then we simply wait to communicate the gospel until some later point in their life when we perceive they are ready and able to understand. If we under-contextualize, then we simply hand them a copy of Wayne Grudem's *Systematic Theology* and send them on their way. Walking in the fear of the Lord means wisely considering how we might steward this opportunity to effectively share the gospel with little kids.

Conclusion

Wherever your church is, you will need to understand how to exegete your ministry and your surrounding culture in order to faithfully and effectively contextualize like Jesus. Similar to exegeting a biblical text, *cultural exegesis* involves asking the right questions and discerning the right answers. Thus, faithful and effective cultural exegesis asks: What are the cultural idols? What are the cultural values? Who does the culture listen to? What are the cultural hero stories? What is beloved? What is despised? What is celebrated? What are the common distractions and comforts? What does the cultural fear? How does the culture communicate? How does the culture live? When a Jesus-centered church understands the ways the culture would answer these questions, it is then in a place to make the necessary changes in practice in order to reach the culture with its theology.

Hinduism will always be centered in India. Islam will always be centered in the Middle East. Christianity, on the other hand, has had its center in the Middle East, Europe, North America, and—if things continue as they are—it will soon be in the Global South. Inherently, Christianity is a contextualizing religion. It is a "go and tell" religion with a message that adapts to its context with the remarkable brilliance of God's design. He does not disdain cultural differences; rather, He delights in them when they are shaped by His gospel. The Jesus-centered church understands how to faithfully contextualize to its surrounding culture while effectively proclaiming its message, the gospel.

The Jesus-centered church is a church that is known for more than great preaching and leadership. It is known for reaching and discipling the particular people in its community. Churches don't "reach" people in general; they reach specific people with specific cultural preferences and identifications. And so the church needs to know these and how to communicate to them meaningfully.

Bottom line, the Church needs to be serious about reaching people. And if a church is going to be serious about reaching people, it must likewise be serious about understanding people, which means contextualizing. Therefore, like Jesus, the mission of the Jesus-centered church depends upon faithful and effective contextualization.

CHAPTER 12

JESUS-CENTERED MINISTRY

A minister may fill his pews, his communion roll, the mouths
of the public, but what that minister is on his knees in secret
before God Almighty, that he is and no more.

~ JOHN OWEN[1]

THERE COMES A POINT IN every relationship when you have the "DTR."

DTR stands for "define the relationship" and is used to describe a heart-level conversation between a couple, sometimes for the good and sometimes not. In reality, a DTR is necessary for any healthy relationship. It clarifies expectations and terms. It provides an honest sense of evaluation and status. It gives insight into how (and if) things should move forward. In fact, the DTR usually stands as a marker in the life of the relationship, whether in terms of progress or cessation. In either case, there is greater clarity.

In a sense, Jesus called His disciples together in Matthew 16 to have a little DTR. They had walked with Jesus, learned from His teaching, experienced His miracles, and witnessed His healings. The good news of the kingdom was going forth, and Jesus' public ministry was gaining traction.

But where was all this going? There was talk of Him in religious circles, and common people were filled with a variety of curiosities about Him. But who was Jesus . . . really? What was the purpose of His ministry? And what did His disciples have to do with it?

Those were the kinds of questions swirling around as Jesus and the disciples ventured into Caesarea Philippi, where a conversation would unfold with life-changing implications for His disciples then and now.

A region wrought with idolatry and pagan worship, Caesarea Philippi was teeming with false gods. Herod the Great had erected a temple for pagan worship of the god "Pan," and the city was formally named "Paneas" in his honor. Philip the Tetrarch had then renamed the city to pay homage to Caesar Augustus, as well as himself. It was here, in the very heart of falsehood and misrepresentation, that Jesus chose to have a conversation that would define His identity, His mission, and the nature of His relationship with His disciples.

Jesus' Identity

It began with a simple question: "Who do people say that the Son of Man is?"

This was a safe question, demanding little vulnerability from the disciples. The nature of the inquiry had more to do with the word on the street. "What are you hearing about Me as you walk through the markets? What are the pundits and talking heads saying about Me?" All it demanded was a relay of information.

And this is just what the disciples did. Their answer reflected what they had gathered over the years—that people had different ideas about Jesus. Some thought He must be another one of the prophets;

some thought He was a gifted teacher; others said He was obviously a man of God. Good answers.

But Jesus did not relent. The first question was safe; the second question was aimed directly at the heart: "But who do you say that I am?"

If the first question was a shotgun approach covering a widespread target audience, this one was a sniper shot. Direct and focused. There was no room for the disciples to maneuver around it. They themselves had walked with Him; they had been up-close witnesses to His work—the most "up-close" of all. This was obviously a question they should've already thought long and hard about, and should've arrived at a very personal answer.

In true form, Peter spoke up: "You are the Messiah, the Son of the living God!" Peter's confession was astounding. He defined Jesus' identity as the Messiah and Son of God—the anointed one, the long awaited hope of Israel who would fulfill every promise and prophecy of the Old Testament. Peter's long-held understanding, along with the rest of Israel, was that the Messiah would come in triumphant victory and justice, ending oppression and restoring God's kingdom in Jerusalem. But Peter was now convinced there was more to Him than that. Jesus, he said, was the unique Son of God. He identified Him as deity.

Jesus responded by blessing this confession and blessing Peter for making it. But as we will see, the disciples still held misguided expectations of what it meant for Jesus to be the Christ, and therefore what it meant for them to be Christians.

Jesus' Mission

On the heels of Peter's confession, the text says that Jesus moved the conversation from His identity to His mission: "From then on Jesus began to point out to His disciples that He must go to Jerusalem and suffer many things from the elders, chief priests, and scribes, be killed, and be raised the third day" (Matt. 16:21 HCSB).

This was different. Suffering didn't seem to be congruent with the work of the Messiah. Peter and his friends, along with all of Israel, were hoping for glory and prosperity. But this reeked of shame and death. It didn't fit with the expectations. Again, this is why a DTR is so crucial. Frustrations are birthed from unmet expectations. And Peter, elated about the identity of Jesus, had vastly different expectations about His mission. Jesus was clarifying expectations.

Peter's frustration and confusion boiled over into a rebuke. He had just confessed that Jesus is Messiah, but now he was going to tell Jesus how to do His job. Before we are quick to point the finger of disappointment at Peter, think of how often we find ourselves doing the very same thing. Oftentimes when our life takes an unexpected turn, we question the very Lord we confess—like Peter did, who spoke up and said, "Oh no, Lord! This will never happen to You!" (Matt. 16:22 HCSB). Although Peter had correctly identified Jesus' identity, he did not understand the nature of Jesus' mission. So in contrast to the blessing that Peter had just received, he now received a stern rebuke: "Get behind Me, Satan! You're an offense to Me because you're not thinking about God's concerns, but man's" (v. 23 HCSB). This reply from Jesus is so forceful and strong, it takes us aback. Peter's thinking obviously needing some rewiring because his perception of life and ministry was astonishingly off-based.

Parents are well aware of teaching moments—times along the way of raising your children when you have a unique opportunity to speak into a situation and teach. We want to be teaching as we go, but there are certain opportunities when our kids might be more receptive to hear. In this case, we can imagine Peter was primed for someone to lead him out of his fog. And he was not alone. Although Peter was the one who spoke, we can be sure the others were thinking the same thing. Now was the time for Jesus to bring the DTR full circle. They knew He was the Messiah and the Son of God, but they needed more clarity. They needed to know the full picture because their preconceived ideas were misguided.

The Messiah was going to be triumphant and provide release from oppression, but not in the way they thought. Yes, there was going to be glory, but the crown would come by way of a cross. And His disciples would follow suit.

Jesus' Disciples

The DTR was nearing its conclusion as Jesus explained the nature of the disciples' relationship to Christ's identity and mission: "If anyone wants to come with Me, he must deny himself, take up his cross, and follow Me. For whoever wants to save his life will lose it, but whoever loses his life because of Me will find it. What will it benefit a man if he gains the whole world yet loses his life? Or what will a man give in exchange for his life?" (Matt. 16:24–26 HCSB).

Jesus' paradigm for life and ministry is based on paradoxical intuition. This is not how we normally think, feel, or dream about life. In fact, our hearts lead us in the very opposite direction. Jesus said to the disciples that anyone and everyone who follows Him will be marked by a death to self. Jesus invoked the imagery of a cross, a clear foreshadowing of His own life mission, and declared that the cross would also be the mark of His people.

Consider how astounding this call truly is. Dietrich Bonheoffer, a German pastor and martyr during World War II, succinctly stated the mark of gospel-centered ministry: "When Christ calls a man, he bids him come and die."[2] This was the invitation of the Messiah to His disciples—a strange invitation, but not a morbid one. For Jesus continued by saying that those who accept His invitation to die will experience true life. Again, here is the paradox: life comes through death. Our attempts at self-preservation or holding on to our concepts of life and vitality prove to be empty of both life *and* vitality. The math just doesn't add up. We might gain everything we thought we ever wanted only to find out that it has cost us our soul. The call to take up our cross and follow Jesus is actually a loving invitation to experience the fullness of life.

And it is a mark of gospel-centered ministry.

Yes, this loving invitation is collectively extended to the Church. Think of how many churches merely exist rather than live, survive rather than thrive. The call to life for a church is a radical call of faith. It is a call for a church to believe God when He says the crown of glory comes through the cross. It is a call for the church's thinking and planning and structuring and operating and overall ministry to reflect God's thinking, not man's thinking. The natural proclivity of a church is a drift toward self-preservation rather than the radical abandonment of self. Jesus' twist on this natural, human philosophy, then, is easier preached than practiced.

How can gospel-centered ministry mark our churches? We can be confident that our gatherings are filled with people who, like Peter, are eager to believe in Jesus as the Christ, the Son of God, but are unclear about what this entails. Just as the Lord redirected the heart of Peter, He continues to call the Church to take up its cross and follow Him. But before we can lead our people here, we need to be sure our own hearts are first aligned to this call.

John the Baptist explained the formula for gospel-centered ministry: "He must increase, but I must decrease" (John 3:30 HCSB). Sadly, many churches today have unwittingly prescribed a different principle for success. There is a tremendous increase in the role and visibility of pastors and an unfortunate decrease of Jesus. It is far too common to see Jesus used as a means to our own selfish ends, co-opting His name to catapult ourselves onto the platform. We forget that real glory is gained through abandoning self, so we make the shameless trade for a glory that fades and is fickle. The attention can be intoxicating, creating an insatiable desire for more.

This attention seems to be irrespective of church size or notoriety. It can happen in a church of two hundred as easily as a church of two thousand . . . or *twenty* thousand. It is a simple stroke of the ego, an affirming feeling that we are needed. In the small creaks and crevices of our heart, the roots of self-inflated pride begin to grow.

Pride, however, is antithetical to gospel-centered ministry. The only thing we have truly earned is separation from God for all of eternity. Anything less than this is grace. Therefore, we cannot operate in a posture of pride. Humility must be the air we breathe.

How can the church nurture an atmosphere of gospel-centered ministry? How does the priestly function in a Jesus-centered culture manifest itself? We want to highlight three primary ways that God lovingly removes our self-sufficiency, reminds us of grace, and emboldens us for the call of gospel-ministry: prayer, suffering, and celebration.

The Primacy of Prayer

Prayer reveals the posture and priorities of our churches. Gospel-centered ministry, evidenced by taking up our cross and following Christ, means crucifying selfish ambition, pride, and self-sufficiency as a church. It means growing in the grace of humility and seeking to know the heart of God. Our ministry, therefore, flows out of the foundation of prayer. Prayer (or the lack thereof) is a litmus test regarding our beliefs about self-sufficiency and dependence.

Prayer is a declaration of dependence. Prayer is an invitation to intimacy. Prayer is a response to grace. Corporate prayer is a collective cry of intercession and petition for God to move in our midst, heal our brokenness, save the lost, restore the wayward, receive our worship, enliven our preaching, forgive our sins, and unify our hearts to fear His name.

The Lord has proven Himself faithful to His people, both in Scripture and throughout history, when they have humbled themselves before Him in prayer. He has granted us access to Himself through Christ and exhorted us in the Scriptures to continually approach Him with petitions. He has kept His people near to Him in dependence and protected them with infinite graces. So in prayer, we experience a deep growth in intimacy and love for Him, as well as an overwhelming realization of His love for us. As a church, prayer should mark our milestones and deepen our resolve in the gospel call.

The leaders of the church must demonstrate through prayer that we are insufficient. Our worship services must make clear that we cannot do what needs to be done, that the pastor is incapable of transforming or persuading or bringing people from death to life. *Prayer makes that statement*—not as a perfunctory transition between sections of the worship service, and not as a hustled-up prayer with the pastor before services begin. Transitional prayer and prayer before services are good and necessary, but if we are not inviting our people into prayer as a deliberate matter of worship, then we are failing to remind them of our need. We are sending a subtle and discreet message that we have this under control. The service may be planned and well rehearsed. Everything can be presented, preached, and performed with the utmost precision and excellence. But without prayer, we will find ourselves missing the only piece that really matters—the power of the Holy Spirit.

Do we invite our people to humble themselves and pray with us? Is there a public/corporate component of confessing our need for the Spirit to do what only the Spirit can do? If the power of the Holy Spirit did not move in your services, would anyone know or recognize the difference?

Martin Luther wrote in his exposition of the Sermon on the Mount, "He [God] also wants to indicate that because of all the temptations and hindrances we face, nothing is more necessary in Christendom than continual and unceasing prayer that God would give his grace and his Spirit to make the doctrine powerful and efficacious among us and among others."[3] Prayer precedes effective ministry.

If we are honest, we will acknowledge how much of our ministry is dependent upon us rather than the Spirit. The way in which we minister reveals this. We get caught up in the routine of doing ministry, spending less time asking to be filled for ministry. In short, this is a sign that we believe by our actions that we can accomplish what the Bible says can only be accomplished by God. Gospel-centered ministry means we recognize our inability to accomplish what needs to be accomplished; therefore we are driven to prayer—not only by our desperation and need, but also because we have been adopted into the family of God and are invited into His presence.

So what does the gospel have to do with prayer and the Church? According to John Calvin, "just as faith is born from the gospel, so through it our hearts are trained to call upon God's name [Romans 10:14–17]. And this is precisely what [Paul] has said a little before; the Spirit of adoption, who seals the witness of the gospel in our hearts [Romans 8:16], raises up our spirits to dare show forth to God their desires, to stir up unspeakable groanings [Romans 8:26], and confidently cry, 'Abba! Father!' [Romans 8:15]."[4] Prayer is more than the desperate cries of the weak; it is an overflow of affection. Calvin notes that the reality of the gospel trains our hearts to call upon the name of the Lord. Prayer, then, is a relational exercise that we grow in more and more as we grow in the grace of the gospel.

We all know that prayer can be laborious at times and challenging to our wandering minds. We lose focus and have difficulty maintaining consistency, but the importance of prayer cannot be overstated. Prayer has a drawing, wooing effect. As we enter into the secret places through prayer, we are reminded of God's love for us in Christ, which is essential in the ministry of the Church.

Ask yourself: Where does prayer fit in the life of your church? Are people invited to participate? How central is prayer in your ministries and the day-to-day working of your church? How do the church staff and leadership pray and stand in the gap on behalf of the church? Where are the sick prayed over and the needy cared for in prayer? The people of the church will be taught the primacy of prayer by the priority it is given in the ongoing life of the church.

Prayer mediates the tension that all ministries must maintain: our feeble weakness and inability, coupled with our loving adoption as sons and daughters. In the end, the call to prayer is a confession of need and a desire for greater affections for Jesus. We need Him to do what we cannot, and we desperately desire to grow in our affections for Him. To that end, we will labor in prayer in our churches as watchmen on the walls.

Suffering and Sanctification

Suffering reminds us of our smallness. Though we all lack control, power, and abilities, we can easily lose sight of this fact during stretches of life when success and accomplishment seem to come easily by our own hand. Pain, however, reveals our humanness.

When discussing the topic of suffering, we are never without an audience because suffering affects everyone in one way or another. As we consider gospel-centered ministry, the hardships and toils we all face are another way that God chisels, molds, and prepares us for the call to lay down our lives for the sake of the gospel.

Suffering is the result of the fall of humanity recorded in Genesis 3. As sin entered the world through our first parents, the universe fractured. What was once perfect and harmonious was now perverse and distorted. But the effects of sin reached beyond humanity to affect the creation as well. The depravity of humanity combined with the corruption of creation makes for a relentless assault of reminders that life is not how it should be. Every natural disaster and every divorce serve as reminders that something is wrong. Suffering interrupts our false pretenses that all is well. Every gut-wrenching case of abuse, every barren womb, every diagnosis of cancer, and every seed of racial hatred is a painful cry that the world in which we minister reeks with suffering and despair.

To avoid these realities is akin to burying our heads in the sand, to live in a false Utopia. The answer to the problem of suffering is not to avoid it or run from it, but to understand it in light of the gospel. Suffering affects each of us in three ways: suffering as the result of *living in a fallen world* (infertility, natural disasters, etc.), suffering as the result of my *personal sin* (addictions, anger, racism, etc.), or suffering as the result of *someone else's sin* (victims of abuse, hate, anger, etc.). Our churches are filled with people in every category. There is not enough room in this chapter to give a full theological and practical treatment of sin and suffering, but, suffice it to say, nobody is immune from it. So how does suffering relate to gospel-centered ministry? Suffering reminds us of our smallness. Perhaps more effective than anything else, suffering makes us decrease and Jesus increase.

Suffering loosens the grip we have on the world and its fading glories and causes us to hold more tightly to the person and promises of Jesus. It strips us of self-reliance and causes us to trust the mercies of a loving God, the One who tempers the heart amid hardship with sustaining hope.

A beautiful mystery in all of this is how God takes what was meant for evil and actually turns it for our good. The promise of Romans 8:28 serves as a warm blanket to the suffering soul: "We know that all things work together for the good of those who love God: those who are called according to His purpose" (HCSB). Through the painful loss that inevitably occurs by means of suffering, the opportunity also exists for glorious gain. We get more of Him. Through suffering.

The Church has the opportunity and responsibility to prepare her people for the reality of suffering. Sadly, many churches have concocted prosperity-driven theologies and have misled their people to believe that suffering and hardship is a result of insufficient faith and lack of genuine belief. Other churches have avoided the topic altogether in favor of sharing pragmatic messages centered on how to get better at this or that. In those types of settings, the Bible becomes a road map to life rather than the account of a faithful God who has redeemed a desperate people.

Much of the Church is driven by the whims of a consumerist-thinking and fear-of-losing people, so the difficult realities are often avoided. But is there anything more intensely practical than a stout understanding of suffering? Flimsy theological foundations and a lack of intentional shepherding of our people toward the biblical reality of suffering only lead to devastating results. In fact, an inept theology of suffering in the life of the church will eventually *compound* suffering, not provide hope in the midst of it. A right understanding of suffering in this world engenders a greater love for our hope in the next, which better frees us to serve in this one. Suffering better equips us to minister.

At The Village Church (where Matt and Josh pastor), suffering has become a persistent reality. In the early days of the church, suffering seemed to be more on the periphery, not as close and personal as it is now. On Thanksgiving morning 2009, however, Matt had a seizure that ultimately revealed a malignant brain tumor. The diagnosis was stifling and the prognosis was sobering, but God was working through all of it.

Thankfully, the Lord had prepared us for this trial through a strong belief in the gospel and the theological foundation that was already laid. In one sense the suffering was shocking, but in another it was not. Suffering is universal. This truth has continued to unfold as we have walked through a deluge of trials, losses, and painful hardships as a church and staff. Suffering is no longer an idea or theological conviction; it is a very personal reality for our body.

He loves us so much that He will bring (or allow) circumstances and situations into our lives that bind us to Him. This is motivated by His mercy and compelled by His gracious love. In seasons of suffering, we often walk by faith with blurry understanding, but this much is clear: He will never leave us or forsake us. Although we may be saddled with confusion, He liberates our hearts with more grace. Think how often when apprising someone else's suffering we say, "I could not weather that storm." Yet we fail to account for the special grace given to them to bear it. Again, He loves us and has forever promised to sustain us for all eternity.

At The Village, God continues to prove Himself faithful in our sufferings. The result of these hardships is that the gospel has become clearer and more valuable to us. Our grip on the things of the world has been loosened, and we long more for the return of Christ than we ever did before the hardships. Good fruit is often wrought through painful seasons.

The interplay between gospel-centered ministry and suffering is clear for several reasons. First, *suffering enlightens us to the life of the Savior.* Our Lord suffered. He understood the pain of loss as He wept over the death of a friend. He walked in personal mistreatment and was the innocent victim of abuse. He knew the emotional suffering of ridicule, mockery, and abandonment. He knew the physical suffering of beatings, lashings, and hanging on a cross. So not only do we better understand the sufferings of Jesus as we walk through our own sufferings, but we better understand Jesus' ministry to us in the midst of our suffering.

The book of Hebrews says that Jesus is our great and empathetic high priest: "Therefore, since we have a great high priest who has passed through the heavens—Jesus the Son of God—let us hold fast to the confession. For we do not have a high priest who is unable to sympathize with our weaknesses, but One who has been tested in every way as we are, yet without sin. Therefore let us approach the throne of grace with boldness, so that we may receive mercy and find grace to help us at the proper time" (Heb. 4:14–16 HCSB). He understands our suffering because of His own suffering. Just as Jesus' suffering allows Him to personally empathize with us in our suffering, so our suffering prepares us to minister to others in their suffering.

The apostle Paul writes in 2 Corinthians 1:3–7:

> Praise the God and Father of our Lord Jesus Christ,
> the Father of mercies and the God of all comfort. He
> comforts us in all our affliction, so that we may be
> able to comfort those who are in any kind of affliction,
> through the comfort we ourselves receive from God. For
> as the sufferings of Christ overflow to us, so through
> Christ our comfort also overflows. If we are afflicted, it
> is for your comfort and salvation. If we are comforted, it
> is for your comfort, which is experienced in your endur-
> ance of the same sufferings that we suffer. And our hope
> for you is firm, because we know that as you share in
> the sufferings, so you will share in the comfort. (HCSB)

What a beautiful promise! Our suffering is not in vain. God uses it to allow us to identify with the hurts of others. And as we experience the comfort of God in our trials, we are better able to comfort others. Suffering comes full circle and is redeemed by the comfort of God. Our ministry becomes more robust, more well-rounded, and more realistic as we endure our own suffering and enter into the sufferings of others.

A second feature of suffering and ministry is found in the biblical truth that *we are strong through our weakness.* The apostle Paul's thorn in the flesh, which he repeatedly asked to be removed from him, was allowed by God to remain for the sake of Paul's humility in ministry. It reminded him of his weakness and limitations.

> Therefore, so that I would not exalt myself, a thorn
> in the flesh was given to me, a messenger of Satan to
> torment me so I would not exalt myself. Concerning
> this, I pleaded with the Lord three times to take it away
> from me. But He said to me, "My grace is sufficient
> for you, for power is perfected in weakness." There-
> fore, I will most gladly boast all the more about my
> weaknesses, so that Christ's power may reside in me.
> So I take pleasure in weaknesses, insults, catastrophes,

persecutions, and in pressures, because of Christ. For
when I am weak, then I am strong. (2 Cor. 12:7–10
HCSB)

Suffering was a constant companion in the life of the apostle
in order that he might decrease while Jesus would increase. The
gospel transforms suffering from a morbid consequence of the fall
to a redeemed opportunity for experiencing the power and grace of
God in a new way. In fact, this relationship is further expounded in
Philippians 3:10–11: "My goal is to know Him and the power of His
resurrection and the fellowship of His sufferings, being conformed to
His death, assuming that I will somehow reach the resurrection from
among the dead" (HCSB). Over and over again throughout the New
Testament we see a positive link between suffering well, ministering
effectively, and being conformed into the image of Christ. The Church
cannot afford to turn a blind eye to these truths or simply teach about
suffering reactively. We must be proactive in our proclamation about
the purpose and opportunity of suffering for the sake of the gospel.

The Necessity of Celebration

Finally, God prepares us and empowers us to minister more effectively through the joy of celebration. Creating a culture of celebration actually prepares us and propels us further into gospel-centered
ministry.

When our hearts are enjoined in celebration, we are turning our
attention toward something or someone else. In short, we are focused
on something other than ourselves. As we think about John the
Baptist's illustration of Jesus increasing and him decreasing, we see
that celebration has a role to play in this. If gospel-centered ministry is
marked by the measured increase of Jesus, then we need to be a people
who celebrate Jesus and the fruit of His Spirit.

Gospel-centered ministry must highlight and point out the evidences of grace that surround us daily.[5] This is the constant reminder that God is at work in our midst. The fact that God is working among us reveals His grace toward us—a fact that should be celebrated. This could be something as seemingly small as an encouragement from a friend or a confession of sin, or as noticeably significant as baptism and salvation. All of these are noteworthy because they are indicators of the work of the Spirit. To overlook any of these is to become accustomed to them and miss the underlying significance in front of us: God is at work!

When we point this out and make it explicit, then we are accomplishing two things. *First, we are celebrating the work of God.* Our hearts are lifted in praise, declaring that He is faithful to move among us. This breaks us out of the monotony of routine to show that God has broken through. And because He does this daily, we should regularly highlight and celebrate them.

Second, we are teaching others to be on the lookout for grace. We are teaching, in effect, how to look for the evidences of grace. We are reminding our people, friends, and family that God has not left us but is constantly moving and working and involved in our lives.

The net effect of celebration is that we become smaller as God and His works become bigger. We celebrate that God is bringing those who are in darkness to the light. We celebrate that He is turning the hearts of the fathers toward their children. We celebrate that there is a growing love for God's Word. Whenever and wherever we see the Spirit of the Lord working and moving in our ministry and our church, then it should be noted and celebrated.

Now, this does not mean that every instance should become a sermon illustration or a weekend video, but it does mean that celebration should be infused into the normal culture of the ministry of the church. Not only should celebration be encouraged and modeled corporately, but it should also be encouraged personally. In the quiet places of our hearts we should make room to celebrate God's infinite graces to us on a daily basis—because each time we properly celebrate the work of God, we are nudging our hearts away from self-sufficiency and self-importance. Each celebration is a subtle reminder that it's not about us.

Third, celebration should also propel us to long for more of God's Spirit. As our hearts are enlivened with joyous celebration, we should eagerly anticipate God to move in our midst. We should be on the lookout for more evidences of grace. Gospel-centered ministry is burdened to see the power of the gospel unleashed to transform lives. It is weighted down with sober excitement to see the evidences of grace around us. You know your ministry is marked by the gospel when the eagerness for celebration is wrapped in humility, not entitlement. We have tasted and seen that the Lord is good, and we long to multiply this experience a thousandfold. Celebration creates a healthy appetite for the Spirit of God.

How can the Church nurture an atmosphere of gospel-centered ministry? Through *prayer, suffering,* and *celebration*. These are the primary means God uses to remove our self-sufficiency, remind us of grace, and embolden us for the call of gospel-ministry. This call is both sobering and joyous. It is shaping, sanctifying, and challenging. But this is the call Jesus has made on the lives of all who follow Him. We are to decrease so that He might increase.

Redefining Success

Jesus changes the game. In so many ways gospel-centered ministry is counterintuitive to our natural thinking. We have already seen that Jesus says life only comes through death, and that gain only comes through loss. The game is to decrease so that Jesus can increase. Again, none of this comes naturally.

We have also talked about three ways that God presses His priorities on His people and forms us for gospel-centered ministry: prayer, suffering, and celebration. We now want to close the chapter—and the book—by discussing how all of this redefines our view of success in ministry.

Nobody ventures into life aiming for failure. Everyone wants to be successful. But what is success? In the context of ministry, it is important to have a healthy and biblical idea of success because our view of success in ministry will fuel our strategies and metrics. It will influence our celebration and serve to bolster our perseverance. A right desire for the future leads to right ambitions in the present.

We live in an age of productivity and efficiency. The clash of capitalism, competition, and a post-Industrial Revolution culture creates an environment that is always pushing the boundaries and expectations. In many ways, this cultural cocktail has fueled the growth of our of nation and resulted in unprecedented prosperity. The American Dream has become an iconic mantra embedded into the very fabric of who we are as a people. To pretend this has not affected the way we view success in the Church would be foolish.

In many respects, then, the Church has become reductionistic in how she views success. The marketplace evaluates success by looking at the bottom line of a balance sheet, the stock price, and so forth—and the Church has tended to follow suit. We have deemed a church successful based on a few clear-cut metrics, but these don't always tell the whole story. Metric dashboards are helpful and necessary, but they don't seem to capture the essence of our biblical mandate. We are called to make disciples of all nations, not simply make converts. Discipleship is long, slow, and messy. In short, it's harder to measure.

The challenge that we will face when evaluating our weaknesses is overcorrection. Most of us will swing the pendulum too far in another direction and simply create a new issue down the road for another generation. The hope in this section is to raise the awareness level of three issues: ministry is inefficient, people are our metric, and the formation of Christ is the end goal.

Ministry Is Inefficient

As much as we plan and prepare and strategize and implement, ministry will always be inefficient. At the root of the call to ministry is a call to shepherd and love people toward godliness. And this is never a straight line. Life cannot be mechanized into a program, and there are no assembly lines for life change. Prayer is inefficient. Discipleship is inefficient. These things have no measurable end and are hard to show on a metric dashboard; rather, they are to be the persistent climate of the Church until Christ calls us home. We are not arguing that we should abandon metrics, but just better understand the limitations of them.

Our drive for efficiency, productivity, and pragmatism leads us to spend more time honing best practices than wading through the murky waters of life change. Yes, the Church should devote attention to best practices and should strive for improvement and excellence, but all in proper priority. At the heart of our ministry we must be convinced that our best practices can only take us so far. Therefore, as we recognize the limitation of best practices, then we begin to reprioritize our approach to ministry.

It is imperative for the Church and her leadership to understand this practically. Sure, most would espouse the inefficiency of ministry theologically but then get frustrated when it plays itself out this way practically. The reality of the sanctification process is that it zigs and zags while taking a few steps forward and a few steps back. This is the story of your life—as well as our lives and the lives of our most sincere church members. We need to account for this in the measurement of our church health. It is unrealistic and an unnecessary burden to place on the church to think that our people will grow unfettered from gutter to glory.

The People Metric

The Church must be a place where it is okay not to be okay. The culture of the Church needs to be a safe place for the weary, weak,

and wobbly. Of all places, we should welcome those who are honest
about their burdens, frustrations, and pitfalls. Our people cannot be
honest about their shortcomings in the marketplace. The Church
provides the release valve of grace that we all desperately need, leadership included.

J. I. Packer writes:

> The church, however, is a hospital in which nobody
> is completely well, and anyone can relapse at any time.
> Pastors no less than others are weakened by pressure
> from the world, the flesh, and the devil, with their lures
> of profit, pleasure, and pride . . . pastors must acknowl-
> edge that they the healers remain sick and wounded and
> therefore need to apply the medicines of Scripture to
> themselves as well as to the sheep whom they tend in
> Christ's name.[6]

It is far too common for the church to expend precious energies
masquerading and upholding images rather then walking in transparency and authenticity. Ministry is messy because life is messy, and
nobody is excluded from the mess. If it is not okay not to be okay in
a church, then what are we doing? Where is the gospel? The hope we
have in Christ is that it is okay not to be okay, but He is leading us
to greater levels of health and maturity. Give your people the grace to
grow and an example to follow.

Proverbs 14:4 says, "Where there are no oxen, the feeding trough
is empty [clean], but an abundant harvest comes through the strength
of the ox" (HCSB). If we want an abundant harvest, then the ox is
necessary. But with the ox comes the mess and hassle of upkeep and
care. We cannot have the ox and clean stables; the two are mutually exclusive. Ministry is inefficient and messy, and we cannot place
onerous metrics of grace-less growth on our people that do not take
this reality into account. The church should enjoy the fruit of steady
growth, discipleship, conversions, and baptisms while understanding

the call to be faithful to a process that in reality is often slower and messier than we like.

Christlikeness Is the Goal

Finally, behind all the numbers are people. Behind every statistic is a story. Behind every point of quantitative data is a qualitative narrative that needs to be recovered. So a balance needs to be introduced into the success equation. The discussion about metrics needs to include the vastly overlooked qualitative element; it needs to include who and where our people actually are in their walk with the Lord.

A biblically informed definition of success has almost nothing to do with the acquisition of material things, the achievement of personal comfort, or entertainment. Success for the believer and for the church is defined in relationship to Jesus Christ and His mission. Christ came to seek and save that which was lost; He calls a people unto Himself. We were once far off and have now been brought near through the blood of Christ. He creates a new humanity with transformed perspectives and ambitions.

The death and resurrection of Christ and the overall mission of God in the world now defines what success looks like for us. Simplistically, our desire for success should be in accordance with Romans 12:1–2, in making ourselves a "living sacrifice" that we might be "transformed" into His image.

Do we look like the Savior? Have we been transformed by His grace to love radically, give generously, suffer willingly, walk humbly, and engage missionally? Is the fruit of God's Spirit evident in our hearts: love, joy, peace, patience, kindness, goodness, faithfulness, gentleness, and self-control? (Gal. 5:22).

Success has been redefined as we have been transformed. In this new, Jesus-centered list, prosperity means an endowment of Christ-saturated thoughts, relationships, and actions, not just a certain annual budget or weekend attendance. Conformity to the image of Christ now compels us, not the creaturely comforts of a fading glory (2 Cor. 5:14). The success we are now pursuing is not elusive; rather, it is eternally ours because it has been purchased by the sufficient blood of Christ and secured by the seal of the Holy Spirit (Eph. 1:7, 14). The "American Church Dream" is a cheap substitute compared to the rich treasure of knowing Christ (Phil. 3:7–10).

The gospel reality awakens us to pleasures evermore and causes us to abandon our prior delusions of grandeur to readily accept the inheritance that is imperishable, undefiled, and unfading, kept in heaven for those who believe (1 Pet. 1:3–5). In short, a successful church is motivated and empowered by the gospel to remain faithful to Christ and His mission of making disciples.

The DTR that Jesus had with His disciples proved to be pivotal. This conversation defined His identity, His mission, and the nature of His relationship with His disciples. And through this one conversation, He also redefined success. Jesus promised that He would establish His kingdom, but He would do so by humbling Himself and ultimately dying on the cross.

And He now invites us—His disciples—to follow in His steps. The DTR has clarified the relationship and the invitation stands. Will we join Him in Jesus-centered living, working, and ministry?

We must.

We were called for this . . . and nothing other. To Him be all glory as He does His great work through us.

CONCLUSION

On this rock I will build My church.

~ Matthew 16:18 (HCSB)

God has always preserved his people.

When we read the Old Testament, we clearly see God preserving Israel, His covenant people. Two Jewish celebrations are beautiful reminders of His special relationship with His people: Passover and Purim.

Passover remembers God's amazing deliverance of His people from Egyptian slavery. God struck down the Egyptians through awe-inspiring plagues revealing that He alone is God. He parted the Red Sea and ensured His people's liberation. Purim is the Jewish holiday remembering God's provision for His people through ordinary events chronicled in the book of Esther. The book of Exodus chronicles the foundation for Passover, and Esther, the foundation for Purim. In the book of Esther, God guides the heart of an evil human king to place Esther in the role of queen who will one day stand up for her people.

In the book of Esther, God's name is not mentioned. And intentionally so. The author was using a literary device to teach God's people that often God works in the ordinary details of life. Often His work is not pronounced with plagues and parting of seas. Sometimes, He is silent. But His silence must not be mistaken for absence. He is always working, always involved in the preservation of His people.

Regardless of a believer's view of eschatology, he holds to the conviction that Christ's Church will prevail. His plans will not be thwarted. The gates of Hades will be pushed further and further back until people from every tribe, tongue, and nation are included in the glorious Creature of the Word.

And why will His Church prevail?

His Church is built on the rock—the reality that He is the Christ. The Church is formed on the gospel, God's righteousness given to us in Christ. The Church finds her power in the gospel and penetrates the kingdom of darkness through the grace and mercy found in the gospel.

The Creature thrives because the gospel is sufficient. Just as the gospel is sufficient for both an individual's justification and maturation, the gospel is sufficient for the Church's birth and sustenance.

The Church will thrive despite the floundering of some churches. Some churches and church leaders will flounder because the gospel will no longer be of first importance, will no longer be that on which they take their stand. They will move to another gospel, another set of beliefs, which is really no gospel at all. Subsequently, they will lose their first love, their power, and their foundation.

As we face struggles, trials, criticism, persecution, and difficulties, be assured that in the grand story, the Creature is victorious with Christ. Christ delivers on His promise to protect and prosper His bride, His Creature.

NOTES

Chapter 1

1. Martin Luther, *Three Treatises Paper,* 2nd ed. (Philadelphia, PA: Augsburg Fortress Publishers, 1990), 238.

2. *Ante-Nicene Fathers,* ed. Allan Menzies, vol. 3, *Latin Christianity: Its Founder, Tertullian* (Edinburgh: T&T Clark; Grand Rapids: Eerdmans); http://www.ccel.org/ccel/schaff/anf03.vi.ii.xii.html.

3. Martin Luther, *Lectures on Romans,* trans. and ed. Wilhelm Pauck, The Library of Christian Classics, vol. 15 (Philadelphia, PA: Westminster, 1961), 128.

4. Special thanks to Jeremy Treat for his exegetical work on this section.

5. Michael S. Horton, *The Christian Faith: A Systematic Theology for Pilgrims on the Way* (Grand Rapids, MI: Zondervan, 2011), 761.

6. Martin Luther, *Three Treatises Paper,* 2nd ed. (Philadelphia: Augsburg Fortress Publishers, 1990), 238

7. Horton, *The Christian Faith,* 752–53.

8. Martin Luther, preface, Commentary on the Epistle to the Galatians, 1535. Abridgement and paraphrase by Timothy Keller.

9. Wolfhart Pannenberg, *Systematic Theology,* vol. 2, trans. Geoffrey Bromiley (Grand Rapids, MI: Eerdmans, 1994), 462–63.

Chapter 2

1. Martin Luther, *Treatise on Good Works,* parts X, XI, 1520; http://www.ccel.org/ccel/luther/good_works.v.html.

2. I think this is actually a Tim Keller paraphrase of Luther, quoted in his *Gospel in Life* (Grand Rapids, MI: Zondervan, 2010), 73.

3. David Clarkson, *Works of David Clarkson*, vol. 2 (Pennsylvania, PA: Banner of Truth, 1988), 299–333.

4. Christopher Coppernoll, *Secrets of a Faith Well Lived: Intimate Conversations with Modern-Day Disciples* (West Monroe, LA: Howard Books, 2001), 213.

5. For an example of church discipline, see John Piper; http://www.desiring-god.org/resource-library/seminars/gravity-and-gladness-on-sunday-morning-part-1.

Chapter 3

1. Paul David Tripp, *Instruments in the Redeemer's Hands: People in Need of Change Helping People in Need of Change* (Phillipsburg, NJ: P&R Publishing, 2002), 164.

2. D. A. Carson, *Love in Hard Places* (Wheaton, IL: Crossway, 2002), 61.

3. See http://www.thevillagechurch.net/mediafiles/conflictanddiscipline.pdf.

4. *Ante-Nicene Fathers,* ed. Allan Menzies, vol. 9, *Latin Christianity: Its Founder, Tertullian* (Edinburgh: T&T Clark; Grand Rapids: Eerdmans); http://www.ccel.org/ccel/schaff/anf03.vi.ii.xii.html.

Chapter 4

1. Martin Luther, *On Christian Liberty,* in *First Principles of the Reformation of Dr. Martin Luther,* ed. Henry Wace and C.A. Buchheim, 1883 (London: William Clowes and Sons, 1520); http://www.ccel.org/ccel/luther/first_prin.i.html.

2. Martin Luther, *Commentary on Genesis,* WA 44,6; cited by Gustaf Wingren, *Luther on Vocation* (Evansville, IN: Ballast Press, 1994), 9.

3. There seems to be no citation for this quote. It's attributed to Augustine, Luther, and Dorothy Day, and Day may be the most likely. It was popularized by Campolo in *Letters to a Young Evangelical* when he attributed it to Augustine.

Chapter 5

1. Charles Spurgeon, "A Sermon and a Reminiscence," *Sword and the Trowel,* March 1873.

2. Joseph Pearce, "J. R. R. Tolkien: Truth and Myth," *Lay Witness,* (September 2001).

3. Ibid.

4. Rodney Stark, *Cities of God: The Real Story of How Christianity Became an Urban Movement and Conquered Rome* (San Francisco, CA: Harper Collins, 2007), 67.

5. This term comes from James Davison Hunter, *To Change the World: the Irony, Tragedy, and Possibility of Christianity in the Late Modern World* (New York: Oxford University Press, 2010).

Chapter 6

1. Thomas Manton, of *Works of Thomas Manton,* vol. 3 (Lexington, KY: Sovereign Grace Publishers, 2002), 28.

2. Sasha Shtargot and Janine Bennetts, "Death on Everest Divides Climbers," *Age,* May 25, 2006, http://www.theage.com.au/articles/2006/05/24/1148150327071.html.

3. Jesper Kunde, *Corporate Religion* (London: Prentice Hall, 2000), 4.

4. John P. Kotter, *Leading Change* (Boston, MA: Harvard Business Press, 1996), 148.

5. Pastor Josh Moody's *No Other Gospel* is an excellent look at the gospel in Galatians. In his book and teaching, he uses the phrase "any supplement to the gospel supplants the gospel." Josh Moody, *No Other Gospel: 31 Reasons from Galatians Why Justification by Faith Alone is the Only Gospel* (Wheaton, IL: Crossway, 2011).

6. We are grateful to Pastor Jeremy Pace for the illustration. He masterfully developed and trains church leaders using the theology-philosophy-practice house metaphor.

7. Jeremy Treat provided this illustration for us, a great example of a foundation with nothing built on it.

8. A. W. Tozer, *Of God and Men,* found in *From the Library of A. W. Tozer* by James Stuart Bell (Bloomington, MN: Bethany House, 2011), 327.

9. John Calvin, *Institutes of the Christian Religion,* 2.15.1 [p. 305].

Chapter 7

1. Charles Spurgeon, from the sermon "Christ's Triple Character" (6/16/1878; Sermon #2787), www.spurgeongems.org/vols46-48/chs2787.pdf.

2. It should be noted that these are minor differences between preaching and teaching, but they are not fundamental ones. We can parse out these differences by degree, but not in kind. For instance, Paul exhorts Timothy and Titus to "teach sound doctrine," and we read in Acts of Paul and Barnabas "teaching and proclaiming the Word of the Lord." Often the two are interwoven so tightly that to tease them apart is ultimately unnecessary. In the end,

it is difficult to make cut-and-dried distinctions based on a comprehensive study of the two.

3. *Kerysso* is used more than sixty times in the New Testament.

4. R. H. Mounce, "Preaching," *New Bible Dictionary*, 3rd ed., ed. J. D. Douglas (Downers Grove, IL: InterVarsity Press, 1996), 950.

5. *Euangelizomai* is used more than fifty times in the New Testament.

6. Mounce, "Preaching," *New Bible Dictionary*, 950.

7. Martin Luther, *Luther's Works,* vol. 41: Church and Ministry III (Minneapolis, MN: Fortress Press, 1966), 150.

8. John Stott, *Between Two Worlds: The Art of Preaching in the Twentieth Century* (Grand Rapids, MI: Eerdmans 1994), 125–26.

9. James Montgomery Boice, "The Foolishness of Preaching," in *Feed My Sheep: A Passionate Plea for Preaching,* ed. Don Kistler (Morgan, PA: Soli Deo Gloria Publications, 2001), 38–44.

10. Mike Bullmore, "A Case for Expositional Preaching," *Nine Marks EJournal* (May/June 2007), http://www.9marks.org/ejournal/biblical-case-expositional-preaching.

11. Michael Lawrence, *Biblical Theology in the Light of the Church: A Guide for Ministry* (Wheaton, IL: Crossway, 2010), 197.

12. John Scott, *Between Two Worlds: The Challenge of Preaching Today* (Grand Rapids, MI: Eerdmans, 1982), 7.

Chapter 8

1. John Calvin, *Institutes of the Christian Religion,* 3.6.4 [p. 688]).

2. Sally Lloyd-Jones, *The Jesus StoryBook Bible: Every Story Whispers His Name* (Grand Rapids, MI: Zondervan, 2007), 103–7.

3. Tedd Tripp, *Shepherding a Child's Heart* (Wapwallopen, PA: Shepherd Press, 1995), 4.

4. Richard Baxter, "The Duties of Parents for Their Children," *A Christian Directory,* 449.

5. We are grateful to Pastor Chris Farley for his work, *Gospel-Powered Parenting.* He deserves the credit for the thinking behind offensive and defensive parenting/ministry. Chris Farley, *Gospel-Powered Parenting: How the Gospel Shapes and Transforms Parenting* (Phillipsburg, NJ: P&R Publishing, 2009).

6. Thomas Chalmers quote paraphrased by Chris Farley taken from Gospel Powered Parenting, 24. He attributes it to Chalmers's sermon "The Expulsive Power of a New Affection."

7. Jonathan Edwards, "Seeking After Christ," in Owen Strachan and Douglas Allen Sweeney, *Jonathan Edwards on Beauty*, vol. 2 of *The Essential Edwards Collection* (Chicago, IL: Moody Publishers, 2010), 78.

8. Ed Clowney, *The Unfolding Mystery: Discovering Christ in the Old Testament* (Phillipsburg, NJ: P&R Publishing, 1988), 11.

9. See http://alvinreid.com/archives/2172.

10. A. N. Wilson, *Tolstoy: A Biography* (city: W. W. Norton and Company, 2001).

11. William Yount, *Created to Learn* (Nashville: B&H Publishing Group, 1996), 65.

12. Richard Dunn, *Shaping the Spiritual Lives of Students* (Downers Grove, IL: InterVarsity Press, 2001).

Chapter 9

1. A. W. Tozer, The Knowledge of the Holy (New York, NY: HarperOne, 1978).

2. This section is indebted to A. D. Clarke, "Leadership," in *New Dictionary of Biblical Theology*, eds. Desmond T. Alexander and Brian S. Rosner (Downers Grove, IL: InterVarsity Press, 2000).

3. The ability to teach and protect sound doctrine is a distinguishing qualification for the pastor/elder. The other qualifications are the same for elders and deacons. Church leadership should be inundated with leaders who are steeped in the gospel. And, the pastors/elders should be gifted teachers who can rightly divide the Word in both proclamation of truth and refutation of error.

4. This does not mean that a leader cannot disqualify himself from leadership temporarily or permanently. There are some sins, although forgiven, that carry the consequence of removal for the leader.

5. P. J. Buys, "The Fear of God as a Central Part of Reformed Spirituality," http://web.archieve.org/web/20070101182437.

Chapter 10

1. C. S. Lewis, *Mere Christianity* (1952; New York, NY: Harper Collins, 2001), 199.

2. A video of Kevin Durant playing frat flag football, http://www.youtube.com/watch?v=IOIa2Ol6SXo.

3. Jonathan Edwards, *Sermons and Discourses, 1734–1738,* ed. M. X. Lesser (WJE Online Vol. 19), 588.

4. Atul Gawande, *The Checklist Manifesto* (New York, NY: Metropolitan Books, 2009), 80.

5. *Works of Jonathan Edwards*, volume II, section II.

6. D. A. Carson, *Themelios*, 34, no. 1 (April 2009).

7. This is actually C. S. Lewis quoting Samuel Johnson, "Dr. Johnson," as saying: "People need to be reminded more often than they need to be instructed." C. S. Lewis, *Mere Christianity* (1952; New York, NY: Harper Collins, 2001), 82.

8. Take from C. J. Mahaney with Kevin Meath, *The Cross Centered Life* (Sisters, OR: Multnomah Books, 2002), 54.

Chapter 11

1. Robert Coleman, *The Master Plan of Evangelism,* 2nd edition (Grand Rapids, MI: Revell Books, 2010).

2 Gailyn Van Rheenen, "Contextualization and Syncretism," *Monthly Missiological Relection* 38:5.

3. Charles Colson and Ellen Vaughn, *Being the Body*, expanded ed. (Nashville, TN: Thomas Nelson, 2004), 371.

Chapter 12

1. John Owen cited in I.D.E. Thomas, *A Puritan Golden Treasury* (Edinburgh: Banner of Truth, 1977), 192.

2. Dietrich Bonhoeffer, *The Cost of Discipleship* (New York: Touchstone, 1959).

3. David Scaer, "Luther on Prayer," *Concordia Theological Quarterly* 47, no. 4 (October 1983), 305–6.

4. John Calvin, *Institutes of the Christian Religion*, 3.20.1.

5. The idea of highlighting the "evidence of grace" is due to the influence of C. J. Mahaney based on a message he delivered at the Resurgence Conference in Seattle in 2008.

6. J. I. Packer, *A Quest for Godliness: The Puritan Vision of the Christian Life* (Wheaton, IL: Crossway Books, 1990), 65.

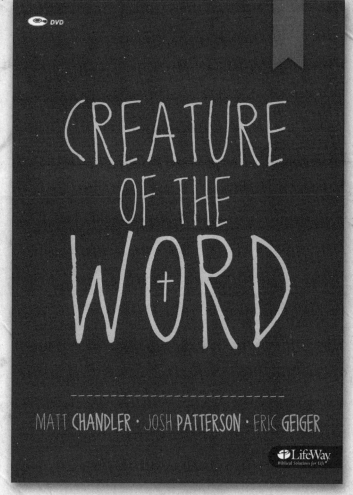